HOMELESS IN AMERICA

HOW COULD IT HAPPEN HERE?

ISSN 1536-5204

HOMELESS IN AMERICA

HOW COULD IT HAPPEN HERE?

Melissa J. Doak

INFORMATION PLUS® REFERENCE SERIES
Formerly Published by Information Plus, Wylie, Texas

THOMSON

GALE

Detroit • New York • San Francisco • San Diego • New Haven, Conn. • Waterville, Maine • London • Munich

THOMSON

GALE

Homeless in America: How Could It Happen Here?
Melissa J. Doak
Paula Kepos, Series Editor

Project Editor
John McCoy

Permissions
Margaret Abendroth, Edna Hedblad,
Emma Hull

Composition and Electronic Prepress
Evi Seoud

Manufacturing
Drew Kalasky

ISBN 0-7876-5103-6 (set)
ISBN 1-4144-0418-2
ISSN 1536-5204

This title is also available as an e-book.
ISBN 1-4144-0477-8 (set)
Contact your Thomson Gale sales representative for ordering information.

Printed in the United States of America
10 9 8 7 6 5 4 3 2 1

TABLE OF CONTENTS

PREFACE

Homeless in America: How Could It Happen Here? is part of the *Information Plus Reference Series*. The purpose of each volume of the series is to present the latest facts on a topic of pressing concern in modern American life. These topics include today's most controversial and most studied social issues: abortion, capital punishment, care for the elderly, crime, the environment, health care, immigration, minorities, national security, social welfare, women, youth, and many more. Although written especially for the high school and undergraduate student, this series is an excellent resource for anyone in need of factual information on current affairs.

By presenting the facts, it is Thomson Gale's intention to provide its readers with everything they need to reach an informed opinion on current issues. To that end, there is a particular emphasis in this series on the presentation of scientific studies, surveys, and statistics. These data are generally presented in the form of tables, charts, and other graphics placed within the text of each book. Every graphic is directly referred to and carefully explained in the text. The source of each graphic is presented within the graphic itself. The data used in these graphics are drawn from the most reputable and reliable sources, in particular from the various branches of the U.S. government and from major independent polling organizations. Every effort has been made to secure the most recent information available. The reader should bear in mind that many major studies take years to conduct, and that additional years often pass before the data from these studies are made available to the public. Therefore, in many cases the most recent information available in 2005 dated from 2002 or 2003. Older statistics are sometimes presented as well if they are of particular interest and no more recent information exists.

Although statistics are a major focus of the *Information Plus Reference Series*, they are by no means its only content. Each book also presents the widely held positions and important ideas that shape how the book's subject is discussed in the United States. These positions are explained in detail and, where possible, in the words of their proponents. Some of the other material to be found in these books includes: historical background; descriptions of major events related to the subject; relevant laws and court cases; and examples of how these issues play out in American life. Some books also feature primary documents or have pro and con debate sections giving the words and opinions of prominent Americans on both sides of a controversial topic. All material is presented in an even-handed and unbiased manner; the reader will never be encouraged to accept one view of an issue over another.

HOW TO USE THIS BOOK

It is a sad but undeniable fact that in the midst of the tremendous wealth of the United States there are still many people who cannot afford a place to live. For some, this is a temporary condition, lasting months or years, but many who become homeless find it extremely difficult to earn enough money to afford housing again. Many organizations, both public and private, work to assist the homeless and the potentially homeless, but all studies agree that there are far more in need of help than ever receive it. This book explores these and other issues, presenting the statistics and facts that illuminate the overall state of the homeless in the United States and the state of those programs that aid them.

Homeless in America: How Could It Happen Here? consists of seven chapters and three appendices. Each of the chapters is devoted to a particular aspect of homelessness in the United States. For a summary of the information covered in each chapter, please see the synopses provided in the Table of Contents at the front of the book. Chapters generally begin with an overview of the basic facts and background information on the chapter's topic, then proceed to examine subtopics of particular interest. For example, Chapter 2: The Demographics of Homelessness begins by discussing the difficulties involved in counting the homeless and consequently the small number of authoritative studies on the subject. It then moves on to look at the estimated number of homeless people in the United States and trends in the overall homeless population over time. The next section describes the characteristics of the homeless population. Covered, for instance, is the level of education of homeless people, whether they are alone or part of a homeless family, and the genders, races, and ethnicities of this population. While demonstrating that the homeless are highly diverse, the chapter gives special attention to segments that are over-represented among the homeless (e.g., single men). The demographics of the child and teenaged homeless population are also examined in detail. The chapter than examines the typical duration of a spell of homelessness and how likely it is that a formerly homeless person will become homeless again. The chapter concludes with a look at the rural homeless population. Readers can find their way through a chapter by looking for the section and subsection headings, which are clearly set off from the text. They can also refer to the book's extensive index if they already know what they are looking for.

Statistical Information

The tables and figures featured throughout *Homeless in America: How Could It Happen Here?* will be of particular use to the reader in learning about this issue. These tables and figures represent an extensive collection of the most recent and important statistics on homelessness, housing, and related issues—for example, graphics in the book cover the percentage of the homeless who are children; changes in the homeless population and services for the homeless by city; the number and types of homeless assistance programs by region; and the decline in publicly subsidized housing since 1998. Thomson Gale believes that making this information available to the reader is the most important way in which we fulfill the goal of this book: to help readers to understand the issues and controversies surrounding homelessness in the United States and to reach their own conclusions.

Each table or figure has a unique identifier appearing above it for ease of identification and reference. Titles for the tables and figures explain their purpose. At the end of each table or figure, the original source of the data is provided.

In order to help readers understand these often complicated statistics, all tables and figures are explained in the text. References in the text direct the reader to the relevant statistics. Furthermore, the contents of all tables and figures are fully indexed. Please see the opening section of the index at the back of this volume for a description of how to find tables and figures within it.

Appendices

In addition to the main body text and images, *Homeless in America: How Could It Happen Here?* has three appendices. The first is the Important Names and Addresses directory. Here the reader will find contact information for a number of government and private organizations that can provide further information on homelessness. The second appendix is the Resources section, which can also assist the reader in conducting his or her own research. In this section, the author and editors of *Homeless in America: How Could It Happen Here?* describe some of the sources that were most useful during the compilation of this book. The final appendix is the detailed Index, which facilitates reader access to specific topics in this book.

ADVISORY BOARD CONTRIBUTIONS

The staff of Information Plus would like to extend their heartfelt appreciation to the Information Plus Advisory Board. This dedicated group of media professionals provides feedback on the series on an ongoing basis. Their comments allow the editorial staff who work on the project to make the series better and more user-friendly. Our top priorities are to produce the highest-quality and most useful books possible, and the Advisory Board's contributions to this process are invaluable.

The members of the Information Plus Advisory Board are:

- Kathleen R. Bonn, Librarian, Newbury Park High School, Newbury Park, California

- Madelyn Garner, Librarian, San Jacinto College— North Campus, Houston, Texas

- Anne Oxenrider, Media Specialist, Dundee High School, Dundee, Michigan

- Charles R. Rodgers, Director of Libraries, Pasco-Hernando Community College, Dade City, Florida

- James N. Zitzelsberger, Library Media Department Chairman, Oshkosh West High School, Oshkosh, Wisconsin

COMMENTS AND SUGGESTIONS

The editors of the *Information Plus Reference Series* welcome your feedback on *Homeless in America: How Could It Happen Here?* Please direct all correspondence to:

Editors
Information Plus Reference Series
27500 Drake Rd.
Farmington Hills, MI 48331-3535

CHAPTER 1
THE NATURE OF HOMELESSNESS

Homelessness is a complex social problem. According to the National Coalition for the Homeless in "How Many People Experience Homelessness?" (http://www.nationalhomeless.org/numbers.html, September 2002), one-half to three-quarters of a million people lack a place to sleep on any given night in the United States, and 3.5 million will be homeless at some time during the year. Social researchers—educators, sociologists, economists, and political scientists—have studied homelessness in the past and present and have determined that homelessness is caused by a combination of poverty, misfortune, illness, and behavior.

HISTORICAL ATTITUDES TOWARD THE HOMELESS

Views of homelessness have changed over time. The condition is recognized by most people in the twenty-first century to be a result of poverty or structural flaws in society. In earlier times the homeless were typically blamed for their own predicament, with their condition assigned to laziness, drunkenness, or crime. That view persists somewhat to this day for those whose drug addiction is seen to contribute to their homelessness. Distinctions, however, have always been made. The English Poor Laws of 1601, for example, distinguished between the "worthy" and "unworthy" poor. The so-called worthy poor—widows, the elderly, the disabled, and children—were not held responsible for poverty and homelessness and sometimes received aid when aid was available. Others, however, were viewed as morally suspect—lazy, criminal, or promiscuous (Linda Gordon, "Welfare and Public Relief," *Reader's Companion to U.S. Women's History,* New York: Houghton Mifflin, 1998).

English colonists bound for North America in the seventeenth and eighteenth centuries brought the English traditions with them. Some thought that the community should intervene to reduce homelessness but still believed that for most people homelessness was the consequence of weakness or flawed character. The colonists established community poorhouses (or workhouses), where the homeless and people unable to care for themselves could reside. Poorhouse residents were put to work doing hard or unpleasant tasks, the hope being that such labor would reform the shiftless, and they would be eager to find other employment that would sustain them.

Poorhouses, however, failed to reduce homelessness, and by the early 1900s, the horrors of large institutions like poorhouses and asylums had become so obvious that reformers pushed for "outdoor" relief programs—aid to people within their homes. By that time the United States was becoming more and more urban and industrial, but factory work paid low wages for long hours. When people lost their homes, they often ended up on the city streets.

Attitudes toward the homeless began to change early in the twentieth century. Social scientists began studying social problems—including homelessness—systematically for the first time. They discovered that most of the homeless either worked or wanted to work, but had problems finding employment that paid enough to cover housing.

Beliefs about homelessness changed further during the Great Depression (1929–41). After the stock market crash of 1929, Americans faced a decade of hard times worse than any they had known before. Millions of people lost their jobs, many lost their homes, and most of those who still had work struggled to make ends meet. A severe drought struck the central United States in the 1930s, destroying the livelihoods of millions of farmers, and they streamed out of the so-called dust bowl of the Great Plains states. Widespread hardship experienced throughout the country produced sympathy for the homeless and led to demands that government come to their aid. President Herbert Hoover, who advocated minimal federal involvement in solving such problems, came under severe criticism, and most historians agree that his stance was at least in part a cause of his defeat in the 1932 presidential election.

The subsequent administration of President Franklin D. Roosevelt passed a number of laws intended to reduce homelessness and poverty as part of its New Deal program. The Social Security Act of 1935 established programs that channeled funds directly to the elderly and to children of single mothers—two groups that had previously suffered most from poverty and homelessness. The United States Housing Act of 1937 established housing and home loan programs for low-income people.

The New Deal laws marked a turning point in attitudes toward the homeless. More resources were added in the 1960s by further legislation, especially the formation of the Department of Housing and Urban Development in 1965. With new laws and bureaucracies in place, American society acknowledged that people could become poor and homeless because of circumstances beyond their control, and that the government should help such people.

This basic idea has continued to guide federal policy, although the shape and implementation of programs has continuously changed. Other political priorities drew attention away from the plight of the poor and homeless during the 1970s and early 1980s. Funding for many programs was cut or frozen. The late 1980s and early 1990s saw renewed interest in the problem, and new ideas surfaced on how best to help people in need.

DEFINING HOMELESSNESS
A Legislative Definition

During a period of growing concern about homelessness in the mid-1980s, the first major piece of federal legislation aimed specifically at helping the homeless was adopted: the Stewart B. McKinney Homeless Assistance Act of 1987 (PL 100-77), today known as the McKinney-Vento Homeless Assistance Act. Part of the act officially defined a homeless person as:

1. An individual who lacks a fixed, regular, and adequate nighttime residence; and

2. An individual who has a primary nighttime residence that is:

A. A supervised publicly or privately operated shelter designed to provide temporary living accommodations (including welfare hotels, congregate shelters, and transitional housing for the mentally ill);

B. An institution that provides a temporary residence for individuals intended to be institutionalized; or

C. A public or private place not designed for, or ordinarily used as, a regular sleeping accommodation for human beings.

A Broader Definition

The government's definition of a homeless person focuses on whether a person is housed. Broader definitions of homelessness take into account whether a person has a home. Martha Burt and her colleagues at the Urban Institute reported in *Helping America's Homeless: Emergency Shelter or Affordable Housing?* (Washington, DC: Urban Institute Press, 2001) that as late as 1980, the Census Bureau identified people who lived alone and did not have a "usual home elsewhere"—in other words, a larger family—as homeless. Home in this sense describes living within a family, rather than having a roof over one's head.

The Urban Institute researchers also stated that homeless people themselves, when interviewed in the 1980s and 1990s, drew a distinction between having a "house" and having a "home." Even when homeless people had spent significant periods of time in a traditional shelter, like an apartment or rented room, if they felt those houses were transitional or insecure, they identified themselves as having been homeless while living there. These answers, according to the authors of *Helping America's Homeless*, "reflect how long they have been without significant attachments to people."

Burt and other homeless advocates have disagreed with the narrow government definition of a homeless person, which focuses on a person's sleeping arrangements. They assert that the definition should be broadened to include groups of people who, while they may have somewhere to live, do not really have a home in the conventional sense. Considerable debate has resulted over expanding the classification to include people in situations such as the following:

- People engaging in prostitution who spend each night in a different hotel room, paid for by clients

- Children in foster or relative care

- People living in stable but inadequate housing (having no plumbing or heating, for example)

- People doubled up in conventional dwellings for the short term

- People in hotels paid for by vouchers to the needy

- Elderly people living with family members because they cannot afford to live elsewhere

Official definitions are important because total counts of the homeless influence levels of funding authorized by Congress for homeless programs. With the availability of federal funds since the passage of the McKinney Act, institutional constituencies have formed that advocate for additional funding, an effort in which more expansive definitions are helpful.

TABLE 1.1

Main causes of homelessness, as reported by big city mayors, 2004

Number of positive survey responses	Causes of homelessness	Cities replying in the affirmative that the listed cause of homelessness was one of the main or primary causes in their city
24	Lack of affordable housing	Boston, Burlington, Cedar Rapids, Charleston, Charlotte, Chicago, Cleveland, Denver, Detroit, Louisville Metro, Miami, Nashville, New Orleans, Norfolk, Philadelphia, Phoenix, Portland, St. Paul, Salt Lake City, San Antonio, San Francisco, Santa Monica, Seattle, and Trenton
21	Mental illness or the lack of needed services	Boston, Burlington, Cedar Rapids, Cleveland, Denver, Detroit, Kansas City (MO), Louisville Metro, Miami, Nashville, New Orleans, Norfolk, Phoenix, Portland, St. Paul, Salt Lake City, San Antonio, San Francisco, Santa Monica, Seattle, and Trenton
20	Substance abuse and the lack of needed services	Burlington, Charleston, Denver, Detroit, Kansas City (MO), Louisville Metro, Los Angeles, Miami, Nashville, New Orleans, Norfolk, Phoenix, Portland, St. Paul, Salt Lake City, San Antonio, San Francisco, Santa Monica, Seattle, and Trenton
16	Low-paying jobs	Boston, Burlington, Charleston, Charlotte, Cleveland, Denver, Louisville Metro, Miami, Nashville, New Orleans, Philadelphia, Phoenix, Providence, Salt Lake City, San Antonio, Seattle
13	Unemployment	Boston, Cedar Rapids, Chicago, Cleveland, Denver, Kansas City (MO), Los Angeles, Nashville, New Orleans, Norfolk, Portland, Providence, San Antonio, Trenton
12	Domestic violence	Boston, Burlington, Denver, Detroit, Miami, Nashville, New Orleans, Norfolk, Salt Lake City, San Antonio, Seattle, and Trenton
7	Poverty	Kansas City (MO), Nashville, New Orleans, Providence, St. Paul, San Antonio, Seattle
5	Prisoner reentry	Boston, Cleveland, Los Angeles, Norfolk, Phoenix

Cities whose mayors participated in the survey:

Boston, MA	Denver, CO	New Orleans, LA	San Antonio, TX
Burlington, VT	Detroit, MI	Norfolk, VA	San Francisco, CA
Cedar Rapids, IA	Kansas City, MO	Philadelphia, PA	Santa Monica, CA
Charleston, NC	Louisville Metro, KY	Phoenix, AZ	Seattle, WA
Charlotte, SC	Los Angeles, CA	Portland, OR	St. Paul, MN
Chicago, IL	Miami, FL	Providence, RI	Trenton, NJ
Cleveland, OH	Nashville, TN	Salt Lake City, UT	

SOURCE: Adapted from Eugene T. Lowe, "Main Causes of Homelessness," in *Hunger and Homelessness Survey: A Status Report on Hunger and Homelessness in America's Cities, 2004*, U.S. Conference of Mayors-Sodexho USA, December 2004, http://www.usmayors.org/uscm/hungersurvey/2004/onlinereport/HungerAndHomelessnessReport2004.pdf (accessed February 2, 2005)

CAUSES OF HOMELESSNESS

In 2004 the United States Conference of Mayors, a nonpartisan organization of cities with populations higher than 30,000, surveyed the mayors of major cities on the extent and causes of urban homelessness, and most of the mayors named the lack of affordable housing as a cause of homelessness. (See Table 1.1.) The next three causes identified by mayors, in rank order, were mental illness or the lack of needed services (twenty-one of twenty-seven), substance abuse and lack of needed services (twenty), and low-paying jobs (sixteen). The lowest ranking cause, cited by five mayors, was prisoner reentry (release from incarceration). Other causes cited were unemployment (thirteen of twenty-seven), domestic violence (twelve), and poverty (seven).

As evident in the findings of the Conference of Mayors survey, homelessness is a complex social problem arising from three fundamental and interacting causes: lack of means, medical conditions, and behavioral problems.

COUNTING THE HOMELESS

Methodology

An accurate count of the U.S. homeless population has proved to be a problem for statisticians. The most formidable obstacle is the nature of homelessness itself. Typically, researchers contact people in their homes using in-person or telephone surveys to obtain information regarding income, education levels, household size, ethnicity, and other demographic data. Since homeless people cannot be counted "at home," researchers have been forced to develop new methods for collecting data on these transient groups. Martha Burt explored this issue for the U.S. Department of Housing and Urban Development (HUD) and the U.S. Department of Health and Human Services (DHHS) and published a table of the most common methods of data collection for homeless people. (See Table 1.2.)

If each and every person without a home could be counted it would be the most accurate way to establish the number of homeless people. Such a count is almost impossible. One way to estimate the number of homeless people is to search records at homeless service provider locations. Alternatively, sampling of those records combined with projections, called "probability-based methods," can be used to count the number of homeless. Another way to count the homeless is to count the number of homeless at one particular time in one particular place. This "snapshot" method estimates the number of homeless at any one time. Longitudinal studies are a way to estimate the proportion of people in a population who may become homeless at some point in their lives. These studies follow individuals over a period of time to determine if they become homeless (Anita Drever, "Homeless Count Methodologies: An Annotated Bibliography," Institute for the Study of Homelessness and Poverty, February 1999).

TABLE 1.2

Common methods for collecting planning information

Method	Usual places to find people for study	Usual period of data collection and of estimate	Probable complexity of data collected
Full counts and other non-probability methods			
Analysis of agency records	Specific agency	Varies; usually not done to develop a population estimate	Whatever the agency routinely records in its case documents
Simple count, involving significant amounts of data by observation or from minimal agency records	Shelters, streets	1 night; point-in-time estimate	Enumeration, + very simple population characteristics (gender, adult/child, race)
Simple count with brief interview	Shelters, meal programs, streets	1 night; point-in-time estimate	Enumeration + basic information as reported by respondent
Screener, counts and brief interviews for anyone screened in, plus unduplication using unique identifiers	Service agencies of all types	Several weeks or months; point-in-time and period prevalence estimate	Enumeration + basic information as reported by respondent
Complete enumeration through multiple agency search and referral followed by extensive interview (also unduplication)	Service agencies and key informants	Several weeks or months; point-in-time and period prevalence estimate	Usually extensive
Probability-based methods			
Block probability with substantial interview	Streets	Several weeks or months; point-in-time estimate	Usually extensive
Other probability approaches	Abandoned buildings, conventional housing in poor neighborhoods	Several days or weeks; point-in-time estimate	Enumeration + basic information as reported by respondent
Service-based random sampling	Usually homeless assistance programs	Several weeks, months, or years; point-in-time estimate	Usually extensive
Shelter and other service tracking systems that allow unduplication across all services in a jurisdiction overtime	Service agencies	On going; point-in-time or period prevalence for periods of any length	Whatever the system collects, but usually simple data for administrative purposes
Other interesting methods			
Surveys of the housed population	At home	Multi-year; produces period prevalence for periods asked about	Basic information as reported by respondent
Longitudinal studies	Shelters, soup kitchens, streets	Multi-year; does not produce a population estimate	Extensive information, collected from the same person at several points in time

SOURCE: Martha R. Burt, "Table 3. Common Methods for Collecting Planning Information," in "Demographics and Geography: Estimating Needs," *Practical Lessons: The 1998 Symposium on Homelessness Research*, edited by Linda B. Fosburg and Deborah L. Dennis, U.S. Department of Housing and Urban Development and the U.S. Department of Health and Human Services, August 1999, http://aspe.os.dhhs.gov/progsys/homeless/symposium/1-demograp.htm (accessed February 2, 2005)

COMPARING METHODS AND RESULTS. As Table 1.2 reveals, methods vary in scope and design. Different designs will produce different results even if the intention is the same—namely to enumerate the homeless population. Table 1.3 shows results of surveys conducted by the Association of Gospel Rescue Missions (AGRM) in 1994, 2003, and 2004. The data presented in Table 1.3 are based on the "snapshot" method—counts of a population at a point in time. AGRM counted all people receiving homeless services during one specific night in each year. Table 1.4 shows results from an Urban Institute study conducted in 1996. Data in Table 1.4 are based on a sample of seventy-six geographical areas selected by the Urban Institute as being representative of all service providers in the United States. The Urban Institute then compared its results by demographic characteristics to the total population as enumerated by the U.S. Census.

The male/female ratios in the AGRM study are quite different from the Urban Institute's study, with AGRM finding that males were more than three-quarters of the homeless (77% in 2004), whereas the Urban Institute's study showed that males were just over two-thirds of the homeless population (68% in 1996). (See Figure 1.1.) Both studies showed that males outnumbered females among the homeless, but the proportions were different. The Census Bureau estimated that in July 2003, women outnumbered men in the U.S. population by a small margin—50.8% of the population were female and 49.2% male.

The Official Count: The U.S. Census Survey

The official U.S. census, which takes place at ten-year intervals, is intended to count everyone in the United States. The results of the census are critical for determining how much federal money goes into different programs and to various regions of the country. Representation of the population in Congress is also based on the census. Since the U.S. Census Bureau counts people in their homes, counting the homeless presents special challenges.

A PROBLEM OF METHODOLOGY. In 1990 census officials, on what was known as Shelter and Street Night, or

TABLE 1.3

Demographic overview of homeless population, 1994–2003

	2004	2003	1994
Gender			
Male	77%	77%	82%
Female	23%	23%	18%
Age groups			
Under 18	9%	10%	8%
18–25	10%	10%	12%
26–35	18%	19%	29%
36–45	30%	31%	29%
46–65	29%	26%	18%
65+	4%	4%	4%
Race/ethnic groups			
Caucasian	44%	48%	42%
African-American	40%	36%	44%
Hispanic	10%	10%	12%
Asian	1%	1%	2%
Native American	5%	5%	4%
Women/children/families			
Couples	16%	12%	20%
Women with children	60%	57%	60%
Men with children	7%	5%	5%
Intact families	16%	26%	15%
Other information			
Veterans—male	23%	23%	28%
Veterans—female	3%	3%	N/A
Served in Korea	5%	6%	N/A
Served in Vietnam	41%	41%	N/A
Served in Persian Gulf	12%	11%	N/A
Homeless less than 1 year	62%	65%	56%
Never before homeless	35%	37%	N/A
Homeless once before	26%	26%	N/A
Homeless twice before	18%	17%	N/A
Homeless 3+ times before	21%	20%	N/A
More than 6 month resident	72%	71%	67%
Harder to find work today than 6 months ago	58%	61%	N/A
Lost government benefits in last 12 months	20%	22%	N/A
Prefer spiritual emphasis in services	80%	79%	N/A
Comes to the mission daily for assistance	78%	N/A	N/A
In long-term rehab—male	35%	31%	30%
In long-term rehab—female	25%	21%	28%

SOURCE: "Data from the 2004 AGRM Fall Snapshot Survey of the Homeless," Association of Gospel Rescue Missions, 2004, http://www.agrm.org/statistics/snap04_data.html (accessed February 2, 2005)

TABLE 1.4

Basic demographic characteristics of homeless and formerly homeless individuals, 1996

Characteristics	Currently homeless clients (N=2938)	Formerly homeless clients (N=677)	U.S. adult population
Sex			
Male	68(%)	54(%)	48(%)
Female	32	46	52
Race/ethnicity			
White non-Hispanic	41	46	76
Black non-Hispanic	40	41	11
Hispanic	11	9	9
Native American	8	2	1
Other	1	2	3
Age			
17	1	0	NA
18–21	6	2	7
22–24	5	2	5
25–34	25	17	21
35–44	38	36	22
45–54	17	26	17
55–64	6	11	11
65 and older	2	6	17
Education/highest level of completed schooling			
Less than high school	38	42	18
High school graduate/G.E.D.	34	34	34
More than high school	28	24	48
Marital status			
Never married	48	45	23
Married	9	9	60
Separated	15	14	[a]
Divorced	24	25	10
Widowed	3	6	7
Living situation			
Client ages 17 to 24			
Clients in families			
Men	*	*	NA
Women	3	1	NA
Single clients			
Men	5	2	NA
Women	4	1	NA
Client ages 25 and older			
Clients in families			
Men	2	3	NA
Women	9	13	NA
Single clients			
Men	62	50	NA
Women	16	30	NA
Veteran status	23	22	13

Note: Numbers do not sum to 100 percent due to rounding.
NA=Not available.
*Denotes values that are less than 0.5 but greater than 0 percent.
[a]Included in "married."
NSHAPC stands for National Survey of Homeless Assistance Providers and Clients.

SOURCE: Martha R. Burt et al., "Table 3.1. Basic Demographic Characteristics, by Homeless Status," in *Homelessness: Programs and the People they Serve: Findings of the National Survey of Homeless Assistance Providers and Clients*, Urban Institute, December 1999, http://www.huduser.org/publications/homeless/homelessness/ch_3b.html#fig3.1 (accessed February 2, 2005)

S-Night, counted homeless persons found in shelters, emergency shelters, shelters for abused women, shelters for runaway and neglected youth, low-cost motels, Young Men's Christian Associations (YMCAs) and Young Women's Christian Associations (YWCAs), and in subsidized units at motels. Additionally, they counted people found in the early morning hours sleeping in abandoned buildings, bus and train stations, all-night restaurants, parks, and vacant lots (Diane F. Barrett et al., "The 1990 Census Shelter and Street Night Enumeration," U.S. Census Bureau, 1992). The results of this count were released the following year in the Census Bureau publication, "Count of Persons in Selected Locations Where Homeless Persons Are Found." Homeless advocates criticized the methods and results as inadequate and charged that they provided a low estimate of homeless people in the United States. In response, according to Annetta and Denise Smith in *Emergency and Transitional Shelter Population: 2000* (U.S. Census Bureau, October 2001), the Census Bureau emphasized

FIGURE 1.1

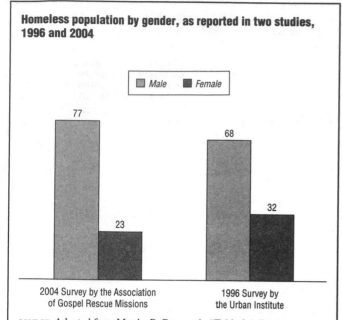

Homeless population by gender, as reported in two studies, 1996 and 2004

Male ☐   Female ■

77   23
2004 Survey by the Association
of Gospel Rescue Missions

68   32
1996 Survey by
the Urban Institute

SOURCE: Adapted from Martha R. Burt et al., "Table 3.1. Basic Demographic Characteristics, by Homeless Status," in *Homelessness: Programs and the People they Serve: Findings of the National Survey of Homeless Assistance Providers and Clients*, Urban Institute, December 1999, http://www.huduser.org/publications/homeless/homelessness/ch_3b.html#fig3.1 (accessed February 2, 2005); and Association of Gospel Rescue Missions, "Data From the 2004 AGRM Fall Snapshot Survey of the Homeless," 2004, http://www.agrm.org/statistics/snap04_data.html (accessed February 2, 2005)

that S-Night "should not be used as a count of people experiencing homelessness." S-Night results were not a reflection of the prevalence of homelessness over a given year, but rather a count of homeless persons identified during a single night, a "snapshot," like the census itself.

CENSUS ACCUSED OF UNCONSTITUTIONALITY. The National Law Center on Homelessness and Poverty alleged that the methodology of the S-Night count was unconstitutional. In 1992 the Law Center, the U.S. Conference of Mayors, the cities of Baltimore and San Francisco, fifteen local homeless organizations, and seven homeless people (the plaintiffs) filed suit in the federal district court in Washington, D.C. They charged the Census Bureau with excluding segments of the homeless population in the 1990 population count by not counting those in hidden areas and by not allocating adequate funds for S-Night.

In its suit, the Law Center cited an internal Census Bureau memorandum that stated, in part, "We know we will miss people by counting the 'open' rather than 'concealed' (two studies showed that about two-thirds of the street population sleep concealed)." Studies funded by the Census Bureau indicated that up to 70% of the homeless street population in Los Angeles were missed, as

were 32% in New Orleans, 47% in New York City, and 69% in Phoenix. Advocates were greatly concerned that this underrepresentation would negatively affect the funding of homeless initiatives.

In 1994 the district court dismissed the case, ruling that the plaintiffs' case was without merit. The court ruled that failure to count all the homeless was not a failure to perform a constitutional duty; the Constitution does not give individuals a right to be counted or a right to a perfectly accurate census. The court stated that the "methods used by the Bureau on S-Night were reasonably designed to count as nearly as practicable all those persons residing in the United States and, therefore, easily pass constitutional muster." In 1996 the U.S. Court of Appeals upheld the district court's finding (United States Court of Appeals, for the District of Columbia Circuit, Argued October 6, 1995, Decided August 9, 1996, No. 94-5312, *National Law Center on Homelessness and Poverty, et al., Appellants v. Michael Kantor, et al., Appellees*, Appeal from the United States District Court for the District of Columbia, 92cv2257).

CENSUS 2000 LIMITS INFORMATION. The Bureau of the Census undertook a special operation, called Service-Based Enumeration (SBE), for the 2000 census. From March 27 through March 29, 2000, census workers focused solely on counting the homeless population at the locations where they were most likely to be found. For the SBE, the Census Bureau released the following schedule:

- Monday, March 27, 2000—Emergency and transitional shelters, hotels, motels, or other facilities. Enumerators will leave blank questionnaires for residents who usually stay at the shelter, but who are away at the time of the enumeration.

- Tuesday, March 28, 2000—Soup kitchens, regularly scheduled mobile food vans.

- Wednesday, March 29, 2000, from 4 A.M. to 7 A.M. only—Outdoor locations. Census workers will complete the census forms for each person at an outdoor location.

The SBE methods were considered an improvement over the methods used in the 1990 census survey. Homeless citizens and advocates alike expected to see an increase in the number of homeless persons reported by the Census Bureau in the 2000 census as compared with the count reported for the 1990 census. Expectations that the higher population counts would translate into higher funding levels for services to the homeless were also raised.

An Associated Press story dated June 27, 2001, reported that the U.S. Census Bureau would not be

TABLE 1.5

City data on homelessness, 2003–04

City	Percent increase in requests for emergency shelter	Percent increase in requests by families for emergency shelter	Shelter beds	Transitional housing units	Family break–up for shelter?	Family leave during day?	Percentage need unmet	Turn away families?	Turn others away?
Boston	0.5	1	increased	decreased	yes	yes	10	yes	yes
Burlington	−10	0.6	same	same	no	no	32	yes	yes
Cedar Rapids	15	−2	same	same	yes	yes	3	yes	yes
Charleston	12	−17	same	increased	no	no	0	no	no
Charlotte	4	4	same	same	yes	yes	15	yes	yes
Chicago	−2.3	10	same	same	no	no	0	no	no
Cleveland	2	2	increased	same	no	no	0	no	no
Denver	20	20	same	same	no	yes	25	yes	yes
Detroit	21	23	same	increased	no	yes	10	yes	yes
Kansas City	9	na	increased	increased	no	no	49	yes	yes
Los Angeles	16	13	increased	same	yes	yes	54	yes	yes
Louisville Metro	−25	−21	same	increased	yes	no	100	yes	yes
Miami	10	20	same	same	yes	yes	10	yes	yes
Nashville	7	15	same	increased	yes	no	10	yes	yes
New Orleans	na	22	same	same	yes	yes	10	yes	yes
Norfolk	−2	15	same	decreased	yes	yes	29	yes	yes
Philadelphia	8.5	−1.4	increased	increased	no	no	0	no	no
Phoenix	0	0	decreased	decreased	no	no	28	yes	yes
Portland	4	1	increased	increased	yes	yes	18	yes	yes
Providence	24	6	same	increased	yes	yes	15	yes	yes
Salt Lake City	17	23	same	same	no	no	29	yes	yes
San Antonio	12	17	increased	increased	yes	no	8	yes	yes
San Francisco	na	−20	decreased	increased	no	no	0	yes	no
Santa Monica	−3	50	same	same	yes	yes	0	yes	yes
Seattle	na	0	increased	increased	yes	yes	0	yes	yes
St. Paul	20	4	same	same	no	yes	1	no	yes
Trenton	15	18	increased	increased	yes	no	6	yes	yes

na=Not available

SOURCE: Eugene T. Lowe, et al., "City Data on Homelessness," in *Hunger and Homelessness Survey: A Status Report on Hunger and Homelessness in America's Cities, A 27–City Survey, December 2004*, The U.S. Conference of Mayors, December 2004, http://www.usmayors.org/uscm/hungersurvey/2004/onlinereport/HungerAndHomelessnessReport2004.pdf (accessed February 2, 2005)

releasing a specific homeless count because of the liability issues raised after the 1990 census. The Census Bureau stated that it would have only one category showing the number of persons tabulated at "emergency and transitional shelters." The people who, in 2000, were counted at domestic-violence shelters, family crisis centers, soup kitchens, mobile food vans, and targeted non-sheltered outdoor locations (i.e. street people, car dwellers, etc.) during the March 2000 SBE night were to be included in the category of "other non-institutional group quarters population." This category was overly inclusive; it included, for instance, students living in college dormitories. The homeless portion of the category could not be extracted.

Rather than release counts of all homeless people, the Census Bureau published *Emergency and Transitional Shelter Population: 2000,* a special report on people sleeping in shelters. Census Bureau officials said the homeless people they did find during the exhaustive, three-day SBE count were included in total population figures for states, counties, and municipalities. Researchers voiced concern that the numbers teased from these data sets would be flawed.

People involved in the receipt or delivery of services to the homeless were worried that their programs would suffer from the lack of SBE night information. A detailed homeless count was thought to be essential for city officials and advocacy groups to plan budgets for shelters and other homeless outreach programs. Results from the U.S. Conference of Mayors 2004 study illustrated the negative impact that inadequate information and funding can have on the delivery of human services. (See Table 1.5.) For example, the needs of 54% of homeless people for shelter could not be met in Los Angeles due to lack of resources. Homeless program funding for most cities was already strained. Two-thirds of cities surveyed in 2004 showed increased requests for emergency shelter services.

Only Estimates Are Available

The actual number of homeless people is unknown. The Urban Institute estimated that 3.5 million people were homeless at some point of time during the year 1996 (*America's Homeless II—Populations and Services,* Urban Institute, February 1, 2000). The 2000 Census counted 170,706 individuals in emergency and transitional

TABLE 1.6

Population in emergency and transitional shelters, 1990 and 2000

Area	1990		2000	
	Number	Percent	Number	Percent
United States	178,638	100.0	170,706	100.0
Region				
Northeast	60,077	33.6	52,369	30.7
Midwest	27,245	15.3	28,438	16.7
South	42,407	23.7	42,471	24.9
West	48,909	27.4	47,428	27.8
State				
Alabama	1,530	0.9	1,177	0.7
Alaska	447	0.3	558	0.3
Arizona	2,735	1.5	2,312	1.4
Arkansas	489	0.3	754	0.4
California	30,806	17.2	27,701	16.2
Colorado	2,554	1.4	2,281	1.3
Connecticut	4,194	2.3	2,291	1.3
Delaware	313	0.2	847	0.5
District of Columbia	4,682	2.6	1,762	1.0
Florida	7,110	4.0	6,766	4.0
Georgia	3,930	2.2	4,774	2.8
Hawaii	854	0.5	747	0.4
Idaho	461	0.3	703	0.4
Illinois	7,481	4.2	6,378	3.7
Indiana	2,251	1.3	2,384	1.4
Iowa	989	0.6	1,013	0.6
Kansas	940	0.5	587	0.3
Kentucky	1,284	0.7	1,626	1.0
Louisiana	1,559	0.9	1,986	1.2
Maine	419	0.2	458	0.3
Maryland	2,507	1.4	2,545	1.5
Massachusetts	6,207	3.5	5,405	3.2
Michigan	3,784	2.1	4,745	2.8
Minnesota	2,253	1.3	2,738	1.6
Mississippi	383	0.2	572	0.3
Missouri	2,276	1.3	2,164	1.3
Montana	445	0.2	477	0.3
Nebraska	764	0.4	913	0.5
Nevada	1,013	0.6	1,553	0.9
New Hampshire	377	0.2	523	0.3
New Jersey	7,470	4.2	5,500	3.2
New Mexico	667	0.4	934	0.5
New York	32,472	18.2	31,856	18.7
North Carolina	2,637	1.5	3,579	2.1
North Dakota	279	0.2	178	0.1
Ohio	4,277	2.4	5,224	3.1
Oklahoma	2,222	1.2	1,478	0.9
Oregon	3,254	1.8	3,011	1.8
Pennsylvania	8,237	4.6	5,463	3.2
Rhode Island	469	0.3	634	0.4
South Carolina	973	0.5	1,528	0.9
South Dakota	396	0.2	414	0.2
Tennessee	1,864	1.0	2,252	1.3
Texas	7,816	4.4	7,608	4.5
Utah	925	0.5	1,494	0.9
Vermont	232	0.1	239	0.1
Virginia	2,657	1.5	2,692	1.6
Washington	4,565	2.6	5,387	3.2
West Virginia	451	0.3	525	0.3
Wisconsin	1,555	0.9	1,700	1.0
Wyoming	183	0.1	270	0.2
Puerto Rico	445	*	586	*

*Not applicable.

SOURCE: Annetta C. Smith and Denise I. Smith, "Table 1. Population in Emergency and Transitional Shelters for the United States, Regions, States, and Puerto Rico: 1990 and 2000," in *Emergency and Transitional Shelter Population: 2000*, Census 2000 Special Reports, CENSR/01-2, U.S. Census Bureau, October 2001, http://www.census.gov/prod/2001pubs/ censr01-2.pdf (accessed February 12, 2005).

shelters, down from 178,638 individuals in 1990. (See Table 1.6). The Census Bureau expressly stated that this number was not a total count of the homeless. The U.S. Department of Housing and Urban Development estimated in 2005 that 150,000 people were chronically homeless—homeless for a year or more—and stated that this population was only about 10% of all homeless individuals, putting the homeless population at 1.5 million people (News Release, U.S. Department of Housing and Urban Development, HUD No. 05-007, January 25, 2005).

PUBLIC INTEREST IN HOMELESSNESS

Interest in and attitudes towards homelessness in America have changed over time. The mid- to late 1980s was a period of relatively high concern about homelessness. In 1986 the American public demonstrated concern over the plight of the homeless by initiating the Hands Across America fundraising effort. Some six million people locked hands across 4,152 miles to form a human chain across the country, bringing an outpouring of national attention and concern to the issue. In 1986 popular comedians Robin Williams, Whoopi Goldberg, and Billy Crystal hosted the Home Box Office (HBO) comedy special *Comic Relief* to help raise money for the homeless. The show was a success and became an annual event. Magazines, art shows, books, and songs turned the nation's attention toward homelessness. Well-funded research studies came out by the dozens. The country was awash in statistical information regarding the homeless. All of these activities pointed to the widely held belief that people became homeless because of circumstances outside of their control.

By 2005, however, national concern about homelessness had faded somewhat. One could only see *Comic Relief* in reruns. The annual fundraiser ran out of steam in 1996 with the exception of a revival show two years later. No resurgence of public interest in the homeless problem appeared in the twenty-first century, although the problem remained, and the U.S. Conference of Mayors reported in 2004 that the demand for services continued to increase. "The Real Face of Homelessness," in the January 20, 2003, issue of *Time*, explored a change in the national mood about homelessness. In New Orleans, for instance, park benches in certain areas had been removed in order to prevent street people from sleeping on them. A campaign was launched in Philadelphia to discourage giving money to panhandlers. In Orlando, Florida, people could be jailed for sleeping on the sidewalk. In San Francisco, Proposition N ("Care Not Cash") reduced county housing support payments from $395 to $59 a month. According to a *Time*/Cable News Network (CNN) poll, also cited in the article, 36% of the 1,006 adults polled favored making panhandling illegal, and 47% thought it should be illegal to sleep in public places.

When asked, Americans still stated that they were troubled by the existence of homelessness. A February 2005 survey of 1,001 adults by the Associated Press/Ipsos-Public Affairs found that nine out of ten adults considered homelessness a very serious or somewhat serious problem. However, only half of adults surveyed believed that chronic homelessness was caused by external circumstances (56%), and more than a third (38%) believed that homeless people were responsible for their homelessness.

Research studies, once so plentiful, were outdated by 2005, but some well-funded research centers and organizations continued to study the homeless population. A look at leading organizations follows.

The Urban Institute

The Urban Institute is a nonprofit policy research organization located in Washington, D.C. The Institute conducts research projects, publishes newsletters and books regarding social issues, and evaluates government programs. It is dedicated to examining society's problems and developing methods to solve them. The Institute's work is designed to help improve government decisions and increase citizens' awareness of important social issues. Funding comes from a variety of government, corporate, and private organizations and people.

The Urban Institute study *Homelessness: Programs and the People They Serve,* published in December 1999, was a landmark in homelessness research. The program was designed specifically to update a 1987 Institute study. The survey was based on a statistical sample of seventy-six metropolitan and nonmetropolitan areas, including small cities and rural areas. It provided relevant information about homeless service providers and examined the characteristics of people who use the services. The analysis presented information about homelessness in national, urban, suburban, and rural areas. It was still one of the most comprehensive research studies available on the subject of homelessness in America in 2005.

The U.S. Conference of Mayors

The U.S. Conference of Mayors organization includes more than 1,000 cities with populations of at least 30,000. Since 1982 the U.S. Conference of Mayors has conducted and published an annual survey that assesses emergency services—food, shelter, medical care, and income assistance—in the nation's largest cities. The survey tracks the increases or reductions in the demand for emergency services from year to year,

including services for the homeless. This study has become one of the leading sources of homelessness research today.

The National Coalition for the Homeless (NCH)

The National Coalition for the Homeless (NCH) is an advocacy group of homeless persons, activists, service providers, and people dedicated to ending homelessness. NCH serves as a national clearinghouse for information and works as a referral resource to enhance the public's understanding of homelessness. NCH believes that homelessness can be eliminated through public education, legislative advocacy, and grassroots movements.

Other Organizations

Homes for the Homeless (HFH) is a New York City–based program designed to find long-term solutions for homeless people in New York. HFH created an innovative and successful program—a network of residential, educational, and employment training centers called the American Family Inns—which has been used as a model for permanent solutions to homelessness. HFH is affiliated with the Institute for Children and Poverty, and together they conduct research studies to uncover strategies for fighting poverty and homelessness.

The National Alliance to End Homelessness (NAEH) is a nationwide federation of public, private, and nonprofit organizations operating on the assumption that homelessness can be ended. Alliance members work to advance the implementation of practical, community-based solutions to homelessness.

The National Law Center on Homelessness and Poverty states that its mission is "to alleviate, ameliorate and end homelessness by serving as the legal arm of the nationwide movement to end homelessness," and works to protect the rights of homeless people and to end homelessness in America. It uses three main strategies to achieve this goal: impact litigation, policy advocacy, and public education. The Law Center conducts research studies and distributes the results by publishing fact sheets and a monthly newsletter.

HOMELESS SERVICES

A substantial number of organizations provide services to homeless people across the country. Faith-based organizations have been providing assistance to the needy throughout history, including programs for the homeless. Many secular nonprofits (organizations with no religious affiliation) also provide such assistance. Since 1987, with the passage of the McKinney Act, federal funding targeted for homelessness has been available. It reached a peak of $1.5 billion in 1995, up

TABLE 1.7

Homeless assistance programs by sponsorship, type, and urban or rural status, 1996

Areas and program types	Total number of programs	Percentage by sponsor type			
		Faith-based non-profit	Secular non-profit	Government	For-profit
All program types	39,664	31.8	47.3	13.4	0.6
Central cities					
All	19,388	36.8	45.9	9.9	0.7
Housing	7,894	28.7	53.8	9.6	0.8
Food	6,018	63.4	28.3	2.6	0.2
Health	1,379	7.5	56.8	29.1	0.7
Other	4,097	23.5	53.0	14.6	1.2
Suburbs					
All	7,694	35.1	48.0	7.4	1.1
Housing	3,230	24.2	53.6	8.7	1.8
Food	3,020	53.0	40.0	2.6	0.4
Health	251	2.9	51.0	32.0	2.6
Other	1,192	26.2	52.9	11.0	0.4
Rural areas					
All	12,583	21.9	48.9	22.6	0.2
Housing	4,754	15.5	56.6	18.6	NA
Food	3,965	37.6	49.1	10.3	0.7
Health	1,110	1.8	11.1	68.4	NA
Other	2,754	18.3	50.7	28.6	NA

NA=Not available.
Rows may not added to 100 percent because programs that did not identify their source of sponsorship in the survey are not listed.

SOURCE: Laudan Y. Aron and Patrick T. Sharkey, "Table 1a. NSHAPC Programs by Urban/Rural Status," in *The 1996 National Survey of Homeless Assistance Providers and Clients: A Comparison of Faith-Based and Secular Non-Profit Programs*, The Urban Institute and the U.S. Department of Health and Human Services, March 2002, http://aspe.hhs.gov/hsp/homelessness/NSHAPC02/report.htm (accessed February 9, 2005)

TABLE 1.8

Homeless assistance programs by sponsorship, type, and region, 1996

Regions and program types	Number of programs	Percentage by sponsor type			
		Faith-based non-profit	Secular non-profit	Government	For-profit
All programs	39,664	31.8	47.3	13.4	0.6
Northeast					
All programs	7,097	28.6	53.6	10.1	0.6
Housing	2,870	16.4	61.3	12.9	0.6
Food	2,401	53.1	37.2	3.6	0.5
Health	306	6.6	69.1	14.1	0.7
Other	1,521	17.4	62.1	14.5	0.7
South					
All programs	11,101	39.0	40.7	13.6	0.5
Housing	4,309	30.0	50.3	10.3	1.1
Food	4,113	58.1	32.2	6.1	NA
Health	863	4.7	26.9	57.0	0.1
Other	1,817	33.5	43.5	17.9	0.1
Midwest					
All programs	11,853	31.6	43.7	16.2	0.5
Housing	4,678	24.5	47.6	16.9	0.4
Food	3,945	54.6	34.3	6.7	0.8
Health	736	2.8	39.7	35.5	NA
Other	2,494	16.8	52.6	24.0	0.4
West					
All programs	9,333	25.8	54.6	12.4	1.0
Housing	3,892	21.2	62.9	8.0	1.0
Food	2,478	42.4	51.0	1.7	0.2
Health	816	6.0	34.7	53.8	1.7
Other	2,147	22.3	51.3	17.2	1.6

NA=Not available.
Rows may not added to 100 percent because programs that did not identify their source of sponsorship in the survey are not listed.

SOURCE: Laudan Y. Aron and Patrick T. Sharkey, "Table 1b. NSHAPC Programs by Region of the Country," in *The 1996 National Survey of Homeless Assistance Providers and Clients: A Comparison of Faith-Based and Secular Non-Profit Programs*, The Urban Institute and the U.S. Department of Health and Human Services, March 2002, http://aspe.hhs.gov/hsp/homelessness/NSHAPC02/report.htm (accessed February 8, 2005)

from $350 million in 1987. In January 2005 the U.S. Department of Housing and Urban Development announced that President George W. Bush's proposed Fiscal Year 2006 budget contained a record level of funding for homeless programs, $1.4 billion, an increase of 8.5% over the previous year (News Release, U.S. Department of Housing and Urban Development, HUD No. 05-007, January 25, 2005).

The most recent comprehensive study of assistance programs dates to 1996. In that year, according to the Urban Institute, about half of all assistance programs (19,388) were located in central cities, about one-fifth (7,694) in suburban fringe communities, the rest in rural areas. (See Table 1.7.) All told, 39,664 programs operated nationwide, with the largest number in the South and Midwest and the lowest in the Northeast. (See Table 1.8.) Some of these programs were aimed directly at homeless people, such as homeless shelters. Others were programs open to a wider group of needy people but intended also to serve the homeless (for example, free health clinics for the poor).

Homeless services provide assistance in three major areas: housing, food, and health. In 1996, 40% of the programs offered housing assistance through shelters, permanent housing, or housing vouchers. Provision of food through such outlets as soup kitchens, food pantries, and mobile food distribution accounted for 33% of services. Seven percent of the assistance programs were related to health care, which included not only physical and mental health care but also assistance to people with drug and alcohol addictions as well as care for sufferers of human immunodeficiency virus / acquired immunodeficiency syndrome (HIV/AIDS). Nationwide there were 15,878 housing programs, 13,003 food programs, and 2,739 health programs. An additional 8,043 programs provided assistance on an outreach basis, through drop-in centers and programs offering financial help for housing.

The Urban Institute also studied the utilization rates of homeless services. A section of its landmark December 1999 study, *Homelessness: Programs and the People They Serve*, illustrates the scope of food programs; 26% of the surveyed providers expected between 101 and 299 requests daily, and 11% expected more than 300 contacts a day. For walk-in services and health programs, about half this percentage expected the same volume of clients; 5% of walk-in programs and 4% of health programs expected more than 300 people a day. Housing programs served the lowest number of people per day: on average, only 2% of the programs expected 300 contacts a day. Food, health, and walk-in services (such as job counseling) are, by nature, geared toward multiple returns and have high traffic. Housing programs, by contrast, provide single-client service delivery over a longer period of time. Housing programs are also geared specifically toward helping the homeless while many food, health, and walk-in programs are open to a wider group of people.

Secular nonprofit organizations provided nearly half (47.3%) of all homeless services in 1996. (See Figure 1.2.) Secular organizations also ran the majority of housing programs (54.6%) and "other" services (52.2%), including outreach, drop-in centers, and financial/housing assistance. Faith-based organizations were most active in providing food services (53.1% of all such programs), including food pantries, soup kitchens, and mobile food distribution. Government agencies led in the provision of health services (45.3% of all such services).

Special Population Services

Many homeless assistance programs are open to anyone who wants to use them, but other programs are designed to serve only specific groups of people. The population served may be defined in several different ways: men by themselves, women by themselves, households with children, youth by themselves, battered women, or veterans, for example. The Urban Institute study revealed that 42.1% of all homeless service programs named a specific population group as a focus. After meeting the basic needs of food, shelter, and health care, these homeless programs provided for other special needs. When an emergency shelter had a specific focus, it was

FIGURE 1.2

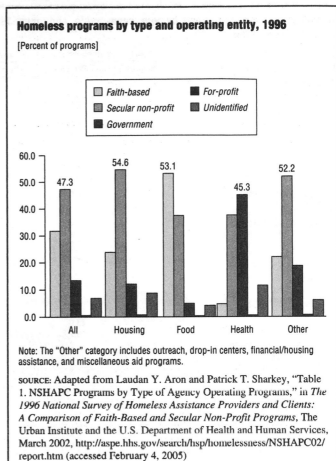

Homeless programs by type and operating entity, 1996

[Percent of programs]

Note: The "Other" category includes outreach, drop-in centers, financial/housing assistance, and miscellaneous aid programs.

SOURCE: Adapted from Laudan Y. Aron and Patrick T. Sharkey, "Table 1. NSHAPC Programs by Type of Agency Operating Programs," in *The 1996 National Survey of Homeless Assistance Providers and Clients: A Comparison of Faith-Based and Secular Non-Profit Programs*, The Urban Institute and the U.S. Department of Health and Human Services, March 2002, http://aspe.hhs.gov/search/hsp/homelessness/NSHAPC02/report.htm (accessed February 4, 2005)

most likely to offer shelter to victims of domestic violence (30.3% of emergency shelters), followed by a focus on chemical dependency (8.6%), on youth (8.3%), or families (5.6%). (See Table 1.9.) The transitional shelters that report specialized assistance programs divide their focus between domestic violence (14%) and chemical dependence (14.4%). Permanent housing programs that target specific population groups focus heavily on those in need of mental health services (15.7% of programs).

TABLE 1.9

Homeless assistance programs by type, sponsorship, and focus, 1996

Program type and focus	Programs by all sponsors		Faith-based non-profit		Secular non-profit		Government	
	Number	Percent	Number	Percent	Number	Percent	Number	Percent
Emergency shelter with	5,320	100%	1,520	100%	3,480	100%	320	100%
No specialization		40.6		63.2		30.4		44.6
Mental health (MH) focus		3.7		2.5		4.1		5.2
Chemical dependency (CD) focus		8.6		15.5		5.3		12.6
MH/CD focus		1.4		2.7		0.9		1.0
HIV/AIDS focus		1.4		1.8		1.3		0.3
Domestic violence focus		30.3		5.2		42.1		20.1
Youth focus		8.3		1.7		11.3		6.8
Family focus		5.6		7.4		4.5		9.3
Transitional shelter with	4,149	100%	1,181	100%	2,535	100%	433	100%
No specialization		43.4		54.8		35.6		57.6
Mental health focus		8.3		3.5		9.6		14.2
Chemical dependency focus		14.4		16.6		15.2		4.2
MH/CD focus		5.2		2.9		6.3		5.2
HIV/AIDS focus		3.1		1.2		4.2		1.7
Domestic violence focus		14.0		7.7		18.2		6.6
Youth focus		4.4		5.6		4.6		0.2
Family focus		7.1		7.6		6.3		10.2
Permanent housing with	1,719	100%	205	100%	980	100%	534	100%
No specialization		63.6		61.6		52.8		84.2
Mental health focus		15.7		8.8		22.1		6.6
Chemical dependency focus		5.2		11.0		5.2		2.9
MH/CD focus		5.8		5.6		7.8		2.2
HIV/AIDS focus		9.8		13.0		12.1		4.2
Soup kitchen with	3,284	100%	2,131	100%	1,057	100%		NA
No specialization		83.2		84.9		79.4		NA
Mental health focus		6.1		4.4		9.8		NA
Chemical dependency focus		6.7		7.6		5.2		NA
Family focus		2.4		2.9		1.6		NA
HIV/AIDS focus		1.5		0.2		4.0		NA

NA=Not available

SOURCE: Adapted from Laudan Y. Aron and Patrick T. Sharkey, "Table 6. What Special Focus Do NSHAPC Programs Have?" in *The 1996 National Survey of Homeless Assistance Providers and Clients: A Comparison of Faith-Based and Secular Non-Profit Programs*, The Urban Institute and the U.S. Department of Health and Human Services, March 2002, http://aspe.hhs.gov/search/hsp/homelessness/NSHAPC02/report.htm (accessed February 4, 2005)

CHAPTER 2

THE DEMOGRAPHICS OF HOMELESSNESS

THE AUTHORITATIVE ESTIMATES

Broad national assessments of homelessness were undertaken by several agencies and organizations during the 1980s and mid-1990s, including *A Report to the Secretary on the Homeless and Emergency Shelters* (Washington, DC: U.S. Department of Housing and Urban Development, 1984), *America's Homeless: Numbers, Characteristics, and Programs that Serve Them* (Martha Burt and Barbara Cohen, Washington, DC: Urban Institute, 1989), and *Homelessness: Programs and the People They Serve, Findings of the National Survey of Homeless Assistance Providers and Clients*, (Martha Burt et al., Washington, DC: Urban Institute Report to the Interagency Council on the Homeless, December 1999). In 2002 Burt and other researchers summarized the difficulty of addressing homelessness without a continuing census or other governmental program to track the homeless population in *Evaluation of Continuums of Care for Homeless People* (Washington, DC: U.S. Department of Housing and Urban Development, May 2002). The report notes that:

> Basically, there are only three sources or original data on which to base estimates of incidence (the number of people homeless on a single day) for the nation as a whole—HUD's 1984 effort (HUD, 1984), the Urban Institute's 1987 study (Burt and Cohen, 1989), and the 1996 National Survey of Homeless Providers and Clients (Burt, Aron, and Lee, 2001). Any national estimates offered by anyone for any years other than 1984, 1987, and 1996 are projections or manipulations of one of these three data sources, and include assumptions of population change or growth that are not grounded in data. HUD's 1984 study was based on a survey of providers, who supplied their best guesses as to the size of the homeless population in their cities. Only the 1987 and 1996 studies are based on statistically reliable samples of homeless people using homeless assistance programs. Using these three data sources, the number

of people homeless at any one time appears to have grown substantially from the mid-1980s until the mid-1990s—from 250,000–350,000 in 1984 (HUD's "most reliable range") to 500,000–600,000 in 1987, to 640,000–840,000 in 1996. Best guesses or projections of the number of people homeless during the course of a year come from various sources. . . . These estimates, using different approaches, nevertheless converge on figures that between 2.5 and 3.5 million people (including children) experience at least one night of homelessness within a given year.

Even these data, considered by the government to be reliable, are based on very small samples. The 1996 data, the most recent and most widely used, were based on interviews with 6,300 homeless program representatives, held in February 1996, and interviews with 4,200 users of homeless programs conducted in October 1996. The total number of people homeless at some point in the year 1996 was derived by projection from this sample. While such methods of estimating are common in statistical analysis, they also show that current knowledge about homelessness is, at best, partial.

HOW NUMBERS ARE USED

The ordinary citizen, hearing of the homeless, envisions people, including children, who live on the street permanently and sleep in cardboard boxes under bridges or in cars. There are, of course, people in this category, but they are the minority among the homeless. HUD has labeled such people the chronically homeless and estimates their number at around 150,000, close to the number of people counted by the Census Bureau as inhabiting emergency and transitional shelters in the 2000 census count (170,706 individuals). Most of the homeless are not chronically homeless but are temporarily without a residence. After some period of homelessness, they find permanent shelter or move in with relatives; people who have moved in with family as well as people who are

TABLE 2.1

Number likely to be homeless at least once during the year, 1996

	New homeless spells begun in last week	Average week estimate	Annual projection
	A	B	C
February 1996	52,000	842,000	3.5 million
October 1996	36,900	444,000	2.3 million

Note: The projection is developed by taking column A times 51 weeks and adding the result to column B. Column B represents the estimated constant population of homeless in any one week. The assumption is that a population of the size shown in column A is continuously passing into and also out of homeless status throughout the year. Data for February were based on the estimates of homeless program employees, data for October on interviews with the homeless.

SOURCE: "Number Likely to be Homeless at Least Once in a Given Year," in *America's Homeless II: Populations and Services*, Urban Institute, February 2000, http://www.urban.org/UploadedPDF/900344_AmericasHomelessll.pdf (accessed February 10, 2005)

"doubled up" are also counted as homeless by some programs and homeless advocates.

A more accurate definition of the homeless population is the group of people who are, on any day, without proper shelter. When agencies or the media cite numbers in the 600,000–800,000 range, they mean the size of the homeless population at any one point in time. Individuals are continuously joining this population while others are leaving it. If all people who are homeless at some point during a given year were counted, the number would reach between 2.5 and 3.5 million individuals, as indicated by HUD in *Evaluation of Continuums of Care for Homeless People*.

The manner in which the annual projections for 1996 were derived is shown in Table 2.1. The data for October, projected from counts of homeless services seekers, show that an estimated 36,900 individuals began spells of homelessness during the week surveyed, while the total number of people in the homeless population in any one week was estimated to be 444,000. The annual projection assumed that each week, 36,900 became homeless and an equal number passed out of the homeless status. Multiplying 36,900 by the fifty-one weeks remaining in the year, and then adding that total to the average homeless population in a week, produced the 2.3 million count of people who were homeless at least once in 1996. The number does not mean that there were 2.3 million homeless during the entire span of 1996.

Counting Children

Sometimes stories in the media cite 600,000 homeless and one million homeless children (see for instance "Are Shelters the Answer to Family Homelessness," *USA Today*, January 1, 2003). Such statements double count the homeless by using two different sources of incompatible data. Under the McKinney-Vento Homeless Assistance Act, the U.S. Department of Education (USDE) is required to file a report on homeless children served by the act. USDE obtains the data from school districts; school districts use different methods of estimation. In its 2000 report to Congress (*Education for Homeless Children and Youth Program*, Washington, DC), USDE estimated that 930,032 children experienced homelessness at some point during the year. This number was much higher than the number of children who were homeless on a particular night during the year.

GROWTH PATTERNS

People living below the poverty threshold decreased between 1984 and 1989 from 33.7 to 31.5 million, according to the U.S. Census Bureau. This population then increased to 39.3 million by 1993, declining after that year to 31.6 million people in 2000 during the boom of the 1990s, and rising again to 35.9 million in 2003. (See Table 2.2.)

Whether using a low or high estimate of the number of homeless people, the number of homeless increased sharply between 1984 and 1987, at the same time that the poverty rate was decreasing. The number of homeless people continued to increase gradually until 1996, even as the poverty rate declined again in the 1990s (see Martha Burt, et al., *Evaluation of Continuums of Care for Homeless People*).

No strong correlation between poverty and homelessness can be seen in this data; however, there is a definite relationship between homelessness and poverty. Most likely, the number of homeless people were underestimated in the early years.

Homeless counts have been based on surveys centered on facilities that provide services to the homeless (such as shelters and soup kitchens). These are permanent sites where some contact with the homeless is possible. The number of such facilities has increased substantially since the passage of the McKinney Act. Shelter and housing for the homeless increased from an estimated 275,000 beds in 1988 to 607,000 beds in 1996; big city food service programs increased from 97,000 meals to 380,100 meals between 1987 and 1996 (*America's Homeless II: Populations and Services*, Washington, DC: Urban Institute, February 2000). With an ever-larger base of support facilities, the ability of researchers to reach more and more precise estimates of populations served has improved.

Trend data on the growth or decline of homelessness, comparable in precision to data collected by the Census Bureau on poverty levels, are still not available. Other but more limited data support the relationship between poverty and homelessness. Data collected by the Census Bureau on the population in emergency and transitional shelters show

TABLE 2.2

Number of people in poverty, 1984–2003

	All people			People in families		
				All families		
	Total	Below poverty level		Total	Below poverty level	
Year		Number	Percent		Number	Percent
All races						
2003	287,699	35,861	12.5	238,903	25,684	10.8
2002	285,317	34,570	12.1	236,921	24,534	10.4
2001	281,475	32,907	11.7	233,911	23,215	9.9
2000	278,944	31,581	11.3	231,909	22,347	9.6
1999	276,208	32,791	11.9	230,789	23,830	10.3
1998	271,059	34,476	12.7	227,229	25,370	11.2
1997	268,480	35,574	13.3	225,369	26,217	11.6
1996	266,218	36,529	13.7	223,955	27,376	12.2
1995	263,733	36,425	13.8	222,792	27,501	12.3
1994	261,616	38,059	14.5	221,430	28,985	13.1
1993	259,278	39,265	15.1	219,489	29,927	13.6
1992	256,549	38,014	14.8	217,936	28,961	13.3
1991	251,192	35,708	14.2	212,723	27,143	12.8
1990	248,644	33,585	13.5	210,967	25,232	12.0
1989	245,992	31,528	12.8	209,515	24,066	11.5
1988	243,530	31,745	13.0	208,056	24,048	11.6
1987	240,982	32,221	13.4	206,877	24,725	12.0
1986	238,554	32,370	13.6	205,459	24,754	12.0
1985	236,594	33,064	14.0	203,963	25,729	12.6
1984	233,816	33,700	14.4	202,288	26,458	13.1

SOURCE: Adapted from "Poverty Status of People by Family Relationship, Race, and Hispanic Origin: 1959 to 2003," in *Historical Poverty Tables*, U.S. Census Bureau, 2003, http://www.census.gov/hhes/poverty/histpov/hstpov2.html (accessed February 10, 2005)

a decline in that population from 178,638 in the 1990 census to a total of 170,706 in the 2000 census. In that period the economy was exhibiting strong growth.

Table 2.3 shows these data together with regional breakdowns of the homeless population. In 2000, 30.7% of the sheltered population were found in the Northeast, a region with 19% of the total U.S. population. The West also had a disproportionate share of homeless people in shelters; 27.8% of the sheltered were found in the region, yet it had only 22.5% of the total population. The Midwest and the South had smaller shares of the sheltered than of their total populations, which might suggest that a greater proportion of people on the coasts were homeless than people in the middle of the country, or it may suggest that a greater proportion of homeless people on the coasts were sheltered.

According to the 2000 census, New York state had 31,856 persons in emergency and transitional shelters. Data for New York City alone, from the Coalition for the Homeless, showed a month-by-month pattern of increasing homelessness during a period of worsening economic conditions. In January 2002, 31,064 people were sheltered; a year later, the number had risen to 38,463. By January 2005 those numbers had dropped somewhat, to 36,599. Over 15,000 of these people were children. While the problem of homelessness had improved somewhat in the previous two years, the number of people housed in shelters for the homeless was still

TABLE 2.3

Population in emergency and transitional shelters, 1990 and 2000

| | Population in shelters | | | | Total 2000 U.S. population |
| | 1990 | | 2000 | | |
Area	Number	Percent	Number	Percent	Percent
United States	178,638	100.0	170,706	100.0	100.0
Region					
Northeast	60,077	33.6	52,369	30.7	19.0
Midwest	27,245	15.3	28,438	16.7	22.9
South	42,407	23.7	42,471	24.9	35.6
West	48,909	27.4	47,428	27.8	22.5

SOURCE: Annetta C. Smith and Denise I. Smith, "Table 1. Population in Emergency and Transitional Shelters for the United States, Regions, States, and Puerto Rico: 1990 and 2000," in *Emergency and Transitional Shelter Population: 2000*, U.S. Census Bureau, October 2001, http://www.census.gov/prod/2001pubs/censr01-2.pdf (accessed February 11, 2005)

extraordinarily high compared with the previous twenty years.

Needs Profiled by Mayors

In *Hunger and Homelessness Survey: A Status Report on Hunger and Homelessness in America's Cities, A 27-City Survey, December 2004*, the U.S. Conference of Mayors presented sixteen years of survey data profiling needs in urban areas. (See Table 2.4.)

Requests for emergency shelter increased in the cities surveyed in 2004 by an average of 6%, with 70% of the

TABLE 2.4

Hunger and homelessness in large urban areas, 1989–2004

Indicator	1989	1990	1991	1992	1993	1994	1995	1996	1997	1998	1999	2000	2001	2002	2003	2004
Hunger																
Increase in demand for emergency food	19%	22%	26%	18%	13%	12%	9%	11%	16%	14%	18%	17%	23%	19%	17%	14%
Cities in which demand for food increased	96%	90%	93%	96%	83%	83%	72%	83%	86%	78%	85%	83%	93%	100%	88%	96%
Increase in demand by families for food assistance	14%	20%	26%	14%	13%	14%	10%	10%	13%	14%	15%	16%	19%	17%	18%	13%
Portion of those requesting food assistance who are families with children	61%	75%	68%	68%	67%	64%	63%	62%	58%	61%	58%	62%	54%	48%	59%	56%
Demand for emergency food unmet	17%	14%	17%	21%	16%	15%	18%	18%	19%	21%	21%	13%	14%	16%	14%	20%
Cities in which food assistance facilities must turn people away	73%	86%	79%	68%	68%	73%	59%	50%	71%	47%	54%	46%	33%	32%	56%	48%
Cities which expect demand for emergency food to increase next year	89%	100%	100%	89%	100%	81%	96%	96%	92%	96%	84%	71%	100%	100%	87%	88%
Homelessness																
Increase in demand for emergency shelter	25%	24%	13%	14%	10%	13%	11%	5%	3%	11%	12%	15%	13%	19%	13%	6%
Cities in which demand increased	89%	80%	89%	88%	81%	80%	63%	71%	59%	72%	69%	76%	81%	88%	80%	70%
Demand for emergency shelter unmet	22%	19%	15%	23%	25%	21%	19%	20%	27%	26%	25%	23%	37%	30%	30%	23%
Cities in which shelters must turn people away	59%	70%	74%	75%	77%	72%	82%	81%	88%	67%	73%	56%	44%	56%	84%	81%
Cities which expect demand for shelter to increase next year	93%	97%	100%	93%	88%	71%	100%	100%	100%	93%	92%	72%	100%	100%	88%	88%
Composition of homeless population																
Single men	46%	51%	50%	55%	43%	48%	46%	45%	47%	45%	43%	44%	40%	41%	41%	41%
Families with children	36%	34%	35%	32%	34%	39%	36%	38%	36%	38%	36%	36%	40%	41%	40%	40%
Single women	14%	12%	12%	11%	11%	11%	14%	14%	14%	14%	13%	13%	14%	13%	14%	14%
Unaccompanied youth	4%	3%	3%	2%	4%	3%	4%	3%	4%	3%	4%	7%	4%	5%	5%	5%
Children	25%	23%	24%	22%	30%	26%	25%	27%	25%	25%	na	na	na	na	na	na
Severely mentally ill	25%	28%	29%	28%	27%	26%	23%	24%	27%	24%	19%	22%	22%	23%	23%	23%
Substance abusers	44%	38%	40%	41%	48%	43%	46%	43%	43%	38%	31%	37%	34%	32%	30%	30%
Employed	24%	24%	18%	17%	18%	19%	20%	18%	17%	22%	21%	26%	20%	22%	17%	17%
Veterans	26%	26%	23%	18%	21%	23%	23%	19%	22%	22%	14%	15%	11%	10%	10%	10%

na=Not available

SOURCE: "Hunger and Homelessness in America's Cities: A Sixteen-Year Comparison of Data," in *Hunger and Homelessness Survey: A Status Report on Hunger and Homelessness in America's Cities: A 27-City Survey, December 2004*, U.S. Conference of Mayors-Sodexho USA, December 2004, http://www.usmayors.org/uscm/hungersurvey/2004/onlinereport/HungerAndHomelessnessReport2004.pdf (accessed February 2, 2005)

cities reporting an increase. The report also stated that the demand for shelter by homeless families grew by slightly more than the 7% expansion of the overall demand. Although demand for shelter continued to be on the rise, it increased at a slower rate than it had since 1997.

An average of 23% of the requests for emergency shelter by all homeless people went unmet in 2004, a decrease from the previous year. More than four out of five cities had to turn people away from shelters at some point during the year. People remained homeless an average of eight months in the survey cities. Almost half (46%) of the city mayors said that the length of time people stayed homeless increased during 2004. Officials in 88% of the cities surveyed expected that requests for emergency shelter by homeless individuals and families would increase in 2005.

Mayors view a lack of affordable housing as the leading cause of homelessness, as cited by twenty-four of twenty-seven cities in the Conference of Mayors survey. In general they see insufficient housing options for low-income people as a root cause of homelessness. In the surveyed cities, applicants waited, on average, twenty months for public housing, and 59% of the surveyed cities had stopped accepting applications for at least one assisted housing program. High housing costs also contribute to the homelessness problem. The city officials estimated that low-income households spent an average of 45% of their income on housing.

Philip Mangano, Executive Director of the Interagency Council on Homelessness, in a keynote address on May 20, 2003, at the Policy Academy in Chicago, blamed the lack of affordable housing on what he called "affluenza." He suggested that the affluenza of the mid-1980s and 1990s caused the destruction of older, affordable housing units and their replacement with "artificial housing and neighborhoods implanted like pacemakers."

The National League of Cities

In 2004 the National League of Cities surveyed a random sample of the nation's municipal elected officials regarding issues and problems they faced in governing American cities. (See Table 2.5.) When asked to indicate whether various conditions had improved or worsened in their cities in the previous year, 20% of

TABLE 2.5

Change in local conditions over past year and assessment of seriousness of problems, 2004

	a) Change in condition since last year			b) Current status of condition		
	Improved	Worsened	No change	Major problem	Moderate problem	Minor/no problem
A. Violent crime	30%	12%	54%	7%	33%	51%
B. Unemployment	18	46	31	17	44	29
C. Impacts of unfunded mandates/preemption	1	63	30	32	44	15
D. City fiscal condition	21	43	31	21	39	30
E. Cable TV rates/broadband availability	20	38	37	10	32	58
F. Family stability	7	19	68	8	35	47
G. Race/ethnic relations	20	9	67	4	32	55
H. Vitality of neighborhoods	40	10	47	7	35	49
I. Police/community relations	44	7	44	4	22	65
J. Overall economic conditions	26	39	31	19	43	28
K. Poverty	6	28	61	13	37	40
L. Volunteerism/community services	36	10	48	3	23	64
M. Availability of quality affordable housing	24	24	46	19	39	33
N. Quality of public education	30	22	44	20	27	43
O. Homelessness	5	20	70	8	25	56
P. City relationships w/community groups	48	7	41	3	19	70
Q. Youth violence and crime	11	21	62	9	37	45
R. Regional/area-wide problem solving	36	17	41	12	40	38
S. Infrastructure	38	25	32	17	44	28
T. Traffic congestion	10	50	35	26	39	26
U. Local environmental quality	20	10	64	5	34	51
V. Federal relations with your city	19	14	61	7	29	54
W. State relations with your city	23	26	46	19	31	41
X. Public school relations with your city	33	10	52	6	23	61
Y. Drugs/alcohol abuse	5	28	60	18	42	30
Z. Vitality of downtown/main street	48	16	30	15	41	34
AA. Availability of child care	15	10	67	8	27	53
BB. Recreation	44	9	42	6	22	62
CC. Civility in public life	19	15	5	95	22	63
DD. Family-friendliness of city	38	4	53	3	13	75
EE. Overall sense of "community"	42	7	46	3	26	62
FF. Efficiency of municipal service delivery	41	8	47	3	21	66
GG. Public transportation/transit service	21	18	55	15	32	43
HH. Cost and availability of health services	8	58	28	38	32	21
II. Homeland Security/Emergency Preparedness	41	9	44	11	36	43
JJ. Availability/Quality of After-school programs	21	13	58	10	33	46

SOURCE: Christiana Brennan and Christopher Hoene, "Specific Local Conditions," in *The State of America's Cities 2004: The Annual Opinion Survey*, National League of Cities, 2004, http://www.nlc.org/content/Files/RMPstateAmerCitiesrpt04.pdf (accessed February 11, 2005)

the officials reported that homelessness had worsened in their cities, while only 5% said homelessness had improved. Eight percent believed homelessness was a major problem in their cities; a quarter believed it was a moderate problem.

A quarter of city officials surveyed stated that the availability of quality affordable housing had decreased in the past year; another quarter believed the availability of housing had increased. Almost one in five thought the lack of affordable housing was a major problem in their cities, and another 39% believed it was a moderate problem. Officials also believed other conditions affecting homelessness had worsened; 46% believed unemployment had worsened, 39% believed overall economic conditions had worsened, and 28% believed poverty had worsened during the previous year. When officials were asked to list the top three "most deteriorated" conditions in their cities (see Table 2.6), homelessness was not even in the top ten, as it had been in previous years, but "availability of quality affordable housing" ranked seventh at 13% percent.

PROFILES OF THE HOMELESS
Gender and Race

Studies of homeless people and surveys of officials knowledgeable about homeless clients conducted in the 1990s and 2000s have shown similar patterns of gender and racial data for the homeless, although the percentages varied from study to study.

Data collected for the 2004 U.S. Conference of Mayors survey showed that in almost all cities surveyed, single males greatly outnumbered single females among the homeless. (See Table 2.7.) Single males were most overrepresented in Nashville, Tennessee (79% of the homeless), followed closely by Santa Monica, California (72%), Miami, Florida (70%), and San Francisco, California (69%). Chicago, Illinois, had the highest proportion of single women among homeless individuals (43%). Women most likely headed the large percentage of single-parent families; for example, in Kansas City, Missouri, 100% of the homeless population belonged to families, and 88% of those families were headed by a

TABLE 2.6

Most deteriorated city conditions, 2004

1. Traffic	27%
2. Unemployment	22%
3. Impacts of unfunded mandates/preemption	22%
4. Overall economic conditions	22%
5. City fiscal conditions	21%
6. Cost and availability of health services	20%
7. Availability of quality affordable housing	13%
8. State relations with your city	13%
9. Infrastructure	11%
10. Drugs/alcohol abuse	10%
11. Quality of public education	8%
12. Youth violence and crime	8%
13. Public transportation/ transit service	7%
14. Violent crime	6%
15. Cable TV rates/broadband availability	6%
16. Regional/area-wide problem solving	6%
17. Vitality of downtown/main street	4%
18. Civility in public life	4%
19. Poverty	4%
20. Vitality of neighborhoods	4%
21. Family stability	3%
22. Federal relations with your city	3%
23. Public school relations with your city	3%
24. Race/ ethnic relations	2%
25. Local environmental quality	2%
26. Availability of child care	2%
27. Homeland security/emergency preparedness	2%
28. Volunteerism	1%
29. Homelessness	1%
30. Recreation	1%
31. Overall sense of "community"	1%
32. Efficiency of municipal service delivery	1%
33. Police/community relations	1%
34. City relations with community groups	0%
35. Family-friendliness of city	0%
36. Availability of quality after-school programs	0%

SOURCE: Christiana Brennan and Christopher Hoene, "Most Deteriorated City Conditions," in *The State of America's Cities 2004: The Annual Opinion Survey of Municipal Elected Officials*, National League of Cities, 2004, http://www.nlc.org/content/Files/RMPstateAmerCitiesrpt04.pdf (accessed February 11, 2005)

single parent. Data from all twenty-seven cities surveyed suggest that homeless adult men are most often not part of family groups, and homeless adult women are most often responsible for one or more children.

The racial composition of the homeless varied from city to city in the Conference of Mayors survey. (See Table 2.7.) Whites were the largest group in Burlington, Vermont (77%), Salt Lake City, Utah (63%), Portland, Oregon (62%), Cedar Rapids, Iowa (61%), Santa Monica (52%), Louisville, Kentucky (44%), Denver, Colorado (39%), and Seattle, Washington (34%). Hispanics were the largest group in San Antonio, Texas (45%). In all other cities surveyed, African-Americans were the largest group among the homeless, with the highest percentages in Philadelphia, Pennsylvania (77%), Chicago (75%), Norfolk, Virginia (73%), and Trenton, New Jersey (72%).

The Association of Gospel Rescue Missions (AGRM), formerly International Union of Gospel Missions (IUGM), has surveyed the homeless population at more than 100 missions serving inner cities. The AGRM surveys are based on large numbers of homeless served. In 2004, for example, 20,500 homeless were surveyed at 154 rescue missions. AGRM data showed that men were 82% of the homeless in 1994 but 77% in 2004. (See Table 1.3 in Chapter 1.) Homeless women have been rising as a proportion of the homeless population at a steady rate for more than a decade.

According to an AGRM survey in 1994, the racial/ethnic composition of the homeless population they served was 42% white, 44% African-American, 12% Hispanic, 2% Asian, and 4% Native American. By 2004 the proportion of white homeless people had risen to 44%; the African-American proportion and Hispanic proportion had dropped to 40% and 10% respectively, and the Asian and Native American proportion had stayed essentially the same. (See Table 1.3 in Chapter 1.)

In the Urban Institute's 1996 survey, 68% of the homeless population were male, and 32% were female. Forty-one percent of the homeless were white, 40% black, 11% Hispanic, 8% Native American, and 1% of other races. (See Table 1.4 in Chapter 1.)

The surveys thus exhibit similar patterns. More of the homeless were male than female, but these proportions have been gradually changing. While in the 1996 homeless survey, 40% of the homeless were African-American, according to the Census Bureau's population estimate for July 2003, only 12.7% of the total population was African-American (National Population Estimates, "Annual Estimates of the Population by Sex, Race and Hispanic or Latino Origin for the United States: April 1, 2000 to July 1, 2003," NC-EST2003-03, U.S. Census Bureau). African-Americans were thus overrepresented among the ranks of the homeless. Hispanic representation among the homeless was near their share of total population (13.7%). Native Americans were homeless in greater proportion to their share of total population (1.2%), and Asians were homeless in lower proportion to their population (4.5%).

Family Structure

According to the 1996 Urban Institute study, 62% of homeless men and 16% of homeless women were single—meaning they were homeless without a spouse or children. (See Table 1.4 in Chapter 1). The 2004 Conference of Mayors survey found that 40% of homeless people were in families with children, 41% were single men, 14% were single women, and 5% were unaccompanied youth. (See Table 2.4.) Since 1989 the proportion of men on their own among the homeless population had declined, while the proportion of families with children had risen. Data from the Conference of Mayors survey show city-by-city estimates of children as a percent of homeless family members. (See Table 2.7.) Values range

TABLE 2.7

Composition of the homeless population, 2003–04

City	Families	Men	Women	Youth	African-American	White	Hispanic	Asian	Native American	Mentally Ill	Substance abusers	Employed	Veterans	Single parent families	Family members who are children
Boston	38	53	8	1	42	39	18	0	1	30	46	44	17	90	59
Burlington	43	34	4	19	8	77	5	0.5	3	20	18	28	3	40	60
Cedar Rapids	62	17	15	6	27	61	2	1	2	43	32	50	13	83	65
Charleston	26	65	8	1	49	46	5	0	0	42	33	69	32	79	30
Charlotte	45	29	23	3	65	23	7	2.5	2.5	28	55	32	25	83	8.2
Chicago	12	44	43	3.5	75	13	3.7	0.4	1.5	31	61	25	2.9	79	67
Cleveland	25	54	20	1	0	0	0	0	4	25	40	20	18	98	70
Denver	58	28	11	3	35	39	21	1	0	30	50	30	14	80	42
Detroit	0	0	0	0	0	0	0	0	0	0	0	0	0	0	0
Kansas City	100	0	0	0	0	0	0	0	0	26	44	0	10	88	61
Los Angeles	41	37	16	5	50	14	33	2	0.1	16	34	16	15	61	39
Louisville Metro	16	56	18	10	43	44	4	1	7	14	11	22	19	38	9.6
Miami	11	70	19	0	46	31	22	1	0.2	0	0	0	0	90	65
Nashville	8	79	13	1	53	42	4	1	0	11	15	12	13	90	50
New Orleans	35	44	16	5	67	29	2	0.5	1	25	42	22	25	65	55
Norfolk	33	56	11	0	73	24	3	0	0	10	15	16	14	91	66
Philadelphia	50	38	12	0	77	13	5	0	0	0	0	0	0	93	69
Phoenix	41	59	0	0	0	0	0	0	0	0	0	0	0	0	0
Portland	39	38	21	2	19	62	14	2	3	18	30	12	8	65	63
Providence	0	0	0	0	0	0	0	0	0	0	0	0	0	0	25
Salt Lake City	51	36	13	0.02	7	63	21	1	3	8	15	0	8	78	62
San Antonio	38	46	12	4	19	35	45	0.5	0.5	19	13	26	13	47	43
San Francisco	4	69	26	1	53	21	23	0.5	0.5	0	0	0	0	60	55
Santa Monica	0	72	28	0	24	52	19	2	3	0	0	0	0	0	0
Seattle	24	46	13	2	29	34	10	2	3	22	26	17	0	78	24
St. Paul	20	60	14	0	47	36	9	1	5	0	0	0	0	78	61
Trenton	45	35	13	1	72	21	6	0	1	7	8	0	0	92	75

SOURCE: "Composition of the Homeless Population," in *Hunger and Homelessness Survey: A Status Report on Hunger and Homelessness in America's Cities: A 27-City Survey, December 2004,* U.S. Conference of Mayors–Sodexho USA, December 2004, http://www.usmayors.org/uscm/hungersurvey/2004/onlinereport/HungerAndHomelessnessReport2004.pdf (accessed February 2, 2005)

from 8.2% of family members in Charlotte, North Carolina, to 75% in Trenton, New Jersey.

The AGRM survey presents data about the family structure of homeless families. (See Table 1.3 in Chapter 1.) According to the survey, 16% of homeless families in 2004 were couples without children; 60% were women with children; 7% were men with children; and 16% were "intact" families—couples with children.

Age

The Urban Institute, in its comprehensive 1996 study (see Table 1.4 in Chapter 1), found that 38% of the homeless were between thirty-five and forty-four years of age, 25% were between twenty-five and thirty-four, and 17% were between forty-five and fifty-four. The AGRM survey for 2004 showed that 18% of the homeless were between twenty-six and thirty-five, 30% were between thirty-six and forty-five, and 29% were between forty-six and sixty-five. (See Table 1.3 in Chapter 1.) The largest group in both surveys was the thirty-five–forty-five group, adults in their middle years.

Education

When the Urban Institute investigated the education of homeless people, it found that 38% had less than a high school diploma, 34% had completed high school, and 28% had some education beyond high school. (See Table 1.4 in Chapter 1.) The homeless were less educated than the population as a whole. In 1996, 18% of the population had less than a high school education, 34% had a high school diploma, and 48% had some education beyond high school.

Military Background

The Urban Institute study also reported that 23% of the homeless were veterans (See Table 1.4 in Chapter 1.) Among homeless men, 33% were veterans; only 13% of the general population were veterans. According to the Veterans Health Administration (VHA), in 1990 veterans were present in shelters at a rate of 149 per 100,000 compared with 126 per 100,000 of other males (*Data on the Socioeconomic Status of Veterans and on VA Program Usage*, Washington, DC, May 2001).

The National Coalition for Homeless Veterans, citing Department of Veterans Affairs (VA) sources, stated on its Web site in 2005 that of homeless veterans, 98% were male and 2% were female. Forty-five percent of homeless veterans had mental illness and half had abused drugs or alcohol. An estimated 299,321 were homeless on any given night; over the course of a year; more than 500,000 were homeless at least one night over the course of a year. The majority were single. Almost half (47%) of homeless veterans served in Vietnam.

The National Coalition for Homeless Veterans conducted a small survey of nineteen homeless veteran service providers to determine the impact of the wars in Iraq and Afghanistan on homeless veteran numbers ("Survey Confirms 'War on Terror' Veterans Are Seeking Homeless Assistance," National Coalition for Homeless Veterans, January 12, 2005). The survey found that those nineteen service providers had served sixty-seven veterans from these wars. Linda Boone, executive director of the organization, stated that these veterans were likely to request assistance sooner and in greater numbers than did veterans of other foreign wars.

CHILDREN AND YOUTHS

Homeless children and youths have always received special attention from the public and from welfare agencies. In the terminology of the nineteenth century, children are considered "worthy" poor, because if they were homeless, they did nothing to deserve that status.

Estimates provided by the U.S. Conference of Mayors provide some indication of the proportion of children and runaway teens (unaccompanied youth) among the homeless population. (See Table 2.4.) In 2004, 40% of the homeless population in the twenty-seven surveyed cities were in family groups. The Conference of Mayors survey did not provide an estimate of the percentage of the homeless who were children in 2004, but in 1998 one-quarter of all homeless people in surveyed cities were children. Between 1989 and 1998, the percentage of children in the homeless population never dropped below 22% and rose to a high of 30% in 1993.

The Conference of Mayors also surveyed the proportion of "unaccompanied youth" in the homeless population; in 2004 these teens made up 5% of the homeless population in surveyed cities. The proportion of unaccompanied youth stayed relatively steady between 3% and 5% between 1989 and 2004, with a low of 2% in 1992 and a high of 7% in 2000. Children and unaccompanied youths made up about 29% of the homeless population throughout the period.

The U.S. Department of Education (USDE) collects estimates of homeless children from selected school district records. The data exclude infants but include some children of preschool age. USDE's tallies showed a total of 930,232 homeless children and youth, 866,899 of whom reported residence status in 2000. (See Table 2.8.) The number of children who lived in shelters (temporary or otherwise), were unsheltered, or had unknown residency was 364,391. All data were for the entire year. These data come close to 1996 estimates on the total population that was homeless during some part of the year. If children represent 29% of the homeless population based on U.S. Conference of Mayors estimates, the range of total

TABLE 2.8

Homeless children and youth, 2000

	Enrollment and attendance				Shelter status reported		
	Estimated number	Enrolled	Attending			Total	% of total
Not specified	9,999			Sheltered		306,404	35.3
Pre-K	257,076	40,265		Doubled-up		301,195	34.7
Elementary	343,340	305,920	271,906	Unsheltered		38,732	4.5
Junior high	155,964	135,785	119,596	Other*		201,313	23.2
High school	163,867	138,794	128,340	Unknown		19,255	2.2
Total	**930,232**	**620,764**	**519,842**	**Total**		**866,899**	**100.0**

*Includes other temporary shelter such as motels.

SOURCE: Adapted from "Table 1. Homeless Children and Youth By Grade Level—Estimated Totals, and Numbers Enrolled and Regularly Attending School," and "Table 2. Primary Nighttime Residence of Homeless Children and Youth," in *Education for Homeless Children and Youth Program, Report to Congress, Fiscal Year 2000*, U.S. Department of Education, Office of Elementary and Secondary Education, 2001, http://www.serve.org/nche/downloads/2000_congress .doc (accessed February 11, 2005)

homeless of all ages was somewhere between 1.2 and 3.2 million people in 2000, depending on whether 364,391 or 930,200 children are counted as homeless.

Table 2.8 also shows that of total children estimated by school districts to be homeless in 2000, only a portion were enrolled and even a smaller number attended school regularly. Among the estimated 343,340 homeless elementary students, 305,920 (89.1%) were enrolled and 271,906 (79.2%) attended regularly. Unfortunately, even when homeless children do attend school, they have less than optimal conditions for educational achievement.

An example of the poor educational achievement of homeless youths is shown in a 2002 study of unaccompanied homeless youths conducted in Monterey County, California. Twenty-one percent of sixteen-year-olds, 22% of seventeen-year-olds, 33% of eighteen-year-olds, 51% of nineteen-year-olds, 59% of twenty-year-olds, and 70% of twenty-one-year-olds were below grade level, according to its findings. Only 13% of the homeless youths in the study had a high school diploma or GED. The remaining 87% were performing below grade level.

The study showed that many homeless youth aged fourteen to twenty-one had been in the foster care system and had become homeless after emancipation. Although this study was only a countywide survey, it confirmed that children formerly in foster care are represented in higher numbers among the homeless than in the population at large. Ten percent of the unaccompanied homeless youths in the Monterey County study were at one time in the foster care system, while only 3% of the general population aged fourteen to twenty-one were ever in foster care.

DURATION AND RECURRENCE

Most homeless people will become homeless again. The Urban Institute's 1996 study showed that 51% of all homeless persons surveyed in that year had been homeless before. The AGRM found in their 2004 survey that 65% of the homeless had been homeless before, 26% had been homeless once before, 18% had been homeless twice before, and 21% had been homeless three or more times before. (See Table 1.3 in Chapter 1).

Thirty-nine percent of homeless studied by the Urban Institute in 1996 had been homeless less than six months; six out of ten had been homeless for more than half a year. Sixty-two percent of the homeless surveyed by the AGRM in 2004 had been homeless less than one year; more than one-third had been homeless for more than a year.

These studies confirm that homelessness is usually a recurring experience and lasts for months at a time, suggesting that programs that help the homeless do not uniformly help clients solve the fundamental problems that can lead to life on the streets.

THE RURAL HOMELESS

Most studies on the homeless have been focused on urban areas, leaving the impression that this problem exists only on city sidewalks. Homelessness is more common in the cities, where the bulk of the population resides, but many areas of rural America also experience the phenomenon. Rural communities have fewer official shelters and fewer public places (heating grates, subways, or train stations, for example) where the homeless can find temporary shelter. Finding the rural homeless is therefore more difficult for investigators of the problem.

In 1996 the U.S. Department of Agriculture (USDA), in *Rural Homelessness: Focusing on the Needs of the Rural Homeless* (Washington, DC, 1996), reported that homeless people in rural areas were more likely to be white, female, married, and currently working than were the urban homeless. They were also more likely to be homeless for the first time and generally had experienced homelessness for a shorter period of time than the urban homeless. Findings also included higher rates of domestic violence and lower rates of alcohol and substance abuse.

The 1996 Urban Institute study determined that 21% of all homeless people in their study lived in suburban areas, and 9% lived in rural communities. This study agreed with the USDA's study on many points. The rural homeless surveyed were more likely to be working, or to have worked recently, than the urban homeless—65% of the rural homeless had worked for pay in the last month. Homeless people living in rural areas were also more likely to be experiencing their first spell of homelessness (60%). In 55% of the cases, the homeless period lasted three months or less.

Patricia A. Post, in *Hard to Reach: Rural Homelessness and Health Care* (Nashville, TN: National Health Care for the Homeless Council, January 2002), argued that rural residents typically deal with a lack of permanent housing not by sleeping on the streets, like their urban counterparts, but by first moving in with a series of friends, secondly moving into abandoned shacks, cars, or campgrounds, and lastly moving to cities in search of employment. They also differ from urban homeless people in many ways: they have less education, typically hold temporary jobs with no benefits, are less likely to receive government assistance or have health insurance, and are more likely to have been incarcerated for a period of time.

Several types of rural areas generate higher-than-average levels of homelessness, including regions that:

- Are primarily agricultural—residents often lose their livelihood because of reduced demand for farm labor or because of a shrinking service sector

- Depend on declining extractive industries, such as mining or timber

- Are experiencing economic growth—new or expanding industrial plants often attract more job seekers than can be absorbed

- Have persistent poverty, such as Appalachia, where the young and able-bodied may have to relocate before they can find work

CHAPTER 3
EMPLOYMENT AND POVERTY AMONG THE HOMELESS

POVERTY AND HOMELESSNESS

There is an undeniable connection between homelessness and poverty. People in poverty live from day to day with little or no safety net for times when unforeseen expenses arise. If a family's resources are very small, expenditures on such necessities as food, shelter, or health care have to be carefully decided and sometimes sacrificed. Should one spend money on food, a visit to the doctor, buying necessary medicines, or paying the rent? In 2005 a full-time job paying minimum wage for forty hours per week provided an income of just $10,712 annually. (The federal poverty guideline for 2005 for one person was $9,570; for two people, $12,830.) Being poor often means that an illness, an accident, or a missed paycheck could be enough to cause homelessness.

Housing costs for such a family may be out of reach, costing from 50%–75% of the family income. According to Ralph da Costa Nunez and Laura M. Caruso in "Are Shelters the Answer to Family Homelessness?" in *USA Today Magazine* (January 1, 2003), low income and high rent payments often result in substandard housing accommodation, doubled-up living, or living on the street or in a public shelter. The necessity of basic sustenance and medical care usually leaves little money left to meet housing needs. People in poverty have further difficulties finding housing if they have previously defaulted on their rent payments or perhaps their house payments, with the end result of homelessness.

MEASURING POVERTY

Defining poverty and counting the poor is a difficult task. The official poverty measure used in the United States was developed during the 1960s by Mollie Orshansky of the Social Security Administration. Called the poverty index, this measure was based on the Department of Agriculture's 1955 Household Food Consumption Survey, which had determined that a family of three

spent approximately one-third of its income on food. The poverty threshold for a family of three was therefore set at three times the cost of the economy food plan, an amount seen as necessary to cover minimal living expenses. A family whose annual before-tax income was below this poverty threshold was "poor." The government has since revised the poverty threshold regularly to account for inflation and changes in the economy.

The Official Poverty Threshold

Table 3.1 shows the 2004 poverty thresholds for families by size and number of children. These amounts include income before taxes but do not include any capital gains or noncash benefits such as public housing, Medicaid, or food stamps. For example, in 2004 a family of five consisting of a father, mother, two related children under age eighteen and an aunt to those children could jointly earn up to $23,108 and still be considered "poor" by the official poverty measure. If, however, all the adults in the family were employed and their annual incomes were as follows: father, $12,000; mother, $8,000; and aunt, $4,000, then the family would have a joint income of $24,000 which is higher than the 2004 poverty threshold figure for a family of five. In 2004 the poverty thresholds ranged from $9,060 for an elderly person living alone to $36,520 for a family of nine or more members with at least one child. The poverty threshold for a family of four was $19,157 (two adults and two related children under eighteen years of age). The threshold for a typical single-parent family with two children was $15,219, almost 50% more than one person would earn working full-time at the federal minimum wage of $5.15 per hour.

Concerns about the Accuracy of the Official Poverty Rate

Social scientists have for years debated about the best and most accurate means of establishing a poverty threshold.

TABLE 3.1

Poverty threshold by size of family and number of related children under 18 years of age, 2004

[In thousands of dollars]

	Related children under 18 years								
Size of family unit	None	One	Two	Three	Four	Five	Six	Seven	Eight or more
One person (unrelated individual)									
Under 65 years	9,827								
65 years and over	9,060								
Two persons									
Householder under 65 years	12,649	13,020							
Householder 65 years and over	11,418	12,971							
Three persons	14,776	15,205	15,219						
Four persons	19,484	19,803	19,157	19,223					
Five persons	23,497	23,838	23,108	22,543	22,199				
Six persons	27,025	27,133	26,573	26,037	25,241	24,768			
Seven persons	31,096	31,290	30,621	30,154	29,285	28,271	27,159		
Eight persons	34,778	35,086	34,454	33,901	33,115	32,119	31,082	30,818	
Nine persons or more	41,836	42,039	41,480	41,010	40,240	39,179	38,220	37,983	36,520

SOURCE: "Poverty Thresholds 2004," U.S. Census Bureau, January 28, 2005, http://www.census.gov/hhes/poverty/threshld/thresh04.html (accessed February 18, 2005)

The central question that arises in debates about measuring poverty is whether to use an absolute or a relative means of updating the poverty rate on an annual or periodic basis. Once established, an absolute poverty measure is updated to account for price changes (inflation) only. A relative poverty measure is one that is updated based on changes in the median or mean income or compensation of the general population. The relative poverty measure adjusts for changing standards of living. The official poverty measure used by the United States is an absolute measure.

In 2001 the "Conveners of the Working Group on Revising the Poverty Measure"—a group of economists, lawyers, professors, and social academics—wrote *An Open Letter on Revising the Official Measure of Poverty* to the Director of the Office of Management and Budget. They wrote to express their concerns over the inadequacy of the official poverty level measurement and proposed a set of guidelines for a revised standard. The letter stated that the current system was one that was established in the 1960s and that it had not been meaningfully adjusted in the years since, despite decades of major changes in the social safety net for low-income families.

Three of the items that were specifically listed in the letter as examples of areas not well accounted for in determining the official poverty rate were:

- Noncash benefits (food stamps, housing assistance, free school lunch programs) that are not included in the calculation of income

- Out-of-pocket medical expenditures that are not included in the calculation of costs

- Out-of-pocket child care costs that are not included in the calculation of costs

The letter criticizes many aspects of the methodology used to determine the official poverty threshold, as did a report published by the National Academy of Sciences in 1995. The debate about how best and most accurately to determine who is and who is not poor has gone on for decades and will likely continue. It is, therefore, worthwhile when reviewing statistics about poverty to keep in mind that they may be skewed by the methods used in calculating them.

WHO ARE THE POOR?

Based on the Official Poverty Rate

An official count of the poor includes all those whose family incomes fall below the poverty threshold figure for that particular size family, as seen in Table 3.1. In 2003, based on those criteria, there were 35.9 million poor in the United States, 12.5% of the population. (See Table 3.2.) Children were poor at a higher rate (17.6%) than were adults aged eighteen to sixty-four (10.8%) or aged sixty-five and older (10.2%).

In 2003 whites had the lowest rate of poverty (10.6%), while African-Americans had the highest rate (24.4%). (See Table 3.2.) People of Hispanic origin also had high poverty rates; more than one in five (22.5%) lived below the poverty threshold. Asian people had a poverty rate slightly below the national rate (11.8%).

In 2003, 7.6 million families, or one in ten of all families, were poor. (See Table 3.2.) Only one in twenty married couple families were below the poverty threshold (5.4%). Male-headed, single-parent families had a rate of poverty of 13.5%, less than half that experienced by female-headed, single-parent families (28%). In other

TABLE 3.2

People and families in poverty, by selected characteristics, 2002 and 2003

[Numbers in thousands, people as of March of the following year]

Characteristic	2002 below poverty		2003 below poverty	
	Number	Percentage	Number	Percentage
People				
Total	**34,570**	**12.1**	**35,861**	**12.5**
Family status				
In families	24,534	10.4	25,684	10.8
Householder	7,229	9.6	7,607	10.0
Related children under 18	11,646	16.3	12,340	17.2
Related children under 6	4,296	18.5	4,654	19.8
In urelated subfamilies	417	33.7	464	38.6
Reference person	167	31.7	191	37.6
Children under 18	241	35.4	271	41.7
Unrelated individual	9,618	20.4	9,713	20.4
Male	4,023	17.7	4,154	18.0
Female	5,595	22.9	5,559	22.6
Race[a] and Hispanic origin				
White alone or in combination	24,074	10.3	24,950	10.6
White alone[b]	23,466	10.2	24,272	10.5
White alone, not Hispanic	15,567	8.0	15,902	8.2
Black alone or in combination	8,884	23.9	9,108	24.3
Black alone[c]	8,602	24.1	8,781	24.4
Asian alone or in combination	1,243	10.0	1,527	11.8
Asian alone[d]	1,161	10.1	1,401	11.8
Hispanic origin (of any race)	8,555	21.8	9,051	22.5
Age				
Under 18 years	12,133	16.7	12,866	17.6
18 to 64 years	18,861	10.6	19,443	10.8
65 years and older	3,576	10.4	3,552	10.2
Nativity				
Native	29,012	11.5	29,965	11.8
Foreign born	5,558	16.6	5,897	17.2
Naturalized citizen	1,285	10.0	1,309	10.0
Not a citizen	4,273	20.7	4,588	21.7
Region				
Northeast	5,871	10.9	6,052	11.3
Midwest	6,616	10.3	6,932	10.7
South	14,019	13.8	14,548	14.1
West	8,064	12.4	8,329	12.6
Residence				
Inside metropolitan areas	27,096	11.6	28,367	12.1
Inside central cities	13,784	16.7	14,551	17.5
Outside central cities	13,311	8.9	13,816	9.1
Outside metropolitan areas	7,474	14.2	7,495	14.2
Work experience				
All workers (16 years and older)	8,954	5.9	8,820	5.8
Worked full-time year-round	2,635	2.6	2,636	2.6
Not full-time year-round	6,318	12.4	6,183	12.2
Did not work at least one week	14,647	21.0	15,446	21.5
Families				
Total	**7,229**	**9.6**	**7,607**	**10.0**
Type of family				
Married-couple	3,052	5.3	3,115	5.4
Female householder, no husband present	3,613	26.5	3,856	28.0
Male householder, no wife present	564	12.1	636	13.5

[a]Data for American Indians and Alaska Natives, and Asian, Native Hawaiian and other Pacific Islanders are not shown separately.
[b]The 2003 and 2004 Current Population Survey (CPS) asked respondents to choose one or more races. White alone refers to people who reported white and did not report any other race category. The use of this single-race population does not imply that it is the preferred method of presenting or analyzing data. The Census Bureau uses a variety of approaches. About 2.6 percent of people reported more than one race in Census 2000.
[c]Black alone refers to people who reported black and did not report any other race category.
[d]Asian alone refers to people who reported Asian and did not report any other race category.

SOURCE: Adapted from Carmen DeNavas-Walt, Bernadette D. Proctor, and Robert J. Mills, "Table 3. People and Families in Poverty by Selected Characteristics: 2002 and 2003," in *Income, Poverty, and Health Insurance Coverage in the U.S.: 2003*, U.S. Census Bureau, Current Population Reports, P60-226, August 2004, http://www.census.gov/prod/2004pubs/p60-226.pdf (accessed February 18, 2005)

words, more than one in four female-headed, single-parent families lived below the poverty threshold in 2003.

Based on Alternate Poverty Measures

The size of the poverty-stricken segment of the U.S. population varies depending on which method of determining the poverty threshold is used to identify the poor population. The U.S. Census Bureau has experimented with ways to measure the numbers of people and families categorized as poor. The experimental methods differ from the official methods in two primary ways. First, they take into account out-of-pocket medical expenses. Second, they make adjustments for different housing costs based on geography, by region and/or metropolitan versus rural residences.

In 2001 the Census Bureau used both official and experimental methods to calculate poverty rates in response to the 1995 National Academy of Sciences recommendations. Figure 3.1 presents poverty rates by age group as calculated by different methods. The official rate of poverty for children under eighteen was higher than the rates produced using experimental methods. Nonetheless, all methods for determining poverty showed a higher rate of poverty for children than for adults aged eighteen to sixty-four years.

The rates for senior citizens showed the most variation between the experimental and official methods for measuring poverty. (See Figure 3.1.) The experimental methods used to study poverty rates make adjustments for medical out-of-pocket expenditures and because the elderly have high out-of-pocket medical expenses, methodologies that adjusted income accordingly resulted in much higher numbers of elderly falling into the ranks of the poor.

Trends in the Poverty Rate

For the most part, the poverty rate is linked to the performance of the U.S. economy. At times when the economy is in recession, the poverty rate increases. In fact, the poverty rate often begins to increase somewhat before a serious economic downturn, and may not begin to decline until some time after a recession ends.

Figure 3.2 demonstrates that during the recession of 1980–82, when many Americans lost their jobs and the economy performed poorly, the poverty rate increased dramatically. In 1979, the year before the recession began, the poverty rate was 11.7%; by 1983 it stood at 15.2%. After the recession of the early 1980s ended, the poverty rate gradually declined. By 1989 it was down to 12.8%, its lowest level since 1979. The United States then endured another recession in 1990–91, and by its end the poverty level was up to 14.2%. While the recession that began in March 2001 ended the following year, the poverty rate and the number of individuals living in poverty continued to rise into 2003.

Poverty Rates by Category

FAMILIES. The Census Bureau's 2004 report on poverty data included poverty rates by family structure. (See Table 3.2.) The recession that started in March 2001 was reflected in rising numbers of people living in poverty across all categories of family structure. The rate of poverty for all families in 2000 was 8.7%; by 2002 it had risen to 10.4% and by 2003 to 10.8%. (For 2000 poverty data, see "Table 1. People and Families in Poverty by Selected Characteristics: 2000 and 2001," in Bernadette D. Proctor and Joseph Dalaker, *Poverty in the United States: Current Population Reports*, P60-219, U.S. Census Bureau, September 2002.) The poverty rate for married couple families in 2000 was 4.7%; by 2002 it had risen to 5.3% and by 2003 to 5.4%. Households headed by single females had a poverty rate of 25.4% of 2000; in 2002, the rate had risen to 26.5% and by 2003, to 28%. The poverty rate of households headed by single males rose from 11.3% in 2000 to 12.1% in 2002 and 13.5% in 2003.

CHILDREN. Almost thirteen million children are in poverty. In 2003 a higher proportion of children lived in poverty (17.6%) than any other age group. (See Figure 3.3.) Over one-third (35.9%) of the people living in poverty were children even though they made up only one-quarter (25.4%) of the population (Carmen DeNavas-Walt et al., *Income, Poverty, and Health Insurance Coverage in the United States: 2003*, U.S. Census Bureau, August 2004).

According to DeNavas-Walt et al., over half (52.9%) of children under six years of age and living in a female-headed, single-parent family lived in poverty. These young children were at particularly high risk of poverty compared to their peers who lived in two-parent households. The poverty rate for children under the age of six living in married-couple households was 9.6%. Overall, children under the age of eighteen who lived in single-parent households were over five times more likely to live in poverty than were children living in married-couple households.

Over the past few decades the child poverty rate has fallen, from a high of 27.3% in 1959 to 17.6% in 2003. (See Figure 3.3.) The decline in poverty for children was not steady but mirrored the fluctuations seen in the poverty rate of adults aged eighteen to sixty-four. The age group that had the most improvement in poverty rates was senior citizens; their rate in 1959 was 35.2% and in 2003 it was 10.2%.

RACE AND ETHNICITY. In 2003 Hispanics and African-Americans were much more likely to be poor than whites. Members of these two populations also had higher rates of

FIGURE 3.1

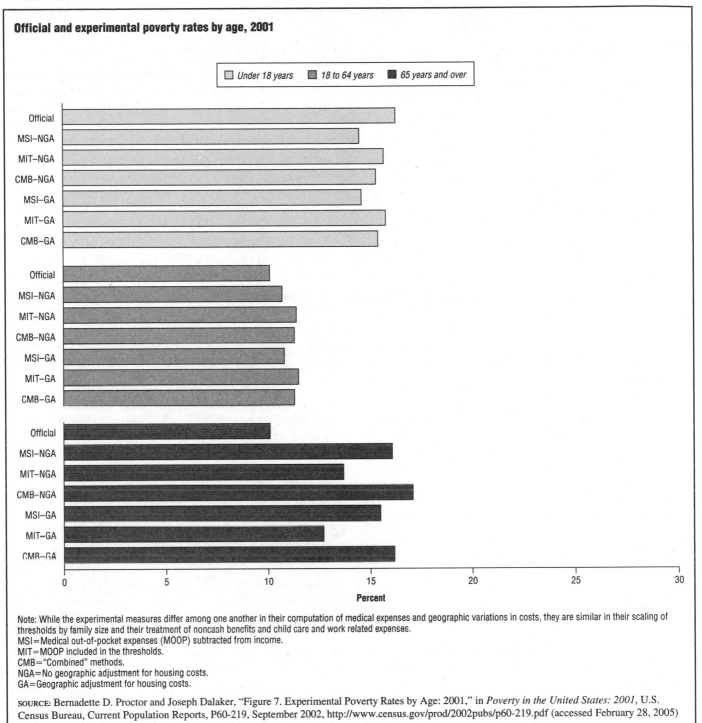

Official and experimental poverty rates by age, 2001

☐ *Under 18 years* ▨ *18 to 64 years* ■ *65 years and over*

Note: While the experimental measures differ among one another in their computation of medical expenses and geographic variations in costs, they are similar in their scaling of thresholds by family size and their treatment of noncash benefits and child care and work related expenses.
MSI=Medical out-of-pocket expenses (MOOP) subtracted from income.
MIT=MOOP included in the thresholds.
CMB="Combined" methods.
NGA=No geographic adjustment for housing costs.
GA=Geographic adjustment for housing costs.

SOURCE: Bernadette D. Proctor and Joseph Dalaker, "Figure 7. Experimental Poverty Rates by Age: 2001," in *Poverty in the United States: 2001*, U.S. Census Bureau, Current Population Reports, P60-219, September 2002, http://www.census.gov/prod/2002pubs/p60-219.pdf (accessed February 28, 2005)

single female-headed households and lower rates of high school graduation, two indicators of increased likelihood of poverty. (See Figure 3.4.) In 2003 the poverty rate for Hispanics (who may be of any race) was 22.5%; 18% of Hispanic families were headed by a single mother, and 43% of the Hispanic population aged twenty-five and older had not graduated from high school. The poverty rate for African-Americans was 24.3%; 32.4% of black families were headed by a

single mother, and one in five African-Americans aged twenty-five and older had not graduated from high school. Non-Hispanic whites and Asian Americans (as reported by DeNavas-Walt et al.) had the lowest rates of poverty by racial group (8.2% and 11.8%, respectively). Only 8.8% of white families were headed by a single mother, and only 10.6% of the white population aged twenty-five and older had not graduated from high school.

FIGURE 3.2

Number in poverty and poverty rate, 1959–2003

[Numbers in millions, rates in percent]

Note: The data points are placed at the midpoints of the respective years.

SOURCE: Carmen DeNavas-Walt, Bernadette D. Proctor, and Robert J. Mills, "Figure 3. Number in Poverty and Poverty Rate, 1959 to 2003," in *Income, Poverty, and Health Insurance Coverage in the U.S.: 2003*, U.S. Census Bureau, Current Population Reports, P60-226, August 2004, http://www.census .gov/prod/2004pubs/p60-226.pdf (accessed February 18, 2005)

FIGURE 3.3

Poverty rates by age, 1959–2003

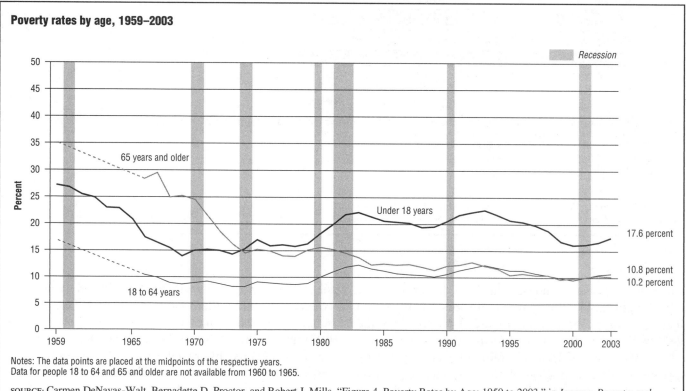

Notes: The data points are placed at the midpoints of the respective years.
Data for people 18 to 64 and 65 and older are not available from 1960 to 1965.

SOURCE: Carmen DeNavas-Walt, Bernadette D. Proctor, and Robert J. Mills, "Figure 4. Poverty Rates by Age: 1959 to 2003," in *Income, Poverty, and Health Insurance Coverage in the U.S.: 2003*, U.S. Census Bureau, Current Population Reports, P60-226, August 2004, http://www.census.gov/prod/ 2004pubs/p60-226.pdf (accessed February 18, 2005)

FIGURE 3.4

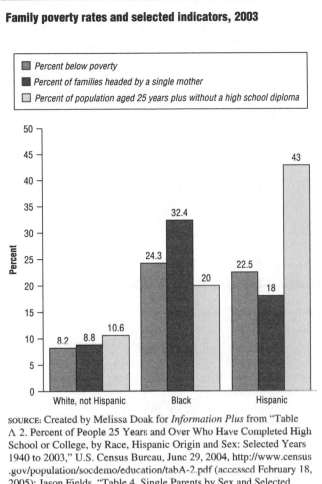

Family poverty rates and selected indicators, 2003

- ■ Percent below poverty
- ■ Percent of families headed by a single mother
- □ Percent of population aged 25 years plus without a high school diploma

SOURCE: Created by Melissa Doak for *Information Plus* from "Table A 2. Percent of People 25 Years and Over Who Have Completed High School or College, by Race, Hispanic Origin and Sex: Selected Years 1940 to 2003," U.S. Census Bureau, June 29, 2004, http://www.census .gov/population/socdemo/education/tabA-2.pdf (accessed February 18, 2005); Jason Fields, "Table 4. Single Parents by Sex and Selected Characteristics: 2003," in *America's Families and Living Arrangements: 2003*, Current Population Reports, P20-553, U.S. Census Bureau, November 2004, http://www.census.gov/prod/ 2004pubs/p20-553.pdf (accessed February 28, 2005); and Carmen DeNavas-Walt, Bernadette D. Proctor, and Robert J. Mills, "Table 3. People and Families in Poverty by Selected Characteristics: 2002 and 2003," in *Income, Poverty, and Health Insurance Coverage in the U.S.: 2003*, U.S. Census Bureau, Current Population Reports, P60-226, August 2004, http://www.census.gov/prod/2004pubs/p60-226.pdf (accessed February 18, 2005)

WORKING STATUS. The poor are often assumed to be the unemployed. People who are unemployed are more likely to be poor but many people who work can be poor as well. People who worked full-time at any point during 2003 had a 2.6% poverty rate. People who worked part-time at any point during 2003 had a 12.2% poverty rate. Those who did not work at all during 2003 had a 21.5% poverty rate. (See Table 3.2.)

Region

Poverty rates vary from one part of the United States to another. All regions saw an increase in poverty rates between 2002 and 2003. (See Table 3.2.) The South had the highest rate of poverty in 2003, 14.1%, up from a rate of 13.8% in 2002. DeNavas-Walt et al.

pointed out that four out of ten (40.6%) poor people lived in the South in 2003, while only 35.9% of Americans lived there. The poverty rate increased in the other regions as well. In the Northeast, the poverty rate increased from 10.9% in 2002 to 11.3% in 2003. In the Midwest, the rate increased from 10.3% in 2002 to 10.7% in 2003. In the West, the rate increased from 12.4% in 2002 to 12.6% in 2003.

Poverty rates also vary by residential area. Inner cities tend to have the highest rates. In 2003 the poverty rate for people living in central cities was 17.5%, up from 16.7% the year before. Rural areas also have a high poverty rate; in 2003 nonmetropolitan areas had a poverty rate of 14.2%, unchanged from the previous year. Suburban poverty rates tend to be the lowest, but even there the rates were rising in the early 2000s; in 2003 the poverty rate in the suburbs was 9.1%, up from 8.9% the year before.

EMPLOYMENT AND WAGES

The poverty rate is established by counting the number of families with before-tax income that is lower than the poverty threshold set for a family that size, so employment and wages are an essential part of the determination.

Household Income

Median annual household income in 2003 was $43,318. Half of all American households earned less than this amount and half earned more. (See Table 3.3.) Not surprisingly, median household income varied greatly according to the composition of the household. The median income for married-couple families in 2003 was $62,405, but for female-headed families with no husband present, it was only $29,307, less than half that of a couple-headed family. Race and ethnicity were also factors. In 2003 Asian households had the highest median income ($55,699). The median income for white, non-Hispanic households was $47,777; for people of Hispanic origin it was $32,997; and for blacks it was $29,689. The median income for all groups except for Asians had fallen from the previous year.

Educational Attainment and Income Level

A strong correlation exists between income level and educational attainment. The poor tend to have less education, and a lower proportion of well-educated people are poor. Table 3.4 presents average earnings by level of highest degree. Generally, the higher the degree a person earns, the higher their average income.

When educational attainment is added to the comparison of family income distribution, a clear and predictable pattern emerges. In 2001 families whose householder had

TABLE 3.3

Money income and earnings by selected characteristics, 2002 and 2003

[Income in 2003 dollars. Households and people as of March of the following year.]

Characteristic	2002		2003		Percentage change in real median income (2003 less 2002)
	Number (thousands)	Median money income (dollars) Value	Number (thousands)	Median money income (dollars) Value	Estimate
Households					
All households	111,278	43,381	112,000	43,318	−0.1
Type of household					
Family households	75,596	53,911	76,217	53,991	0.1
Married-couple	57,320	62,657	57,719	62,405	−0.4
Female householder, no husband present	13,620	29,665	13,781	29,307	−1.2
Male householder, no wife present	4,656	42,667	4,717	41,959	−1.7
Nonfamily households	35,682	25,988	35,783	25,741	−1.0
Female householder	19,662	21,392	19,647	21,313	−0.4
Male householder	16,020	32,123	16,136	31,928	−0.6
Race[a] and Hispanic origin					
White alone or in combination	92,740	45,994	93,196	45,572	[f]−0.9
White alone[b]	91,645	46,119	91,962	45,631	[f]−1.1
White alone, not Hispanic	81,166	47,974	81,148	47,777	−0.4
Black alone or in combination	13,778	29,845	13,969	29,689	−0.5
Black alone[c]	13,465	29,691	13,629	29,645	−0.2
Asian alone or in combination	4,079	53,483	4,235	55,262	3.3
Asian alone[d]	3,917	53,832	4,040	55,699	3.5
Hispanic origin (of any race)	11,339	33,861	11,693	32,997	[f]−2.6
Age of householder					
Under 65 years	88,619	50,644	88,951	50,171	[f]−0.9
15 to 24 years	6,611	28,466	6,610	27,053	[f]−5.0
25 to 34 years	19,055	46,368	19,159	44,779	[f]−3.4
35 to 44 years	24,069	54,747	23,222	55,044	0.5
45 to 54 years	22,623	60,373	23,137	60,242	−0.2
55 to 64 years	16,260	48,284	16,824	49,215	[f]1.9
65 years and older	22,659	23,682	23,048	23,787	0.4
Nativity of the householder					
Native	97,365	44,212	97,840	44,347	0.3
Foreign born	13,912	38,849	14,159	37,499	[f]−3.5
Naturalized citizen	6,423	46,471	6,567	46,049	−0.9
Not a citizen	7,490	34,758	7,592	32,806	[f]−5.6
Region					
Northeast	21,229	46,913	21,017	46,742	−0.4
Midwest	25,630	44,621	25,643	44,732	0.2
South	40,107	40,427	40,742	39,823	[f]−1.5
West	24,313	46,177	24,598	46,820	1.4
Residence					
Inside metropolitan areas	90,075	46,294	90,613	46,060	−0.5
Inside central cities	33,543	37,708	33,717	37,174	[f]−1.4
Outside central cities	56,532	51,879	56,896	51,737	−0.3
Outside metropolitan areas	21,203	35,448	21,387	35,112	−0.9
Shares of household income quintiles and gini index					
Lowest quintile	22,256	3.5	22,400	3.4	[f]−2.9
Second quintile	22,256	8.8	22,400	8.7	−1.1
Third quintile	22,256	14.8	22,400	14.8	—
Fourth quintile	22,256	23.3	22,400	23.4	0.4
Highest quintile	22,256	49.7	22,400	49.8	0.2
Gini index of income inequality	111,278	0.462	112,000	0.464	0.4
Earnings of full-time year-round workers					
Men	58,761	40,332	58,772	40,668	0.8
Women	41,876	30,895	41,908	30,724	−0.6

the least education earned the least, while the majority of families with a highly educated householder earned the highest incomes. (See Figure 3.5.) Of heads of households with less than a ninth-grade education, one-half earned under $25,000, and 24.5% earned under $15,000 in 2001. On the other hand, more than half the families headed by a person with a doctoral degree (54.4%) earned $100,000 or more.

TABLE 3.3

Money income and earnings by selected characteristics, 2002 and 2003 [CONTINUED]

[Income in 2003 dollars. Households and people as of March of the following year.]

Characteristic	2002 Number (thousands)	2002 Median money income (dollars) Value	2003 Number (thousands)	2003 Median money income (dollars) Value	Percentage change in real median income (2003 less 2002) Estimate
Per capita income					
Total[a]	285,933	23,316	288,280	23,276	−0.2
White alone or in combination	235,036	24,511	236,875	24,442	−0.3
White alone[b]	230,809	24,695	232,254	24,626	−0.3
White alone, not Hispanic	194,421	26,727	194,877	26,774	0.2
Black alone or in combination	37,350	15,619	37,651	15,583	−0.2
Black alone[c]	35,806	15,795	36,121	15,775	−0.1
Asian alone or in combination	12,504	23,785	12,905	23,654	−0.5
Asian alone[d]	11,558	24,684	11,869	24,604	−0.3
Hispanic origin (of any race)	39,384	13,796	40,425	13,492	−2.2

Note: "—" represents zero or rounds to zero.
[a]Data for American Indians and Alaska Natives, and Asian, Native Hawaiian and Other Pacific Islanders are not shown separately.
[b]The 2003 and 2004 CPS asked respondents to choose one or more races. White alone refers to people who reported white and did not report any other race category. The use of this single-race population does not imply that it is the preferred method of presenting or analyzing data. The Census Bureau uses a variety of approaches. About 2.6 percent of people reported more than one race in Census 2000.
[c]Black alone refers to people who reported black and did not report any other race category.
[d]Asian alone refers to people who reported Asian and did not report any other race category.

SOURCE: Carmen DeNavas-Walt, Bernadette D. Proctor, and Robert J. Mills, "Table 1. Money Income and Earnings Summary Measures by Selected Characteristics: 2002 and 2003," in *Income, Poverty, and Health Insurance Coverage in the U.S.: 2003*, U.S. Census Bureau, Current Population Reports, P60-226, August 2004, http://www.census.gov/prod/2004pubs/p60-226.pdf (accessed February 18, 2005)

TABLE 3.4

Mean earnings by highest degree earned, 2002

[In dollars. For persons 18 years old and over with earnings. Persons as of March the following year.]

Characteristic	Total persons	Level of highest degree Not a high school graduate	High school graduate only	Some college, no degree	Associate's	Bachelor's	Master's	Professional	Doctorate
All persons[b]	36,308	18,826	27,280	29,725	34,177	51,194	60,445	112,845	89,737
Age									
25 to 34 years old	32,527	19,235	26,278	28,879	30,662	42,623	48,598	75,247	62,190
35 to 44 years old	41,963	22,324	30,259	37,533	37,440	58,267	63,758	123,811	88,818
45 to 54 years old	45,392	21,231	31,251	40,225	39,167	60,680	67,096	126,230	112,538
55 to 64 years old	42,381	24,761	30,893	37,450	34,848	55,057	62,640	132,372	81,166
65 years old and over	36,611	18,949	27,519	29,809	34,331	51,612	61,151	114,981	91,771
Sex									
Male	44,310	22,091	32,673	36,869	42,392	63,503	73,629	138,827	99,607
Female	27,271	13,459	21,141	22,292	27,341	37,909	47,368	61,583	66,426
White[c]	37,376	19,264	28,145	30,570	34,876	52,479	60,787	115,523	92,125
Male	45,793	22,539	33,920	38,095	43,494	65,439	74,426	140,965	103,787
Female	27,512	13,354	21,388	22,452	27,480	37,903	47,209	60,944	64,106
Black[c]	28,179	16,516	22,823	26,711	30,391	42,285	51,974	96,368	69,780
Male	31,790	19,294	25,582	31,858	36,028	47,018	60,647	[a]	[a]
Female	25,131	13,748	20,209	22,455	26,940	38,741	47,765	[a]	[a]
Hispanic[d]	25,824	18,981	24,163	26,459	31,710	40,949	58,814	81,186	[a]
Male	29,084	21,611	27,992	31,545	37,365	46,115	59,901	90,767	[a]
Female	21,008	13,694	18,810	20,707	25,888	35,357	57,447	[a]	[a]

[a]Base figure too small to meet statistical standards for reliability of a derived figure.
[b]Includes other races, not shown separately.
[c]For persons who selected this race group only. The 2003 Current Population Survey (CPS) allowed respondents to choose more than one race. Beginning 2003 data represent persons who selected this race group only and exclude persons reporting more than one race. The CPS in prior years only allowed respondents to report one race group.
[d]Persons of Hispanic origin may be of any race.

SOURCE: "Table 215. Mean Earnings by Highest Degree Earned: 2002," in *Statistical Abstract of the United States: 2004–2005*, U.S. Census Bureau, 2004, http://www.census.gov/prod/2004pubs/04statab/educ.pdf (accessed February 21, 2005)

FIGURE 3.5

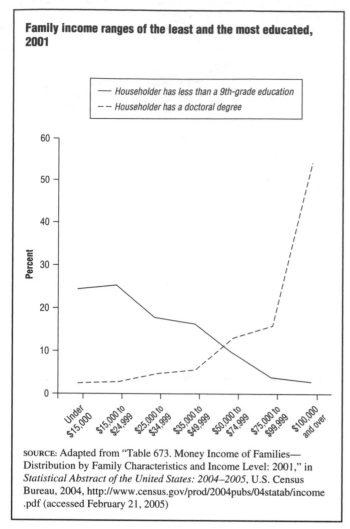

Family income ranges of the least and the most educated, 2001

— Householder has less than a 9th-grade education
-- Householder has a doctoral degree

SOURCE: Adapted from "Table 673. Money Income of Families—Distribution by Family Characteristics and Income Level: 2001," in *Statistical Abstract of the United States: 2004–2005*, U.S. Census Bureau, 2004, http://www.census.gov/prod/2004pubs/04statab/income.pdf (accessed February 21, 2005)

FIGURE 3.6

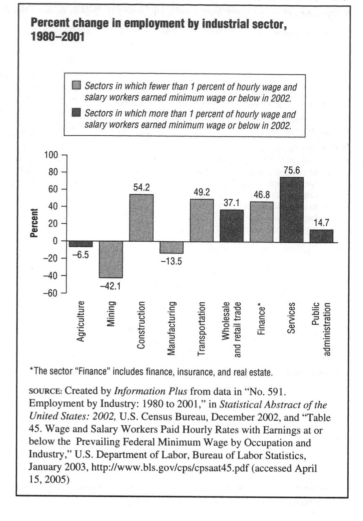

Percent change in employment by industrial sector, 1980–2001

■ Sectors in which fewer than 1 percent of hourly wage and salary workers earned minimum wage or below in 2002.

■ Sectors in which more than 1 percent of hourly wage and salary workers earned minimum wage or below in 2002.

*The sector "Finance" includes finance, insurance, and real estate.

SOURCE: Created by *Information Plus* from data in "No. 591. Employment by Industry: 1980 to 2001," in *Statistical Abstract of the United States: 2002*, U.S. Census Bureau, December 2002, and "Table 45. Wage and Salary Workers Paid Hourly Rates with Earnings at or below the Prevailing Federal Minimum Wage by Occupation and Industry," U.S. Department of Labor, Bureau of Labor Statistics, January 2003, http://www.bls.gov/cps/cpsaat45.pdf (accessed April 15, 2005)

A lack of education leaves a person ill equipped to support him- or herself, or a family, comfortably. Education opens doors and opportunities that are simply not available to the undereducated, especially in an economy that is transitioning from a reliance on manufacturing to a reliance on the information and service industries.

Growth of Jobs in Low Wage Industries

During the 1970s manufacturing industries began closing down plants and moving their production facilities to cheaper labor markets at home and abroad. For much of the twentieth century the United States had been primarily an industrial economy. The last two decades of the century saw the beginning of the nation's transition to what has now been dubbed the information or service economy.

Figure 3.6 shows the change in employment between 1980 and 2001 by industrial sector. The industry that grew the most was the service industry. In 1980 the service sector employed 28.8 million people; by 2001 it had grown to employ 50.5 million, a 75.6% increase.

Industries that pay higher wages than those offered in the services, like mining and manufacturing, shrank during this same period, by 42.1% and 13.5% respectively.

The shift in employment from production work to service work has shifted workers from higher to lower paying jobs. According to the U.S. Bureau of Labor Statistics, average hourly wages earned by people employed in the service industries are much lower than average hourly wages earned in the fields of manufacturing, mining, and construction.

Minimum Wage Jobs

The Bureau of Labor Statistics provides data on which industrial sectors employ the highest percentage of people at minimum wage. Table 3.5 shows the total number of wage and salary workers by occupation and by industry. It also shows the number and percent of those workers who, in 2004, earned at or below the federal minimum wage of $5.15 per hour.

Almost one in ten service workers (9.1%) earned at or below the federal minimum wage, and almost one in five food preparation and service workers (19%) earned

TABLE 3.5

Wage and salary workers paid hourly rates equal to or less than the prevailing minimum wage, by occupation and industry, 2004

[Numbers in thousands]

Occupation and industry	Total	2004 Workers paid hourly rates — Below prevailing federal minimum wage	At prevailing federal minimum wage	Total at or below prevailing federal minimum wage — Number	Percent of hourly-paid workers
Occupation					
Management, professional, and related occupations	13,743	39	27	66	0.7
Management, business, and financial operations occupations	3,750	14	2	16.	4
Management occupations	2,120	12	1	13.	6
Business and financial operations occupations	1,630	2	1	3.	2
Professional and related occupations	9,993	25	25	50	.5
Computer and mathematical occupations	762	—	1	2.	2
Architecture and engineering occupations	952	1	2	3.	3
Life, physical, and social science occupations	414	1	1	2.	5
Community and social services occupations	717	2	1	4.	5
Legal occupations	281	—	—	—	—
Education, training, and library occupations	2,024	8	11	19	1.0
Arts, design, entertainment, sports, and media occupations	777	8	6	13	1.7
Healthcare practitioner and technical occupations	4,065	4	3	7	.2
Service occupations	16,381	1,238	256	1,494	9.1
Healthcare support occupations	2,460	21	12	32	1.3
Protective service occupations	1,823	20	4	25	1.3
Food preparation and serving related occupations	6,236	1,036	147	1,183	19.0
Building and grounds cleaning and maintenance occupations	3,608	63	39	102	2.8
Personal care and service occupations	2,254	97	54	151	6.7
Sales and office occupations	20,650	104	146	250	1.2
Sales and related occupations	7,512	66	76	143	1.9
Office and administrative support occupations	13,139	37	69	107	.8
Natural resources, construction, and maintenance occupations	9,368	24	26	50	.5
Farming, fishing, and forestry occupations	603	10	11	22	3.6
Construction and extraction occupations	5,430	7	6	14	.3
Installation, maintenance, and repair occupations	3,335	6	9	15	.4
Production, transportation, and material moving occupations	13,796	78	66	144	1.0
Production occupations	7,708	36	18	55	.7
Transportation and material moving occupations	6,087	42	47	89	1.5
Industry					
Private sector	64,708	1,423	467	1,889	2.9
Agriculture and related industries	623	9	10	19	3.1
Nonagriculture and related industries	64,085	1,413	457	1,870	2.9
Mining	312	—	1	1.	2
Construction	5,552	10	8	17.	3
Manufacturing	10,388	38	23	61	.6
Durable goods	6,397	20	8	29.	4
Nondurable goods	3,991	18	15	32	.8
Wholesale and retail trade	12,456	85	96	181	1.5
Wholesale trade	2,038	7	10	16.	8
Retail trade	10,418	78	86	165	1.6
Transportation and utilities	2,915	13	7	21.	7
Transportation and warehousing	2,431	12	7	20.	8
Utilities	485	1	—	1.	2
Information	1,472	4	10	15	1.0
Publishing, except Internet	328	—	2	3.	8
Motion pictures and sound recording	204	3	7	10	4.8
Broadcasting, except Internet	228	—	—	—	—
Telecommunications	600	1	1	2.	3
Financial activities	3,453	13	20	33	1.0
Finance and insurance	2,429	8	10	18.	7
Finance	1,581	3	6	9.	6
Insurance	848	5	4	9	1.1
Real estate and rental and leasing	1,025	6	10	15	1.5
Professional and business services	5,461	37	24	61	1.1
Professional and technical services	2,249	5	9	14	.6
Management, administrative, and waste services	3,212	32	15	47	1.5
Education and health services	11,022	76	62	137	1.2
Educational services	1,263	13	21	34	2.7
Health care and social assistance	9,759	62	41	103	1.1

TABLE 3.5

Wage and salary workers paid hourly rates equal to or less than the prevailing minimum wage, by occupation and industry, 2004 [CONTINUED]

[Numbers in thousands]

Occupation and industry	2004				
		Workers paid hourly rates		Total at or below prevailing federal minimum wage	
	Total	Below prevailing federal minimum wage	At prevailing federal minimum wage	Number	Percent of hourly-paid workers
Leisure and hospitality	8,095	1,066	176	1,242	15.3
Arts, entertainment, and recreation	1,198	45	20	65	5.4
Accommodation and food services	6,897	1,021	156	1,177	17.1
Accommodation	1,037	35	9	44	4.2
Food services and drinking places	5,860	986	147	1,133	19.3
Other services*	2,959	71	31	101	3.4
Other services, except private households	2,470	36	27	63	2.5
Other services, private households	489	35	4	39	7.9
Public sector	9,231	60	53	114	1.2
Federal government	1,781	8	11	20	1.1
State government	2,347	15	17	32	1.4
Local government	5,103	37	25	62	1.2

*Includes other industries, not shown separately.
Note: The prevailing federal minimum wage was $5.15 per hour in 2004. Data are for wage and salary workers, excluding the incorporated self-employed. They refer to a person's earnings on their sole or principal job, and pertain only to workers who are paid hourly rates. Salaried workers and other nonhourly workers are not included. The presence of workers with hourly earnings below the minimum wage does not necessarily indicate violations of the Fair Labor Standards Act, as there are exceptions to the minimum wage provisions of the law. In addition, some survey respondents might have rounded hourly earnings to the nearest dollar, and, as a result, reported hourly earnings below the minimum wage even though they earned the minimum wage or higher. Beginning in January 2004, data reflect revised population controls used in the household survey.

SOURCE: "Table 45. Wage and Salary Workers Paid Hourly Rates with Earnings At or Below the Prevailing Federal Minimum Wage by Occupation and Industry," in *Household Data Annual Averages*, 2004, U.S. Department of Labor, Bureau of Labor Statistics, http://www.bls.gov/cps/cpsaat45.pdf (accessed February 21, 2005)

minimum wage or below. (See Table 3.5.) Almost 8% of service workers who worked in private households earned minimum wage or less. Almost one in seven workers (15.3%) in the leisure and hospitality industry earned this little. In contrast, less than 1% of managers and professionals earned minimum wage or less.

The shift from a primarily industrial economy to one primarily engaged in providing services has been one of the leading factors in a shift in the distribution of wealth in the United States.

THE DISTRIBUTION OF WEALTH

While most discussions of poverty focus simply on people who are below the poverty line versus those who are above it, it is important to keep in mind that even among the poor, some people have fewer resources than others. An analysis of changes in the distribution of wealth helps to explain why homelessness and poverty can remain level, even when the economy performs well.

During the 1980s and 1990s the poverty rate declined for the most part. In the first years of each of these decades the number of people in poverty rose but during the rest of the twenty-year period the numbers of people in poverty declined. (See Figure 3.2.) However, the patterns seen in the distribution of wealth underwent a change. Table 3.6 breaks the U.S. population down into five groups based on income, ranging from the fifth of

the population with the lowest incomes to the fifth with the highest incomes. It then displays the percent of total income earned by each fifth of the population in a particular year, as well as the amount earned by those in the top 5% of all Americans (the highest fifth of the highest fifth).

From 1991 to 2001, the highest fifth or quintile of the population increased its income 7.9%, bringing its share of total income from 44.2% to 47.7%. (See Table 3.6.) In each of the other, lower income quintiles the share of aggregate income received declined over the same time period, 1991—2001. The lowest fifth went from 4.5% of all income in 1991 down to 4.2% in 2001. The top 5% of Americans saw their percentage of aggregate income rise 23% during the 1990s, increasing their share from 17.1% to 21% of the nation's income.

As the U.S. economy went through a period of historic growth during the 1990s, every fifth of the population also saw its income rise. (See Figure 3.7.) The richest fifth of the population, however, gained the largest share of the new wealth and increased their overall share of aggregate income while each of the other fifths lost some of its share of the aggregate income. Although it is not accurate to say that the poor got poorer, since their incomes grew, it is true that they became poorer relative to the rich. The 1990s resulted in increased disparity between the rich and the poor.

TABLE 3.6

Share of aggregate income received by each fifth and top five percent of families, 1947–2001

[Percent]

	Lowest fifth	Second fifth	Middle fifth	Fourth fifth	Highest fifth	Top 5 percent
1947	5.0	11.9	17.0	23.1	43.0	17.5
1948	4.9	12.1	17.3	23.2	42.4	17.1
1949	4.5	11.9	17.3	23.5	42.7	16.9
1950	4.5	12.0	17.4	23.4	42.7	17.3
1951	5.0	12.4	17.6	23.4	41.6	16.8
1952	4.9	12.3	17.4	23.4	41.9	17.4
1953	4.7	12.5	18.0	23.9	40.9	15.7
1954	4.5	12.1	17.7	23.9	41.8	16.3
1955	4.8	12.3	17.8	23.7	41.3	16.4
1956	5.0	12.5	17.9	23.7	41.0	16.1
1957	5.1	12.7	18.1	23.8	40.4	15.6
1958	5.0	12.5	18.0	23.9	40.6	15.4
1959	4.9	12.3	17.9	23.8	41.1	15.9
1960	4.8	12.2	17.8	24.0	41.3	15.9
1961	4.7	11.9	17.5	23.8	42.2	16.6
1962	5.0	12.1	17.6	24.0	41.3	15.7
1963	5.0	12.1	17.7	24.0	41.2	15.8
1964	5.1	12.0	17.7	24.0	41.2	15.9
1965	5.2	12.2	17.8	23.9	40.9	15.5
1966	5.6	12.4	17.8	23.8	40.5	15.6
1967	5.4	12.2	17.5	23.5	41.4	16.4
1968	5.6	12.4	17.7	23.7	40.5	15.6
1969	5.6	12.4	17.7	23.7	40.6	15.6
1970	5.4	12.2	17.6	23.8	40.9	15.6
1971	5.5	12.0	17.6	23.8	41.1	15.7
1972	5.5	11.9	17.5	23.9	41.4	15.9
1973	5.5	11.9	17.5	24.0	41.1	15.5
1974	5.7	12.0	17.6	24.1	40.6	14.8
1975	5.6	11.9	17.7	24.2	40.7	14.9
1976	5.6	11.9	17.7	24.2	40.7	14.9
1977	5.5	11.7	17.6	24.3	40.9	14.9
1978	5.4	11.7	17.6	24.2	41.1	15.1
1979	5.4	11.6	17.5	24.1	41.4	15.3
1980	5.3	11.6	17.6	24.4	41.1	14.6
1981	5.3	11.4	17.5	24.6	41.2	14.4
1982	5.0	11.3	17.2	24.4	42.2	15.3
1983	4.9	11.2	17.2	24.5	42.4	15.3
1984	4.8	11.1	17.1	24.5	42.5	15.4
1985	4.8	11.0	16.9	24.3	43.1	16.1
1986	4.7	10.9	16.9	24.1	43.4	16.5
1987	4.6	10.7	16.8	24.0	43.8	17.2
1988	4.6	10.7	16.7	24.0	44.0	17.2
1989	4.6	10.6	16.5	23.7	44.6	17.9
1990	4.6	10.8	16.6	23.8	44.3	17.4
1991	4.5	10.7	16.6	24.1	44.2	17.1
1992	4.3	10.5	16.5	24.0	44.7	17.6
1993	4.1	9.9	15.7	23.3	47.0	20.3
1994	4.2	10.0	15.7	23.3	46.9	20.1
1995	4.4	10.1	15.8	23.2	46.5	20.0
1996	4.2	10.0	15.8	23.1	46.8	20.3
1997	4.2	9.9	15.7	23.0	47.2	20.7
1998	4.2	9.9	15.7	23.0	47.3	20.7
1999	4.3	9.9	15.6	23.0	47.2	20.3
2000	4.3	9.8	15.4	22.7	47.7	21.1
2001	4.2	9.7	15.4	22.9	47.7	21.0

SOURCE: "Table F-2. Share of Aggregate Income Received by Each Fifth and Top 5 Percent of Families, 1947–2001," in *Historical Income Tables—Families*, U.S. Census Bureau, September 2002, http://www.census.gov/hhes/income/histinc/f02.html (accessed February 21, 2005)

SAVINGS ARE DOWN, BANKRUPTCIES ARE UP

One of the risk factors for becoming homeless is the lack of a financial safety net upon which individuals can fall back should something unexpected occur. The loss of a job, and in many cases the concomitant loss of health insurance, is one such occurrence. An accident resulting in the need for expensive medical treatment is another example of the sort of incident that requires a financial safety net. Financial experts stress the importance of maintaining savings that can help see people through this sort of crisis. Yet in the United States, the rate at which Americans save has been declining since the 1980s.

Figure 3.8 provides an overview of the personal savings rate over the period 1970–2004. The Bureau of Economic Analysis defines personal savings as the rate

FIGURE 3.7

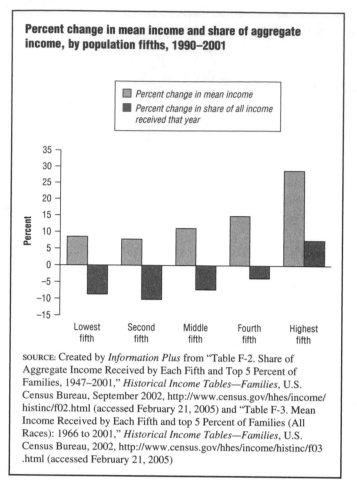

Percent change in mean income and share of aggregate income, by population fifths, 1990–2001

SOURCE: Created by *Information Plus* from "Table F-2. Share of Aggregate Income Received by Each Fifth and Top 5 Percent of Families, 1947–2001," *Historical Income Tables—Families*, U.S. Census Bureau, September 2002, http://www.census.gov/hhes/income/histinc/f02.html (accessed February 21, 2005) and "Table F-3. Mean Income Received by Each Fifth and top 5 Percent of Families (All Races): 1966 to 2001," *Historical Income Tables—Families*, U.S. Census Bureau, 2002, http://www.census.gov/hhes/income/histinc/f03.html (accessed February 21, 2005)

FIGURE 3.8

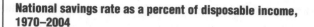
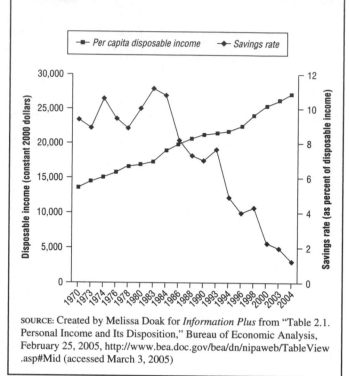

National savings rate as a percent of disposable income, 1970–2004

SOURCE: Created by Melissa Doak for *Information Plus* from "Table 2.1. Personal Income and Its Disposition," Bureau of Economic Analysis, February 25, 2005, http://www.bea.doc.gov/bea/dn/nipaweb/TableView.asp#Mid (accessed March 3, 2005)

at which we save our disposable income (the income remaining after taxes have been paid). Disposable income grew over this period from $13,563 in 1970 to $27,237 in 2004 (based on constant, inflation-adjusted 2000 dollars). The savings rate in 1970 was 9.4% of disposable income, but by 2004 it had dropped to just 1.2%. As people save less, they become more vulnerable to unplanned expenditures that periodically arise in life.

Exacerbating the problem of low savings is rising consumer credit debt. Kim Khan, in "How Does Your Debt Compare?" reported that not only is debt rising, but 43% of American families spend more than they earn each year and average $8,000 in credit card debt (MSN Money, http://moneycentral.msn.com/content/SavingandDebt/P70581.asp, accessed July 2, 2005). Mortgages also skyrocketed in the early 2000s. Because of historically low interest rates, many homeowners over-borrowed. According to the *American Housing Survey for the United States in 2003* (Census Bureau, September 2004), more than 855,000 owners had three or more mortgages on the homes they occupied, and 2.5 million owners had loans equal to or greater than the value of their homes. As a result, bankruptcies and foreclosures were on the rise.

The rise in the number of bankruptcy filings during the late 1990s, a period of strong economic growth, was likely the result of low savings and high credit debt. According to the Federal Reserve, the typical family filing for bankruptcy in 1997 owed more than one and a half times its annual income in short-term, high-interest debt. For example, a family earning $24,000 had an average of $36,000 in credit card and similar debt. Between 1980 and 2002, the number of personal bankruptcy filings rose by an astonishing 435%, from 287,580 in 1980 to 1,539,111 in 2002.

Controversial new bankruptcy regulations were signed into law by President George W. Bush in April 2005, making it more difficult for many to file personal bankruptcy. The new law addresses the uninformed and uneducated use of consumer credit by large numbers of Americans and includes a requirement that the successful conclusion of any personal bankruptcy case be accompanied by credit counseling for the filer, as well as a requirement that some filers repay some of their debt over a period of years, based on means.

UNEMPLOYMENT

The official unemployment rate has been the subject of considerable scrutiny and criticism over the years. Many social and economic researchers believe that the rate misrepresents the actual number of people who cannot find work to support themselves and their families. For example, the official unemployment figures do not count those who have given up searching for work because of failure to find work over a long period of time. The figures also leave out those who are underemployed, such as college graduates who take low-paying jobs or part-time jobs until adequate employment becomes available. It is likely, then, that the true number of people who cannot find adequate employment is higher than official statistics indicate.

Unemployment is a permanent feature of the economy. It can never be entirely eliminated since there will always be people who lose their jobs for various reasons. The transition between a lost job and the next job takes time even in the best of economic times.

The 1990s were a period of economic growth. The decade began with a seasonally adjusted unemployment rate in 1990 of 5.6%. The rate rose to a high of 7.5% in 1992 and then fell to a low of 4% in 2000. A rise in unemployment between 2000 and 2002 (31%) reflected the downturn in the economy that began in 2001 and was exacerbated in the uncertainty that followed the September 11 attacks.

By the end of 2002 the unemployment rate was 5.8%. (See Figure 3.9.) The first two quarters of 2003 saw the unemployment rate continue to rise. By June 2003 it had risen to a high of 6.5%. By August 2003 the unemployment rate had fallen slightly to 6%, but there were signs of a growing number of people dropping off the unemployment registers, having given up the search for a new job. The U.S. Bureau of Labor Statistics reported that in February 2005, eight million people were officially unemployed, or 5.4% of the labor-aged population wishing to work, down from the high of June 2003, but up from the previous month.

UNEMPLOYMENT RATES BY POPULATION SEGMENT. Some segments of American society have experienced more unemployment than other segments. According to the U.S. Bureau of Labor Statistics in *Employment Characteristics of Families* (April 2004), 8.1% of the nation's 75.3 million families reported having an unemployed member at some time during 2003. The proportion of black families with an unemployed member (13.7%) was higher than the proportion for Hispanic (11.1%), Asian (9.4%), or white families (7.1). (See Figure 3.10.)

Underemployed and Discouraged Workers

The U.S. Census Bureau's *Current Population Survey* regularly reports unemployment figures as well as figures for adults who are not in the labor force and a subgroup of people not in the labor force who are discouraged and have stopped looking for work. Dis-

FIGURE 3.9

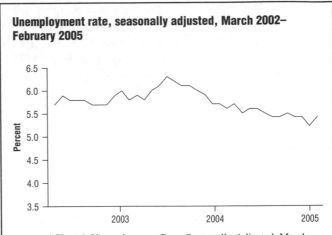

Unemployment rate, seasonally adjusted, March 2002–February 2005

SOURCE: "Chart 1. Unemployment Rate, Seasonally Adjusted, March 2002–February 2005," in *The Employment Situation: February 2005*, March 4, 2005, Bureau of Labor Statistics, http://www.bls.gov/news .release/pdf/empsit.pdf (accessed March 6, 2005)

FIGURE 3.10

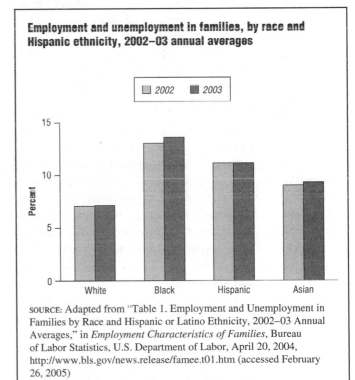

Employment and unemployment in families, by race and Hispanic ethnicity, 2002–03 annual averages

SOURCE: Adapted from "Table 1. Employment and Unemployment in Families by Race and Hispanic or Latino Ethnicity, 2002–03 Annual Averages," in *Employment Characteristics of Families*, Bureau of Labor Statistics, U.S. Department of Labor, April 20, 2004, http://www.bls.gov/news.release/famee.t01.htm (accessed February 26, 2005)

couraged workers give up looking for work specifically because they believe no jobs are available for them. In January 2005 the Bureau of Labor Statistics reported in *Labor Force Statistics from the Current Population Survey*, that 515,000 workers had given up looking for work, up 83,000 over the number reported one year earlier.

WELFARE REFORM AND THE POOR

In 1996 the passage of the Personal Responsibility and Work Opportunity Reconciliation Act (PL 104-193), the most sweeping welfare legislation since the 1960s, ended Aid to Families with Dependent Children (AFDC) and gave the states control over the administration of benefits in the form of Temporary Assistance for Needy Families (TANF) grants. In addition, the law made significant changes to Supplemental Security Income (SSI) and Medicaid.

Returning Local Control

The TANF block grant legislation (the welfare reform initiative) was designed to fulfill two primary objectives:

- To return more control of relief assistance programs to the state governments—this granted the states great flexibility to design whatever mix of services and benefits they thought would reduce dependency and provide for the needy

- To limit the amount of time a person spends on public assistance—specifically, the 1996 law contained a five-year lifetime limit on receipt of federally funded cash assistance and authorized states to impose shorter time limits at their discretion; and required that, by the year 2002, 50% of all recipients who had received cash aid for two years work at least thirty hours a week in order to continue receiving benefits

Many people argued that these were worthy goals. First, they believed local authorities would be better equipped to determine the needs of the people in their area than a distant federal government. Second, they believed the focus on encouraging the poor to work rather than receive public assistance was important because the old system unintentionally discouraged welfare recipients from working, since most welfare recipients could not meet the increased expenses incurred while working (transportation and child care) with their low-paying jobs. Supporters of the reform also pointed out that the welfare-to-work initiative had another, residual benefit: the likelihood that the children of the recipient would be impoverished as an adult were lowered.

However, critics of the reform bill pointed out that local responsibility for the poor has historically proven to result in discriminatory practices and lends itself to subjective and/or punitive practices. The second objective—to put people to work—resembled the deserving/undeserving moral judgments of the poor in the nineteenth century. It was in applying these same qualifications that the poorhouses were born.

These attitudes and their results continue to provide a basis for concern regarding welfare reform. While local control makes it easier to address the specific needs of the poor in particular areas, it also makes it possible for localities to restrict benefits in ways that a nationwide program would never be able to do. The welfare reform laws also contain an inherent assumption that anyone who really wants work can find it, and that anyone who cannot find work within a specified period must not really be trying and therefore does not deserve government aid. This assumption ignores the fact that many people on welfare, and poor people in general, lack the skills or education necessary for most jobs. The homeless, who do not have a fixed address or telephone number and may not have clean clothes for an interview, are especially vulnerable in this system.

LIFE AFTER WELFARE REFORM. Welfare reform proved to be more successful at removing individuals and families from welfare rolls than its many critics expected. Welfare rolls had declined by roughly half since the early 1990s and employment rates had risen for most former (and many current) welfare recipients. How much of these positive results were due to the economic boom of the 1990s, with the accompanying increase in jobs, remains to be determined. Since the economic downturn in 2001, when the most recent recession began, the number of welfare recipients continued to decline from 5.3 million in 2001 to 4.7 million in June 2004, according to the Administration for Children and Families of the U.S. Department of Health and Human Services.

Researchers know that there have been declines in the welfare rolls, but as of yet they do not know what happened to the people who are no longer aid recipients. Major studies are now underway. To get a look at what information is available and what the welfare reform act meant to people whose lives were directly affected, Sheila Zedlewski and Donald Alderson of the Urban Institute analyzed current data and presented the following preliminary results of the AFDC-to-TANF reform measures (*Families on Welfare in the Post-TANF Era: Do They Differ from Their Pre-TANF Counterparts?* Paper presented at the American Economics Association meeting, New Orleans, January 2001). They based their analysis on a comparison of 1,831 families on TANF in 1997 and 850 families in 1999, representing 2.2 million and 1.5 million families, respectively. The characteristics and work activities presented were obtained from interviewing the adult most knowledgeable about the children in the family, usually the mother.

The researchers found:

- The proportion of single mothers on welfare who reported living with partners increased.

- The proportion of African-Americans on welfare who reported living with partners increased.

- The proportion of adults on welfare who worked for pay rose.

- The proportion of recipients who were new entrants to the welfare system was about the same, despite some new state programs that attempt to divert adults from enrolling in TANF.

- Adults on TANF in 1999 were no more disadvantaged than those on TANF in 1997.

- Longer-term welfare recipients were significantly more disadvantaged than the new entrants.

- The proportion of recipients with less than high school education, and therefore less employable, was the same (2%) in 1997 and 1999.

EMPLOYMENT AND THE HOMELESS

It is extremely difficult for the homeless to escape their condition without a job. Yet it is equally difficult for the homeless to find and keep good jobs. Health Care for the Homeless Information Resource Center's newsletter "Employment for Homeless People: What Works, Fall 2000" listed the following barriers:

- Lack of transportation

- Medical and dental problems

- Housing instability

- Mental illness

- Substance abuse

- Domestic violence

- Lack of job skills

- Criminal record

- Lack of child care

- Lack of education

- Diminished self-confidence

In addition, the homeless, like other workers, are subject to the state of the labor market. The availability of jobs and the wages paid for the available jobs often determined whether or not people could remove themselves from homelessness.

Wage Barriers to Exiting Homelessness

Of the homeless respondents from a 1996 study by the Urban Institute, 44% reported working in the previous month. Two percent earned income as self-employed entrepreneurs—by peddling or selling belongings. Forty-two percent of the homeless respondents worked for, and were paid by, an employer.

Advocates for the homeless are concerned that this dependency on wages, combined with the unfavorable labor market conditions, actually supports continued homelessness. Since the majority of homeless people do not have more than a high school education, and since a majority of the low-paying jobs go to those with at least a high school education, advocates worry that the available job opportunities for homeless people provide an insufficient base for exiting homelessness.

WORK FOR THE HOMELESS

It costs money to live. Even homeless people have needs that can only be met with money. From needing something as simple as a toothbrush or a meal, to money for a newspaper or a phone call to a job prospect, homeless people need money to begin to improve their lives. Out of the need to survive, homeless people have come up with a number of ways to earn money, weaving their ventures among local ordinances, public opinion, and the labor market.

Street Newspapers: Bootstrap Initiatives

In the United States, as well as overseas, homeless people are writing, publishing, and selling their own newspapers. *The 2003 North American Directory of Street Newspapers*, published by the National Coalition for the Homeless in September 2003, reported there were over fifty street newspapers across the United States and Canada.

Many street newspaper publishers belong to a professional organization, the North American Street Newspaper Association (NASNA), organized in Chicago in 1996. NASNA holds an annual conference, offers business advice and services, and supports street newspaper publishers in the same way that any professional organization supports its membership. They also lobby the government on homeless issues.

Generally, the street newspapers are loaned on credit to homeless vendors who then sell them for $1 or $2 each. At the end of the workday, the vendor pays the publisher the agreed-upon price and pockets the remainder as profit. For example, Boston's *Spare Change* newspaper publishes 10,000 copies every two weeks. Vendors purchase newspapers for $0.25 each and resell them for $1.00, pocketing $0.75 for each paper sold. New York City's *Street News* gives the vendors thirty free copies, allows them to buy additional copies for $0.25 each, and the papers are sold for $1.25.

This cooperative arrangement among publishers, vendors, and consumers has many benefits:

- Creation of jobs

- Supports the work ethic

- Accommodates the mobility of homeless people

- Provides reliable employment despite crisis living conditions

- Informs the public about homelessness

- Erases stereotypes of the drunken, illiterate, "unworthy" homeless person

- Gives the writers and vendors a sense of accomplishment

- Provides immediate cash to people who desperately need it

Most of the homeless newspaper vendors have not been able to earn enough just from selling newspapers to move themselves from homelessness, but as the quality and availability of these publications grow, homeless people envision the street newspaper industry becoming a means of moving tens of thousands from homelessness.

STREET NEWS, NEW YORK CITY. The earliest known homeless publication, *Street News*, was launched in 1989 by the *New York Times* and the New York Metropolitan Transportation Authority. By 1991, when the publication suffered from a scandal involving misuse of funds, *Street News* was boasting some 25,000 copies per issue, which then fell to 6,000 by 2005. The paper is known for its radical political stance and unusual stories.

SPARE CHANGE, BOSTON. Begun in 1992 as one of the nation's first street newspapers to benefit the homeless, *Spare Change* has been published every other week by the Homeless Empowerment Project (HEP) in Cambridge, Massachusetts. Its stated mission is to "play a role in ending homelessness in our community by providing income, skill development and self-advocacy opportunities to people who are homeless or at risk of homelessness." The newspaper provides a forum for creative expression and advocacy for homeless individuals. Along with the production, distribution, and sale of the street newspaper, HEP operates a training center for teaching computer skills to the homeless. They also sponsor a writer's workshop and promote a speaker's bureau. In June 2005, however, the paper was facing an uncertain future, with an operating loss of $4,000 per issue, according to Jay Fitzgerald in the *Boston Herald* (June 16, 2005).

Day Labor

Regular work, characterized by a permanent and ongoing relationship between employer and employee, does not figure significantly in the lives and routines of most homeless, as it is usually unavailable or inaccessible. Homelessness makes getting and keeping regular work difficult due to the lack of a fixed address, communication, and, in many cases, the inability to get a good night's sleep, clean up, and dress appropriately. Studies have found that the longer a person is homeless, the less likely he or she is to pursue wage labor and the more likely that person is to engage in some other form of work. For those who do participate in regular jobs, in

most cases, the wages received are not sufficient to escape from living on the street.

Day labor, wage labor secured on a day-to-day basis, typically at lower wages and changing locations, is somewhat easier for the homeless to secure. Day labor may involve unloading trucks, cleaning up warehouses, cutting grass, or washing windows. Day labor often fits the abilities of the homeless because transportation may be provided to the work site, and appearance, work history, and references are less important. Equally attractive to a homeless person, day labor usually pays cash at quitting time, thus providing immediate pocket money. Day labor jobs are, however, by definition, without a future. They can provide for daily survival on the street but are not generally sufficient to get a person off the street. Consequently, many homeless turn to shadow work.

Shadow Work

Shadow work refers to methods of getting money that are outside the normal economy, some of them illegal. These methods include panhandling, scavenging, selling possessions, picking up cans and selling them, selling one's blood or plasma, theft, or peddling illegal goods, drugs, or services. A homeless person seldom engages in all of these activities consistently but may turn to some of them as needed. Researchers estimate that 60% of homeless people engage in some shadow work. Shadow work is more common for homeless men than homeless women. Theft is more common for younger homeless persons.

A mixture of institutionalized assistance, wage labor, and shadow work is typical of those who live on the streets. Studies have found that many homeless people are very resourceful in surviving the rigors of street life and recommend that this resourcefulness be somehow channeled into training that can lead to jobs paying a living wage. Some observers suggest, however, that homeless people who have adapted to street life may likely need transitional socialization programs as much as programs that teach them a marketable skill.

Institutionalized Assistance

Institutionalized assistance refers to "established or routine monetary assistance patterned in accordance with tradition, legislation, or organizations" (David Snow et al., *Material Survival Strategies on the Street: Homeless People as Bricoleurs, Homelessness in America*, edited by the National Coalition for the Homeless, Phoenix, AZ: Oryx Press, 1996). This would include institutionalized labor, such as that provided by soup kitchens, shelters, and rehabilitation programs that sometimes pay the homeless for work related to facility operation. The number of people employed by these agencies is a small percentage of the homeless population. In addition, the pay—room, board, and a small stipend—tends to tie the homeless to the organization rather than providing the means to get off the street.

Institutionalized assistance also includes income supplements provided by the government, family, and friends. According to *Material Survival Strategies on the Street*, while a considerable number of the homeless may receive some financial help from family or friends, it is usually small. Women seem to receive more help from family and friends and to remain on the streets for shorter periods of time than men. Cash from family and friends seems to decline with the amount of time spent on the street and with age.

EXITING HOMELESSNESS

According to the 1996 Urban Institute study, homeless people say that the primary reason they cannot exit homelessness is insufficient income. Of those clients surveyed, 54% cited employment-related reasons for why they remained homeless. Nearly a third (30%) cited insufficient income and nearly a quarter (24%) cited lack of a job.

The data from the Urban Institute study showed how little income the homeless earn. Eighty-one percent of the "currently" homeless had incomes of less than $700 in the thirty days before the study; the average income was $367. Most of the homeless in the study were receiving their income from Aid to Families with Dependent Children (now TANF). Of formerly homeless people surveyed, the median income of $470 would amount to an annual income of $5,640, an amount well below the poverty level for a single person ($7,740 in 1996).

These income levels clearly demonstrate the financial difficulty a homeless person encounters in trying to permanently exit homelessness or poverty. However, exiting homelessness—especially by the chronically homeless—requires more than income. Persistent medical assistance, sometimes for an entire lifetime, has to be available for the mentally ill, or people with addiction and substance abuse problems. Furthermore, without programs such as job training, assistance with general education, help with socialization skills, and in many instances counseling, the maintenance of a degree of independent life for the long term can be very difficult for the chronically homeless.

CHAPTER 4
THE HOUSING PROBLEM

A home was at one time defined as a place where a family resided, but as American society changed, so did the definition of home. A home is now considered a place where one or more people live together, a private place to which they have legal right and where strangers may be excluded. It is the place where people keep their belongings and where they feel safe from the outside world. For housing to be considered a home it should be permanent with an address. Furthermore, in the best of circumstances a home should not be substandard but should still be affordable. Many people would agree that a place to call home is a basic human right.

Those people who have no fixed address and no private space of their own are the homeless. The obvious solution to homelessness would be to find a home for everyone who needs one. There is enough housing available in the United States; the problem lies in the affordability of that housing. Most of the housing in the United States costs far more than the very poor can afford to rent or buy. According to Census 2000, the median monthly gross rent for the nation's 35.7 million renter-occupied housing units (one-third of the nation's 105.5 million occupied housing units) was $602, a 5.4% increase over the $571 median for 1990. (See Table 4.1.) Renters in California led the nation in the share of their incomes spent on rent (27.7%). According to the Census Bureau, nine of the nation's ten highest-rent cities are in California, with median gross rents ranging from $985 to $1,272.

Homeownership is well beyond the reach of most low-income families. The National Association of Realtors reported that in January 2005 the median price for all housing types was $189,000, up 10.5% from January 2004, when the median price was $171,000 (Beth Bresnahan, "Existing-Home Sales Hold Steady in January," New York: RISMedia, February 28, 2005).

THE PRIMARY REASON FOR HOMELESSNESS

Research indicates that the primary cause of most homelessness is the inability to pay for housing, caused by some combination of low income and high housing costs. While many other factors may contribute to homelessness, such as a low level of educational achievement or mental illness, addressing these problems will seldom bring someone out of homelessness by itself. The underlying issue of not being able to afford housing will still need to be addressed.

New York University (NYU) researchers conducted a study that showed no real difference exists between homeless people and the rest of society, other than housing affordability issues. Funded by the National Institute of Mental Health (NIMH), the NYU team conducted a five-year study of 564 homeless families. They presented their results in *Predictors of Homelessness among Families in New York City: From Shelter Request to Housing Stability* (November 1998).

The research team found that when homeless families were provided with subsidies that allowed them to afford housing, 80% remained housed in their own residence for at least a year. This was true regardless of their social or personal attributes, such as their education level, race, or sex. This confirms the idea that while many homeless people face difficulties due to their personal backgrounds, these problems are not what drove most of them into homelessness. Furthermore, if given access to affordable housing, most will be able to take advantage of it.

HOUSING THE POOR

When 30% or more of a meager income is spent on housing, hardship is the result. For that reason the federal government's official standard for low-income housing is that rent and utilities should cost no more than 30% of the annual income of someone in poverty. "Low-income housing" is housing that is affordable to those in poverty based on that formula. In 2005 a family of one adult and one child with an annual income of less than $12,830 was

TABLE 4.1

Median gross rent and median gross rent as percent of household income, 1990 and 2000

Area	1990		2000	
	Median gross rent	Median gross rent as percent of household income (1989)	Median gross rent	Median gross rent as percent of household income (1999)
United States	$571	26.4	$602	25.5
Region				
Northeast	$638	26.4	$651	25.9
Midwest	$506	25.4	$533	24.0
South	$517	25.7	$559	25.0
West	$684	27.9	$694	27.1
State				
Alabama	$415	24.8	$447	24.8
Alaska	$714	23.8	$720	24.8
Arizona	$560	27.5	$619	26.6
Arkansas	$418	26.5	$453	24.4
California	$792	29.1	$747	27.7
Colorado	$533	26.1	$671	26.4
Connecticut	$764	26.6	$681	25.4
Delaware	$634	24.7	$639	24.3
District of Columbia	$612	25.4	$618	24.8
Florida	$613	28.0	$641	27.5
Georgia	$553	25.8	$613	24.9
Hawaii	$830	27.4	$779	27.2
Idaho	$422	23.8	$515	25.3
Illinois	$569	25.9	$605	24.4
Indiana	$477	24.3	$521	23.9
Iowa	$429	24.1	$470	23.2
Kansas	$474	24.5	$498	23.4
Kentucky	$408	24.9	$445	24.0
Louisiana	$450	27.9	$466	25.8
Maine	$535	26.8	$497	25.3
Maryland	$700	25.4	$689	24.7
Massachusetts	$741	26.8	$684	25.5
Michigan	$540	27.2	$546	24.4
Minnesota	$539	26.7	$566	24.7
Mississippi	$394	27.1	$439	25.0
Missouri	$470	25.2	$484	24.0
Montana	$396	25.0	$447	25.3
Nebraska	$445	23.7	$491	23.0
Nevada	$650	26.8	$699	26.5
New Hampshire	$701	26.4	$646	24.2
New Jersey	$756	26.3	$751	25.5
New Mexico	$473	26.5	$503	26.6
New York	$620	26.3	$672	26.8
North Carolina	$488	24.4	$548	24.3
North Dakota	$400	23.9	$412	22.3
Ohio	$483	25.3	$515	24.2
Oklahoma	$434	25.4	$456	24.3
Oregon	$521	25.5	$620	26.9
Pennsylvania	$516	26.1	$531	25.0
Rhode Island	$625	27.5	$553	25.7
South Carolina	$482	24.4	$510	24.4
South Dakota	$391	24.6	$426	22.9

TABLE 4.1

Median gross rent and median gross rent as percent of household income, 1990 and 2000 [CONTINUED]

Area	1990		2000	
	Median gross rent	Median gross rent as percent of household income (1989)	Median gross rent	Median gross rent as percent of household income (1999)
Tennessee	$456	25.0	$505	24.8
Texas	$505	24.6	$574	24.4
Utah	$471	23.8	$597	24.9
Vermont	$570	27.1	$553	26.2
Virginia	$632	25.8	$650	24.5
Washington	$569	25.7	$663	26.5
West Virginia	$387	26.8	$401	25.8
Wisconsin	$510	24.9	$540	23.4
Wyoming	$425	23.7	$437	22.5
Puerto Rico	$261	29.4	$297	27.0

Note: The dollars have been adjusted to 2000 dollars using the government's Consumer Price Index (CPI). This means that the effect of inflation has been eliminated.

SOURCE: Robert Bonnette, "Table 2. Median Gross Rent and Median Gross Rent as Percentage of Household Income for the United States, Regions, and States, and for Puerto Rico: 1990 and 2000," in *Housing Costs of Renters: 2000*, Census 2000 Brief, C2KBR-21, May 2003, http://www.census.gov/prod/2003pubs/c2kbr-21.pdf (accessed February 28, 2005)

National Low Income Housing Coalition (NLIHC) quoted a finding by a congressional commission that there were almost two million fewer units of housing affordable to low-income households than there were such households in 2004 (Cushing N. Dolbeare, *Changing Priorities: The Federal Budget and Housing Assistance, 1976–2005*, National Low Income Housing Coalition, 2004).

The poor essentially have two rental options: low-income housing units operated by local public housing authorities and privately owned housing, whose owners accept Section 8 rental assistance vouchers issued by the federal government. In 2002 about 1.5 million families took advantage of the Section 8 vouchers. However, the rents permitted under the voucher program have not kept pace with actual rents in many markets. In his testimony before the House Subcommittee on Housing and Community Opportunity on April 23, 2002, Roy Ziegler of the National Leased Housing Association reported that many Section 8 vouchers go unused because there are not enough rental units available to which the vouchers can be applied.

According to a 1999 report from the U.S. Department of Housing and Urban Development (HUD) (*Waiting in Vain: An Update on America's Housing Crisis*, Washington, DC), in 1998 a family spent an average of thirty-three months on a waiting list for HUD-assisted housing operated by the largest public housing authorities. The situation had improved somewhat by 2003, when the U.S. Conference of Mayors reported that applicants waited an average of twenty months for public housing; however, the survey also revealed that 59% of the surveyed cities had stopped accepting applications for at least one assisted

in poverty; a family of four with two children under age eighteen was in poverty if their income was less than $19,350 (*Federal Register* 70, No. 33, February 18, 2005). Thus, in 2005 low-income housing for a family of two should cost no more than $321 a month; for a family of four it should cost no more than $484 a month.

Not Enough Affordable Units Available

Researchers from every discipline agree that the number of housing units that are affordable to the poor is insufficient to meet needs. A paper published by the housing program (*Hunger and Homelessness Survey: A Status Report on Hunger and Homelessness in America's Cities, A 27-City Survey, December 2004*). High housing costs also contributed to the homelessness problem. The city officials estimated that low-income households spent an average of 45% of their income on housing.

In December 2000 Congress established the bipartisan Millennial Housing Commission (MHC) to examine the role of the federal government in meeting the nation's housing needs. In *Meeting Our Housing Challenges* (Washington, DC, May 2002), the commission stated that "there is simply not enough affordable housing. The inadequacy of supply increases dramatically as one moves down the ladder of family earnings. The challenge is most acute for rental housing in high-cost areas, and the most egregious problem is for the very poor."

The federal government considers a housing cost of 30% or less of current income affordable and appropriate. In 2003 the median monthly housing cost for renter households was $651; the median monthly housing cost as a percent of current income was 30.1%. In other words, half of renters paid more than 30.1% of their income on rent—more than what the federal government considers affordable and appropriate. The median monthly housing cost for owner households was $758; the median monthly housing cost as a percent of current income was 18.2%—lower than that of renters. However, almost a quarter (23.5%) of owners paid above 30% of their income for housing (*American Housing Survey for the United States: 2003*, Census Bureau, September 2004).

The National League of Cities, in its annual opinion survey of municipal elected officials (*The State of America's Cities 2004*), found that 23% of city officials believed that increasing the availability of quality affordable housing should be a priority for the federal government. (See Table 4.2.)

The Joint Center for Housing Studies of Harvard University reported in *The State of the Nation's Housing: 2004* that in 2003, three in ten households had housing affordability problems, spending more than 30% of their incomes on housing. Thirteen percent spent more than half of their income on housing. Two million households were housed in severely inadequate units. The report also stated that affordability problems for renters were on the rise in the early 2000s, with the median share of income spent on rent rising to near 29% by 2003. (See Figure 4.1.)

At Risk of Becoming Homeless

In January 2001 the HUD Office of Policy Development and Research released the results of an in-depth study (*A Report on Worst Case Housing Needs in 1999—New Opportunity Amid Continuing Challenges*). The report found that in the two years between 1997 and 1999, a time of economic prosperity, the number of renter households with

TABLE 4.2

Issues selected by city officials as high priorities for federal attention, 2004

Cost and availability of health services	31%
Overall economic conditions	29%
Impacts of unfunded mandates/preemption	28%
Unemployment	25%
Availability of quality affordable housing	23%
Homeland security/emergency preparedness	18%
Infrastructure	15%
Traffic	12%
Quality of public education	12%
Federal relations with your city	10%

Note: Data reflects percent of city officials listing item as one of the three conditions the federal government and the presidential candidates should devote the most attention to.

SOURCE: Christiana Brennan and Christopher Hoene, "Table 5. High Priority Areas for Federal Attention," in *The State of America's Cities 2004: The Annual Opinion Survey of Municipal Elected Officials*, National League of Cities, 2004, http://www.nlc.org/content/Files/RMPstateAmerCitiesrpt04.pdf (accessed February 28, 2005)

worst-case housing needs declined at least 8% (440,000 households), reversing the preceding ten-year trend of growing worst-case needs. However, there were still nearly five million households in serious need of housing assistance. HUD defines families with "worst-case needs" as those who:

- Are renters

- Do not receive housing assistance from federal, state, or local government programs

- Have incomes below 50% of their local area median family income, as determined by HUD

- Pay more than one half of their income for rent and utilities, or live in severely substandard housing

In other words, these are extremely impoverished people who do not own their housing and can barely afford to pay their housing costs, or can only afford to stay in the very worst housing. Of all the people who had housing, they are the ones closest to being forced into homelessness. HUD found that 10.9 million people inhabited the 4.9 million households in the worst-case housing classification in 1999. This number included 1.4 million elderly and 3.6 million children.

The reduction in the number of worst-case households between 1997 and 1999 was attributed to income growth among low-income renters rather than to growth in the number of affordable rental housing units. The report stated that the number of units affordable and available to renters with extremely low income fell, and also predicted that in the event of an economic slowdown, income growth among low-income renters could very well be reversed. In fact, the study done by the Joint Center for Housing Studies of Harvard University showed that as the country entered a period of recession in 2001, renter affordability problems worsened. (See Figure 4.1.)

FIGURE 4.1

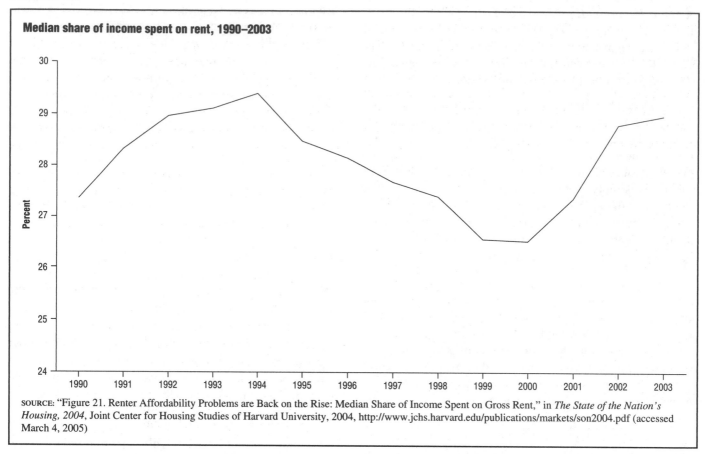

Median share of income spent on rent, 1990–2003

SOURCE: "Figure 21. Renter Affordability Problems are Back on the Rise: Median Share of Income Spent on Gross Rent," in *The State of the Nation's Housing, 2004*, Joint Center for Housing Studies of Harvard University, 2004, http://www.jchs.harvard.edu/publications/markets/son2004.pdf (accessed March 4, 2005)

For as long as worst-case needs have been reported, affordability rather than housing quality has been the main problem facing renters. A household that spends more than 50% of its income on housing is considered severely cost-burdened. *The State of the Nation's Housing: 2004* found that fully half of the households in the bottom fifth of income distribution spent more than 50% of their income on housing. This group spent, on average, only $161 per month on food and $34 per month on health care.

Working Families Struggle to Keep Up

Out of Reach, 2004, a report by the National Low Income Housing Coalition (NLIHC), compared the Fair Market Rent—the U.S. Department of Housing and Urban Development's estimate of what a household seeking modest rental housing must expect to pay for rent and utilities—to the median hourly wage. The hourly wage needed to pay the fair market rent for a two-bedroom apartment is $15.37. However, the median hourly wage in the United States is only $14.00, more than a quarter of people in the United States earn less than $10.00 per hour, and the federal minimum wage was $5.15. The report stated that rents continued to rise faster than did incomes in 2004.

According to *Out of Reach*, in no metropolitan area of the country could a minimum-wage worker afford a two-bedroom apartment. In only four counties in the country could a person earning minimum wage even afford a one-bedroom apartment. In most cities, the housing wage was at least twice the federal minimum wage.

Reasons for the Lack of Low-Income Housing

The major reasons for the lack of low-income housing are declining federal support; bureaucratic red tape, fraud, and waste; and a variety of local factors that affect new construction.

DECLINING FEDERAL SUPPORT. The development and operation of low-income housing units depends on government funding administered by HUD. In *Changing Priorities: The Federal Budget and Housing Assistance, 1976–2005* (National Low Income Housing Coalition, October 2004), Cushing N. Dolbeare argued, "The federal government's high water mark for housing assistance was the mid-1970s, and funding has not come near that level in the years since. Nor will it in the next five years, absent a major policy and funding shift." Between 1976 and 2004, the housing assistance budget authority decreased 48%; in addition, in 1976 low-income housing units were being built, while in 2004, the budget mainly maintains existing units. In fact, due to public housing demolitions, the number of low-income housing units declined by 2004.

FRAUD, WASTE, AND DELAYS HAMPER REHABILITATION. A major HUD goal is to increase the supply of affordable, decent, and safe rental housing, but it has not been particularly successful in this regard. In *Department of Housing and Urban Development: Status of Achieving Key Outcomes and Addressing Major Management Challenges* (Washington, DC, July 2001), the U.S. General Accounting Office (GAO), now Government Accountability Office, the watchdog arm of Congress, noted that HUD programs had been plagued by fraud, waste, and errors.

One of the few federal housing production programs administered by HUD is the Urban Revitalization Demonstration Program, commonly known as HOPE VI. This program provides grants to local public housing authorities, who contract with private developers to rehabilitate public housing. Between fiscal years 1993 and 2001, HUD awarded about $4.5 billion in HOPE VI revitalization grants to 98 public housing authorities for 165 sites. In 2002 Congress charged the GAO with investigating and reporting on progress and HUD's oversight of the projects. In *Public Housing: HUD's Oversight of HOPE VI Sites Needs to Be More Consistent* (Washington, DC, May 2003), the GAO reported that as of December 31, 2002, construction was complete on only fifteen of the 165 sites. About one-quarter (27%) of the planned rehabilitation work had been done but nearly half (47%, or $2.1 billion) of the grant money had been spent. Work had been completed by the deadline on only three of the grants and the construction deadlines had expired on forty-two grants. For fiscal year 2004 the Bush administration proposed eliminating the HOPE VI program; however, the program was funded at $120 million, down 76.7% from the $574 million funded in fiscal year 2003.

LOW PROFIT MARGINS BRING NEGLECT. HUD contracts with private owners limit profits and often limit the monies put back into the property for repairs. The existing housing available to renters at the lowest income levels often suffers from lack of upkeep. Neglected maintenance results in deterioration and sometimes removal from the housing inventory altogether.

According to *The State of the Nation's Housing, 2003*, about 705,000 tenants receiving government housing assistance in 2003 lived in substandard conditions. HUD data showed that during the late 1990s more than one million very-low-income residential units were lost as old buildings were torn down or owners opted out of low-income programs; also lost were 750,000 units available to the next income level (30% of area median income).

FACTORS THAT INHIBIT CONSTRUCTION. Construction of low-income units has been hampered by community resistance, by regulations that increase the cost of construction, and by limits on federal tax credits that make new construction unprofitable.

In his "Dissenting Statement to the Report of the Millennial Housing Commission" (May 30, 2002), Commissioner Robert Rector complained: "It is a simple fact that those cities that have the greatest 'affordability' problems are those that have 'smart growth' or other regulatory policies that severely limit new housing growth. Policies such as restrictive zoning, antiquated building codes, and high impact fees for new construction reduce housing supply and greatly increase costs for everyone in a community."

To many people, the prospect of low-income subsidized housing is synonymous with rising crime, falling property values, and overcrowded classrooms, and it is cause for protest. Resistance to the construction of low-income housing is said to be evidence of a "Not in My Backyard"(NIMBY) way of thinking. *From NIMBY to Good Neighbors: Recent Studies Reinforce that Apartments Are Good for a Community*, a 2003 report from the National Multi Housing Council/National Apartment Association, summarizes research showing that smart growth may depend on the development of more high-density housing, such as apartments.

Developers complain that there is no profit to be made from building and operating low-income housing. The 1986 Low-Income Housing Tax Credit program gave the states $1.25 per capita in tax credits toward the private development of low-income housing. In "A New Era for Affordable Housing" (*National Real Estate Investor*, March 1, 2003), H. Lee Murphy reported on National Council of State Agencies' data indicating that construction peaked in 1994, when 117,100 apartment units were built with the credits. Skyrocketing construction costs brought a decline in new construction, which reached a low of 66,900 units in 2000. In 2001 Congress raised the per capita allotment to $1.75 and provided that the formula would rise each year with inflation. The tax credits financed the construction of 75,000 new units in 2001.

Affordable Housing for the Homeless

In testimony before the House Subcommittee on Housing and Community Opportunity, Committee on Financial Services, on June 21, 2003, Nan P. Roman, President of the National Alliance to End Homelessness, spoke about affordable housing and the homeless. She claimed that for 80% of the homeless, "homelessness is a housing affordability issue." Roman also testified that for the remaining 20%—the chronically homeless who suffer from a variety of disabilities ranging from mental illness to substance abuse, HIV/AIDS, and physical problems—200,000 units of supportive housing such as group homes, multi-family units, or individual homes with programs to address their needs "could end chronic homelessness."

HABITAT FOR HUMANITY

One group dedicated to solving the housing problem one house at a time was the brainchild of Millard and Linda Fuller, who formed Habitat for Humanity International with a group of supporters in 1976. The purpose of this worldwide Christian service organization is to provide simple housing for the needy, built by volunteers assisted by the future homeowner. The homeowner assumes an interest-free, thirty-year mortgage, and materials are funded through donations and fund-raising activities. The idea is to give people assistance accompanied by responsibility.

By March 2005 Habitat for Humanity International had built more than 175,000 houses that sheltered one million people worldwide. Homes in developing countries may cost less than $1,000 to build while the average house in the United States can cost up to $46,600. Not all houses are new; the organization also restores older homes. Many volunteers travel to other countries to build homes. The most famous volunteers, former President Jimmy Carter and his wife, Rosalynn, made their first work trip in 1984 to New York City, sparking widespread interest in the movement. An annual event since that time, the week-long Jimmy Carter Work Project built more than fifty homes in Benton Harbor and Detroit, Michigan, in June 2005.

WHERE THE HOMELESS LIVE

When faced with high rents and low housing availability, many poor people become homeless. What happens to them? Where do they live? Research shows that after becoming homeless, many people move around, staying in one place for a while, then moving on to another place. Many homeless people take advantage of homeless shelters at some point. Such shelters may be funded by the federal government, by religious organizations, or by other private homeless advocates.

Emergency Housing: Shelters and Transitional Housing

Typically, a homeless shelter provides dormitory-style sleeping accommodations and bathing facilities, with varying services for laundry, telephone calls, and other needs. Residents are often limited in the length of their stays and must leave the shelter during the day under most circumstances. Transitional housing, on the other hand, is intended to bridge the gap between the shelter or street and permanent housing, with appropriate services to move the homeless into independent living. It may be a room in a hotel or motel, or it may be a subsidized apartment.

Counting the Homeless in Shelters

The 2000 census showed a decline in the number of people living in homeless shelters since the 1990 census. The Census Bureau counted 170,706 people living in shelters in March 2000, down 4% from the 178,638 people counted ten years earlier. Based on their own experience,

advocates for the homeless denied that there could have been a decline in the numbers. They criticized the Census Bureau's count as flawed, complaining that the survey excluded shelters with fewer than 100 beds and could not provide a full picture of homelessness because it was conducted over only three nights. In its report, *Emergency and Transitional Shelter Population: 2000: Census 2000 Special Reports* (Washington, DC, October 2001), the Census Bureau itself cautioned that its count was not "representative of the entire population that could be defined as living in emergency and transitional shelters."

According to the U.S. Conference of Mayors, in 2003 the number of demands for emergency shelter beds in the twenty-seven major cities surveyed increased since the previous year by an average of 6%. Of all the cities surveyed, 70% reported an increase in demand.

Homeless Youth

In 2002 an attempt to count the number of homeless people in Monterey County, California, was undertaken. Researchers focused on what was called "the fastest growing segment of the homeless population," homeless youth (*Homeless Census and Homeless Youth/Foster Teen Study*, County of Monterey, California, 2002). Based on an actual count and interviews with 2,681 homeless individuals, the researchers estimated that between 8,686 and 11,214 people were homeless in Monterey County at some time during 2002. The majority of those interviewed (65%) were found on the street, 14% were in transitional housing, and 6% were in emergency shelters.

Of the individuals counted, more than one-fifth (21%) were between the ages of fourteen and eighteen. The youths were asked to describe their current living situation. The majority (61%) reported staying temporarily with family or friends. More than one-fifth (22%) reported they were living outdoors, 6.1% were living in a shelter, and 11.5% were living in an automobile/van. This particular segment of the homeless tended to shy away from shelters, especially if they were underage and feared interference from the authorities.

Homeless Children

In accordance with the provisions of the Education for Homeless Children and Youth program, Title VII-B of the McKinney-Vento Homeless Assistance Act (42 USC 11431 et seq.), states that receive funds under the act must submit a report to the U.S. Department of Education regarding the estimated number of homeless children in the state every four years beginning in 2006. According to the previous count (*Report to Congress Fiscal Year 2000*, Washington, DC, 2000), in 2000 there were an estimated 866,899 homeless children in forty-six reporting states. (See Table 4.3.) This number represented an increase of 176% from the 314,449 homeless children reported in

TABLE 4.3

Primary nighttime residence of homeless children, by state, 2000

| State | Primary nighttime residence | | | | | Total |
	Shelter	Doubled-up	Unsheltered	Other	Unknown	
Alabama	2,984	3,243	105	—	—	6,332
Alaska	1,057	548	160	723	3,178	5,666
Arizona[a]	1,288	6,225	841	1,408	1,416	11,178
Arkansas	2,629	1,442	127	190	1,136	5,524
California	61,182	80,058	17,640	130,145	—	289,025
Colorado	1,773	1,976	436	1,326	893	6,404
Connecticut	3,151	—	—	—	—	3,151
Delaware	1,100	—	—	—	—	1,100
Florida	—	—	—	—	—	—
Georgia	14,717	3,287	—	1,619	1	19,623
Hawaii	563	80	388	—	—	1,031
Idaho	218	452	13	45	28	756
Illinois	1,547	14,567	260	—	—	16,374
Indiana	14,060	11,200	1,400	840	1,500	29,000
Iowa	—	—	—	—	—	—
Kansas	2,075	1,175	43	61	20	3,374
Kentucky	1,294	5,798	702	250	292	8,336
Louisiana	10,438	4,873	565	—	—	15,876
Maine	4,913	—	—	—	—	4,913
Maryland	3,618	820	—	1,086	229	5,753
Massachusetts	—	—	—	—	—	—
Michigan	28,900	11,376	2,054	3,043	2,528	47,901
Minnesota	2,396	—	—	—	303	2,699
Mississippi[b]	—	—	—	—	—	—
Missouri	7,264	6,741	5,094	2,277	207	21,583
Montana	1,113	1,127	168	157	170	2,735
Nebraska	5,119	786	94	719	445	7,163
Nevada	192	992	35	485	—	1,704
New Hampshire[c]	4	—	—	—	—	4
New Jersey	6,435	1,064	5	8,940	71	16,515
New Mexico	682	1,264	—	269	—	2,215
New York	9,165	—	—	—	—	9,165
North Carolina	—	—	—	—	—	—
North Dakota	93	130	—	8	1	232
Ohio	7,124	17,809	2,968	—	1,780	29,681
Oklahoma	2,998	3,793	127	—	—	6,918
Oregon	12,540	4,390	2,900	12,000	920	32,750
Pennsylvania	17,000	3,000	1,000	—	—	21,000
Puerto Rico	649	100	100	858	500	2,207
Rhode Island	1,286	53	1	1	2	1,343
South Carolina	1,731	4,219	33	196	36	6,215
South Dakota	2,960	1,246	381		370	4,973
Tennessee	2,300	2,600	275	443	—	5,618
Texas	29,910	90,728	—	29,975	—	150,613
Utah	1,668	3,845	282	2,402	581	8,778
Vermont	—	—	—	—	276	276
Virginia	12,631	2,649	174	572	952	16,978
Washington	15,703	—	—	—	—	15,703
West Virginia	402	2,061	—	355	651	3,469
Wisconsin	2,718	1,220	244	617	55	4,854
Wyoming	150	550	—	—	108	808
Totals	**306,404**	**301,195**	**38,732**	**201,313**	**19,255**	**866,899**

—Data were not provided.
[a]Only 34 school districts responded.
[b]Data were reported by percentage: shelters, 23 percent; doubled-up, 75 percent; unsheltered, 2 percent.
[c]Data were requested but not consistently reported by school district.

SOURCE: "Table 2. Primary Nighttime Residence of Homeless Children and Youth," in *Education for Homeless Children and Youth Program, Report to Congress, Fiscal Year 2000*, 2000, http://www.ed.gov/programs/homeless/rpt2000.doc (accessed February 28, 2005)

forty-eight states in 1997. About two-thirds (67%) were enrolled in school, and the greatest number of those children were in preschool and elementary school. More than one-third (35%) of these children lived in shelters; 35% stayed doubled up with others, presumably family or friends; 25% lived in motels and the like. Most distressing for those concerned about the health and well-being of children was that 38,732 children lived unsheltered. By far the greatest number of unsheltered children (17,640) lived in California.

Illegal Occupancy

Poor neighborhoods are often full of abandoned buildings. Even the best-intentioned landlords cannot afford to maintain their properties in these areas. Many have let their buildings deteriorate or have simply walked away, leaving the fate of the building and its residents in the hands of the government. Despite overcrowding and unsafe conditions, many homeless people move into these dilapidated buildings illegally, glad for what shelter they can find. Municipal governments, overwhelmed by long waiting lists for public-housing and a lack of funds and personnel, are often unable or unwilling to strictly enforce housing laws, allowing the homeless to become "squatters" rather than forcing them into the streets. Some deliberately turn a blind eye to the problem, knowing they have no better solution for the homeless.

The result is a multitude of housing units with deplorable living conditions—tenants bedding down in illegal boiler basements or sharing beds with children or in-laws, or sharing bathrooms with strangers. The buildings may have leaks and rot, rusted fire escapes, and rat and roach infestations. Given the alternative, many homeless people feel lucky to be sheltered.

THE RISK OF SQUATTING. Squatting can leave the homeless vulnerable to legal remedies or public criticism. In December 1999 in Worcester, Massachusetts, a homeless couple had taken up residence in an abandoned building. One of them allegedly knocked over a candle during an argument and the building caught fire. The Worcester fire department was called, and six firefighters were killed. The homeless man and woman were each charged with involuntary manslaughter. The public outcry against the homeless couple, and against homeless people in general, reached national proportions. Frustration ran rampant in the ranks of homeless advocates. Most believed the Worcester couple was guilty of nothing more than trying to stay alive. In an Associated Press story dated December 8, 1999, Nicole Witherbee, policy coordinator for the Massachusetts Coalition for the Homeless, voiced her frustration: "We make laws all the time, they can't panhandle, they can't loiter, we don't have enough shelter beds, so when they go into abandoned buildings it's trespassing. So where is it they're supposed to be?"—underscoring the lack of options and resources homeless people deal with on a daily basis.

CHAPTER 5
FEDERAL GOVERNMENT AID FOR THE HOMELESS

Homelessness is widespread, and many people expect the government to step in to solve such a large-scale problem. What should the role of the government be in combating homelessness? Some people believe it is the duty of the government to take care of all citizens in times of need. Others point out that government help has often been misdirected or inadequate; in some instances, it has even added to the problem. Some people assert that people in trouble should solve their problems themselves. Federal programs for the homeless reflect a consensus that limited government help is important and necessary, but that homeless people also need to help themselves.

A TIMELINE OF GOVERNMENT INVOLVEMENT

Since 1860 the federal government has been actively involved with the housing industry, specifically the low-income housing industry. In 1860 the government conducted the first partial census of housing—by counting slave dwellings. Twenty years later the U.S. census focused on the living quarters of the rest of the population, conducting a full housing census. Since then the federal government has played an increasingly larger role in combating housing problems in the United States:

- 1892—Congress designated $20,000 for a Labor Department study on slum conditions in Baltimore, New York, Chicago, and Philadelphia, the four cities with populations over 200,000 at that time. The study revealed that 14% of the cities' populations, mostly immigrants, lived in slums under crowded conditions. Most of these people spent one-third or more of their income on rent.

- 1908—President Theodore Roosevelt appointed a Housing Commission to study the problems in American slums; among the suggestions made by the panel were broad federal acquisition of slum properties and direct loans from the federal government to finance the renovation and construction of decent, sanitary

housing that the poor could buy or occupy at low interest rates or rents.

- 1925—Borrowing and mortgaging properties reached their highest levels ever to that date. The rate of foreclosures also started to rise, leading to increased homelessness. Although no one knew it at the time, the debts that Americans had run up for their housing would be a major problem just a few years later.

- 1929—Stocks trading at the New York Stock Exchange suffered a tremendous crash in prices. The Great Depression had begun.

- 1932—As many Americans lost their jobs and failing banks called in their loans, homelessness skyrocketed. The Emergency Relief and Construction Act authorized the Reconstruction Finance Corporation to lend government money to corporations to build housing for low-income families.

- 1933—The National Industrial Recovery Act allowed the Public Works Administration (a government-sponsored work program) to use federal funds for slum clearance, the construction of low-cost housing, and subsistence homesteads; close to 40,000 units were produced that year.

- 1937—The United States Housing Act of 1937 established the Public Housing Administration (which was later merged into the Federal Housing Administration [FHA] and the Department of Housing and Urban Development [HUD]) to create low-rent housing programs across the country through the establishment of local public housing agencies.

- 1938—The National Housing Act Amendments were implemented. They allowed the FHA to insure low-income rental projects built for profit.

- 1940—The U.S. Census, reporting on the first comprehensive survey of the nation's housing stock, showed that 18% of housing units needed major repairs, 31% lacked running water, 44% had neither a bathtub nor a shower, and 35% lacked a flush toilet. The worst conditions generally were found in inner-city slums and in the South, where many sharecroppers lived in shacks.

- 1941—The United States entered World War II (1939–45). The economy surged to meet wartime needs, and millions of young men entered the military. As a result, the Great Depression came to a close.

- 1946—The Farmers Home Administration (FmHA) was created under the Department of Agriculture to provide low-income housing assistance in rural areas.

- 1949—The Housing Act of 1949 set the goals of "a decent home and a suitable environment" for every family and authorized an 810,000-unit public housing program over the next six years. Title I of the Act created the Urban Renewal program; Title V created the basic rural housing program under the FmHA, which put the federal government directly into the mortgage business.

- 1961—President John F. Kennedy made decent housing for all Americans a national objective. He wanted to accelerate urban renewal projects to make more mortgage funds available to homebuyers and to provide decent housing for low-income and minority households. Congress responded by passing the Housing Act of 1961, creating a new program for FHA-insured, low-income rental housing. This was the FHA's first direct subsidy program.

- 1965—Congress established the Department of Housing and Urban Development. Its goal was to create a new rent supplement program for low-income households in private housing.

- 1968—The Housing and Urban Development Act was passed in response to President Johnson's "Message to Congress on Housing and Cities." The president declared that America's cities were in crisis and set a national housing goal of twenty-six million new units (six million targeted to low- and moderate-income households) over the next ten years. Congress provided two new options for low- and moderate-income rent subsidy programs and mortgage insurance for low- and moderate-income families with poor credit histories.

- 1970—A massive reorganization of federal housing organizations was completed. FHA was merged into HUD. With this reorganization, the FHA began to provide support for lower-priced housing and directed home ownership and rental opportunity programs for low-income households in inner cities.

- 1973—President Nixon declared a moratorium on housing and community development assistance, suspending all subsidized housing programs.

- 1974—The Housing and Community Development Act of 1974 created a new leased-housing program that included a certificate (voucher) program, expanding housing choices for low-income tenants, and fair-market rent ceilings to control the cost of the program. The voucher program soon became known as Section 8, after the section of the act that established it.

- 1981—The Housing and Community Development Amendments of 1981 required subsidized tenants to pay up to 30% of their income for rent before qualifying for assistance under Section 8 and further limited benefits of public housing programs to the neediest households.

- 1983—The Housing and Urban-Rural Recovery Act of 1983 established rental rehabilitation programs and modified components of the Section 8 program to limit its benefits. Under Section 8, an experimental housing voucher program was established, and new rehabilitation grants and housing development grants were created.

- 1987—The Stewart B. McKinney Homelessness Assistance Act was passed. This was the first federal act aimed directly at helping homeless people. It established new programs and funding for HUD to provide emergency shelter to homeless people and eventually help secure permanent housing for them.

- 1989—The HUD Reform Act of 1989 was enacted. Its intent was to clean up HUD and prevent the misuse of funds that had been plaguing the agency.

- 1990—The National Affordable Housing Act renewed the federal government's commitment to home ownership, tenant-based assistance, and subsidized housing. The Low-Income Housing Preservation and Residential Home Ownership Act demonstrated a federal commitment to permanent preservation of assisted low-income, multi-family housing; the act also repealed the rental rehabilitation grant and the rehabilitation loan program. A special homeless assistance component of the moderate rehabilitation program was retained.

- 1997—The Quality Housing and Work Responsibility Act of 1998 thoroughly reformed public housing initiatives. It removed disincentives for residents to work, provided rental protection for low-income residents, deregulated the operation of public housing authorities, authorized the creation of mixed-finance public housing projects, and gave more power and flexibility to local governments and communities to operate housing programs.

THE MCKINNEY-VENTO HOMELESS ASSISTANCE ACT

Widespread public outcry over the plight of the homeless in the early 1980s prompted Congress to pass the Stewart B. McKinney Homeless Assistance Act of 1987. Congress renamed the act the McKinney-Vento Homeless Assistance Act in 2000 (H.R. 5417) to honor Representative Bruce Vento's service to the homeless. The range and reach of the act has broadened over the years. Most of the money authorized by the act went, initially, toward the funding of homeless shelters. The program also funded a Supportive Housing program, a Shelter Plus Care program, and the Single Room Occupancy program in addition to the Emergency Shelter Grant program. Amendments to the act later enabled funding and other services to support permanent housing and other programs to help the homeless. HUD administers most McKinney-Vento funds.

Program Structure

In 2005 programs administered under the McKinney-Vento Act fell into three distinct categories. A cluster of activities known as the Continuum of Care (CoC) programs provided competitive grants intended to help communities and organizations provide comprehensive services to the homeless. A noncompetitive formula grant program, the Emergency Shelter Grants Program, provided funds for emergency shelters to states, large cities, urban counties, and U.S. territories. The Title V program freed properties for use to house the homeless.

Continuum of Care

According to HUD (*Homeless Assistance Programs,* http://www.hud.gov/offices/cpd/homeless/programs/index.cfm), the concept behind Continuum of Care programs is as follows: "A continuum of care system is designed to address the critical problem of homelessness through a coordinated community-based process of identifying needs and building a system to address those needs. The approach is predicated on the understanding that homelessness is not caused merely by a lack of shelter, but involves a variety of underlying, unmet needs—physical, economic, and social."

Nonprofit groups and local government entities applying for funds under these programs are expected to survey and assess local needs and to write a comprehensive plan for combating homelessness and meeting needs. Grant recipients are required to assess their clients' progress and make changes in the program in response to ongoing evaluation. Three major programs and some additional demonstration and rural efforts have developed over the years.

SUPPORTIVE HOUSING PROGRAM (SHP). The aim of the Supportive Housing Program is to provide housing and services that will enable clients to achieve economic independence and control over their lives. SHP provides up to $400,000 in matching funds for construction of new buildings for housing homeless people; it also provides funding for the acquisition or refurbishing of existing buildings. The program underwrites 75% of the operating cost, including administration, and up to 80% of the cost of support programs. These programs must help clients achieve independence by providing skills training, childcare, education, transportation assistance, counseling, or job referrals. Elements of the program include transitional housing for twenty-four months, permanent housing for the disabled, supportive services without housing, havens for the hard-to-reach and the mentally ill, and other innovative programs to solve problems of homelessness.

SHELTER PLUS CARE (S+C). The Shelter Plus Care Program helps agencies that specifically target the hardest-to-serve homeless: those with mental and physical disabilities living on the street or in shelters, including drug addicts and AIDS sufferers. The program provides for rental assistance funded by HUD and other sources. Housing in this program can be in the form of group homes or individual units with supportive services. Grant funds must be matched with local dollars. Subsidies for projects are available for ten years; assistance to sponsors and tenants is available for five years. Rental assistance includes four types of contracts:

1. Tenant-Based Rental Assistance—Direct contract with a low-income tenant

2. Project-Based Rental Assistance—Building owner contracts

3. Sponsor-Based Rental Assistance—Contracts with nonprofit organizations, and

4. SRO-Based Rental Assistance—Single room occupancy contracts provided by public housing authorities (PHAs)

SINGLE ROOM OCCUPANCY (SRO). Single-room occupancy housing is housing in a dormitory-style building where each person has his or her own private room but shares kitchens, bathrooms, and lounges. Single Room Occupancy Program (SRO) housing is generally the cheapest type of housing available. Funding is intended to encourage the establishment and operation of such housing. Subsidy payments fund a project for a period of ten years in the form of rental assistance in amounts equal to the rent, including utilities, minus the portion of rent payable by the tenants.

OTHER PROGRAM COMPONENTS. Other programs folded under the Continuum of Care designation by HUD include demonstration programs for safe havens for the homeless and innovative homeless programs as well as rural homeless housing programs.

TABLE 5.1

Requirements of four HUD McKinney-Vento programs, 2002

Program requirement	Emergency shelter grants	Supportive housing program	Shelter plus care	Single-room occupancy
Type of grants	Formula grant	Competitive grant	Competitive grant	Competitive grant
Eligible applicants	States Metropolitan cities Urban counties Territories	States Local governments Other governmental agencies Private nonprofit organizations Community mental health centers that are public nonprofit organizations	States Local governments Public housing authorities	Public housing authorities Private nonprofit organizations
Eligible program services	Emergency shelter Essential social services	Transitional housing Permanent housing for people with disabilities Supportive services only Safe havens Innovative supportive housing	Tenant based rental assistance Sponsor based rental assistance Project based rental assistance Single-room occupancy based rental assistance	Single-room occupancy housing
Eligible activities	Renovation/conversion Major rehabilitation Supportive service Operating costs Homelessness prevention activities	Acquisition Rehabilitation New construction Leasing Operating and administrative costs Supportive services only	Rental assistance	Rental assistance
Eligible population	Homeless individuals and families People at risk of becoming homeless	Homeless individuals and families for transitional housing and supportive services Disabled homeless individuals for permanent housing Hard-to-reach mentally ill homeless individuals for safe havens	Disabled homeless individuals and their families	Homeless individuals
Initial term of assistance	1 year	Up to 3 years	5 or 10 years	10 years
Matching funds	States: no match for first $100,000 and dollar-for-dollar match for rest of funds. Local governments: dollar-for-dollar match for all funds.	Dollar-for-dollar match for acquisition, rehabilitation, and new construction grants. Operating costs must be shared by 25 percent in the first 2 years and 50 percent in the third year. A 25-percent match for supportive service grants No match for grants used for leasing or administrative costs.	Dollar-for-dollar match of the federal shelter grant to pay for supportive services	No match required

SOURCE: Stanley Czerwinsky, "Table 3. Requirements of Four HUD McKinney-Vento Programs," in *Homelessness: Improving Program Coordination and Client Access to Programs*, U.S. General Accounting Office, March 2002, http://www.gao.gov/new.items/d02485t.pdf (accessed March 10, 2005)

Emergency Shelter Grants (ESG)

The Emergency Shelter Grants program provides homeless persons with basic shelter and essential supportive services. It can assist with the operational costs of the shelter facility, and for the administration of the grant. ESG also provides short-term homeless prevention assistance to persons at imminent risk of losing their own housing due to eviction, foreclosure, or utility shutoffs.

—*Emergency Shelter Grants*, HUD, February 1, 2005

The ESG is HUD's formula grant program administered as a part of its community planning and development grant program. Recipients of funding are states, large cities, urban counties, and U.S. territories that have filed consolidated community development plans with HUD. ESG is called a formula program because the amounts allocated are based in part on population and poverty levels within the planning entities that participate. ESG funds flow from governmental entities to organizations that actually operate shelters and provide services. Money may be used to help individuals avoid homelessness by providing emergency funds.

Title V

HUD maintains information about and publishes listings of federal properties categorized as unutilized, underutilized, in excess, or in surplus. States, local governments, and nonprofit organizations can apply to use such properties to house the homeless. Title V does not provide funding; it provides properties to agencies for housing use. Groups may apply for funding under the Continuum of Care program to modify, refurbish, or adapt such structures for residential uses.

Consolidations, New Initiatives, and Reorganizations

HUD's programs, particularly those under Continuum of Care, have overlapping objectives yet operate under separate rules and requirements. (See Table 5.1.) The U.S. General Accounting Office (GAO), now Government Accountability Office, an investigative body of the U.S. Congress, studied the McKinney programs in 1999 and concluded that the number of programs and the differences between them create barriers to their efficient use (*Homelessness: Coordination and Evaluation of Programs Are Essential*, Washington, DC, 1999).

HOMELESS ASSISTANCE GRANTS. HUD's program administrators evidently reached much the same conclusions as GAO. In its fiscal year (FY) 2004 budget request to Congress (*Fiscal Year 2004 Budget Summary*, HUD, February 3, 2003) and again in its FY 2005 budget summary (*Fiscal Year 2005 Budget Summary*, February 2, 2004), HUD proposed consolidating its three major programs under Continuum of Care, along with the demonstration and rural assistance programs, into a single Homeless Assistance Grants program. The department believed that this consolidation would facilitate comprehensive delivery of services while reducing administrative expenses, both at HUD and on the part of grant recipients. President George W. Bush's proposed budget for McKinney-Vento assistance programs for FY 2006 was $1,415,000,000, up from $1,241,000,000 in FY 2005.

THE SAMARITAN INITIATIVE. In 2004 HUD proposed that Congress fund a new program called the Samaritan Initiative. The new program targeted an estimated 150,000 individuals HUD considers "chronically homeless." In FY 2005 HUD received $50 million to provide housing for the chronically homeless. The U.S. Department of Health and Human Services and the U.S. Department of Veterans Affairs also provided services for drug abuse and health treatment.

FEDERALLY SUBSIDIZED HOUSING

The national effort to provide housing for those in need is far more massive than would be indicated by the expenditure of about $1.5 billion on assistance to the homeless. HUD's expenditures on public and Native American housing were projected to be $23.8 billion in FY 2005. (See Table 5.2.) If these funds are added to projected expenditures on homeless programs, total spending on subsidized housing in FY 2005 would be $25.3 billion. Of this total, 5.8% is allocated to helping the homeless and 94.2% to ensuring that people do not become homeless. To help people stay housed, the government has housing programs that help poor and low-income people.

Households in Subsidized Housing

In 2002 over 5.1 million families, or 4.6% of U.S. households, lived in subsidized housing. (See Table 5.3.) Of those in subsidized housing, 2.6 million households had income below the officially defined poverty level; these households were 2.3% of all households and just over half of all subsidized households (51%).

The U.S. Census Bureau provides estimates of families living in poverty and of poverty-stricken households (a sector that includes family as well as nonfamily groups and singles). In 2002 there were roughly seventy-five million families in the United States but more than 111 million households. The Census Bureau estimated in

TABLE 5.2

HUD budget authority for homeless and public housing programs, 2002–04

[In millions of dollars]

	Fiscal year 2003	Fiscal year 2004	Fiscal year 2005 (estimate)
Homeless assistance programs			
Homeless assistance grants	1,217	1,260	1,257
Shelter plus care renewals	...	193	193
Samaritan housing program	...	...	50
Emergency food and shelter	...	...	153
Total, homeless	**1,217**	**1,260**	**1,485**
Public and Indian housing			
Housing certificate fund	15,938	16,413	16,909
Public housing capital fund	2,712	2,696	2,674
Revitalization of severely distressed public housing projects	570	149	...
Public housing operating fund	3,577	3,579	3,573
Native American housing block grants	645	650	647
Total, public and Indian housing	**23,425**	**23,493**	**23,756**

SOURCE: Adapted from "Appendix B. Budget Authority by Program," in *Fiscal Year 2005 Budget Summary*, U.S. Department of Housing and Urban Development, February 2004, http://www.hud.gov/about/budget/fy05/budgetsummary.pdf (accessed March 10, 2005)

Statistitcal Abstract of the United States 2004–2005 that in 2002 more than 13.5 million households lived below the poverty level. Elsewhere, the Census Bureau estimated that 7.2 million families (or 9.6% of all families) were living in poverty in 2002 (*Poverty in 2002*, U.S. Census Bureau, September 2003). In 2002 more than 5.1 million households lived in subsidized housing. (See Figure 5.1.) In the 1990–2002 period, those in subsidized housing peaked in 2002. Total households living in subsidized housing increased 18.1%.

Types of Programs

Virtually all government housing programs are targeted to poor or low-income households. For this reason subsidized housing is "means-tested," meaning that the income of those receiving help must be below a certain threshold. The qualifying income level—much like the definition of poverty—changes over time. Beneficiaries of housing assistance never receive cash outright. The benefits are therefore labeled "means-tested noncash benefits."

HUD has operated many different kinds of housing programs, but these can be classified under three headings: public housing owned by the government, tenant-based programs that provide people vouchers to subsidize rent, and project-based programs that underwrite the costs of private owners who, in turn, pledge to house low-income people.

Public housing and voucher programs account for roughly equal proportions of subsidized units. Project-based programs, also known as "private subsidized

TABLE 5.3

Households receiving means-tested noncash benefits, 1980–2002

[In thousands (82,368 represents 82,368,000), except percent. Households as of March of following year.]

Type of benefit received	1980	1990	1995	2000	2002 Below poverty level Total	2002 Below poverty level Number	2002 Below poverty level Percent of total	2002 Above poverty level
Total households	**82,368**	**94,312**	**99,627**	**106,418**	**111,278**	**13,505**	**100**	**97,773**
Receiving at least one noncash benefit	14,266	16,098	21,148	20,131	22,478	7,806	58	14,672
Not receiving cash public assistance	7,860	8,819	13,335	14,465	16,890	5,003	37	11,887
Receiving cash public assistance*	6,407	7,279	7,813	5,667	5,588	2,803	21	2,785
Total households receiving—								
Food stamps	6,769	7,163	8,388	5,563	6,245	3,834	28	2,411
School lunch	5,532	6,252	8,607	7,185	7,930	3,092	23	4,838
Public housing	2,777	4,339	4,846	4,689	5,125	2,593	19	2,532
Medicaid	8,287	10,321	14,111	14,328	16,765	6,182	46	10,583

*Households receiving money from Aid to Families with Dependent Children Program (beginning 2000, Temporary Assistance for Needy Families Program), Supplemental Security Income program or other public assistance programs.
Note: Data covers civilian noninstitutional population, including persons in the armed forces living off post or with their families on post. A means-tested benefit program requires that the household's income and/or assets fall below specified guidelines in order to qualify for benefits. There are general trends toward underestimation of noncash beneficiaries. Households are classified according to poverty status of family or nonfamily householder.

SOURCE: "No. 522. Households Receiving Means-Tested Noncash Benefits, 1980 to 2002," in *Statistical Abstract of the United States, 2004–2005*, U.S. Census Bureau, http://www.census.gov/prod/2004pubs/04statab/socinsur.pdf (accessed March 10, 2005)

FIGURE 5.1

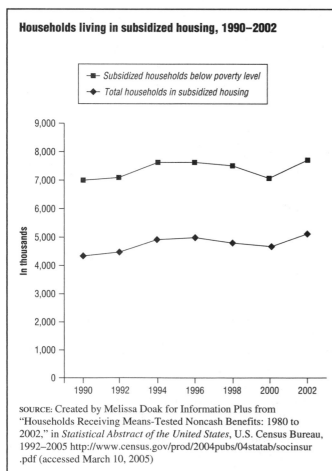

Households living in subsidized housing, 1990–2002

- ■ *Subsidized households below poverty level*
- ◆ *Total households in subsidized housing*

SOURCE: Created by Melissa Doak for Information Plus from "Households Receiving Means-Tested Noncash Benefits: 1980 to 2002," in *Statistical Abstract of the United States*, U.S. Census Bureau, 1992–2005 http://www.census.gov/prod/2004pubs/04statab/socinsur.pdf (accessed March 10, 2005)

projects," account for the most units, but these "private subsidies" take many forms, some quite complicated. A look at the major programs follows.

PUBLIC HOUSING

HUD's FY 2005 budget anticipated funding for 1.2 million public housing units. Public housing has been decreasing in numbers (1.37 million in 1998, for example), in part because of an initiative to remove, modernize, and refurbish many poorly constructed and dilapidated public housing units. An estimated 3,150 public housing authorities manage the 1.2 million units. In FY 2005, $2.7 billion was allocated to fund major repairs and modernization of units and $3.6 billion was allocated for operating costs.

Public Housing Residents

On its Web site HUD provides a data server on public housing residents called *Resident Characteristics Report* (http://www.hud.gov/offices/pih/systems/pic/50058/rcr/index.cfm). As of March 31, 2005:

- Average annual income was $10,725. Only 7% of the public housing population earned more than $25,000 a year.

- Among residents, 31% had wage income, 19% had Temporary Assistance for Needy Families (TANF) income, 54% had Social Security income, and 18% had other income (the same person could have income from more than one source). Four percent had no income from any source.

- The average rental payment was $243 per month.

- Females with children were 38% of families, 18% were elderly and not disabled, and 11% were elderly with a disability. A number of other, overlapping, categories were shown as well, but notably missing was a category for male-headed families with children.

- Half (50%) of heads of households were white, 46% were black, 2% were Asian, and 1% were American Indians or Alaska Natives. One in five heads of household (21%) were of Hispanic origin.

- Nearly half (46%) of households consisted of just one person, 20% of two, 15% of three, 10% of four, 5% of five, 2% of six, and 1% of seven persons. No households had more than seven persons.

- The 932,850 units reporting data had 2,075,079 household members, with an average household size of 2.2 persons.

- Of units occupied, 7% had no bedroom, 34% had one, 30% had two, 23% had three, 5% had four, and 1% had more than five bedrooms.

- Thirteen percent of the population had been in public housing for more than twenty years, 17% for ten to twenty years, 21% for five to ten years, 23% for two to five years, 11% for a year or two, and 16% had moved during the past year. The rest did not report on length of stay.

Public Housing Agencies

Management of public housing is handled by housing agencies (sometimes called authorities) established by local governments to administer HUD housing programs. The Housing Act of 1937 requires that PHAs submit annual plans to HUD but also declares it to be the policy of the United States "to vest in public housing agencies that perform well the maximum amount of responsibility and flexibility in program administration, with appropriate accountability to public housing residents, localities, and the general public."

PHAs thus operate under plans approved by HUD and under HUD supervision, but they are expected to operate with some independence accountable to their residents, local (or state) governments, and the public. Not all PHAs have "performed well," and HUD has been accused of lax supervision. PHAs and public housing generally reflect the distressed conditions of the population living in government-owned housing. PHAs have been charged with neglecting maintenance, tolerating unsafe living conditions for tenants, and with fraudulent or careless financial practices.

Responding to such accounts, Congress created the National Commission on Severely Distressed Public Housing in 1990. In its report, released in August 1992, the Commission concluded that severely distressed public housing was a national problem. The Commission reported that 86,000 (or 6%) of the nation's public housing units were plagued by crime and deteriorated physical conditions in violation of HUD standards. Five years later the National Housing Institute, a not-for-profit advocacy group, charged that HUD still did not know how much, or which parts, of its public housing inventory met its own "troubled housing" definition despite the fact that these troubled properties represented a significant portion of the available low-income housing in the United States (J. Atlas and E. Shoshkes, *Saving Affordable Housing, What Community Groups Can Do and What Government Should Do*, National Housing Institute, 1997).

Troubled housing refers to low-income projects that are badly deteriorated, are located in unsafe neighborhoods, or are in danger of being lost to market-rate housing conversion or foreclosure. In an effort to improve its accountability for the conditions of low-income housing, HUD began to implement a new Public Housing Assessment System (PHAS) in January 2000. PHAS is used to measure the performance of public housing agencies. The four primary PHAS components are:

1. Physical Inspection Indicator—Ensures that PHAs meet the minimum standard of being decent, safe, sanitary, and in good repair

2. Financial Condition Indicator—Oversees the finances of PHAs

3. Management Operations Indicator—Evaluates the effectiveness of PHA management methods

4. Resident Satisfaction and Service Indicator—Allows public housing residents to assess PHA performance

A March 2002 GAO report commissioned by Congress studied the implementation of PHAS and its progress. The study found that HUD had also formed the Public and Indian Housing Information Center, a database that collected additional information not addressed by PHAS, such as compliance and funding. The findings indicated that as of 2002, PHAS's method of evaluation considered only component three, managerial deficiencies, to declare PHAs as troubled. The plans were to incorporate all four components. Table 5.4 shows the number of the then existing 3,167 authorities investigated that would have been classified as troubled if all four PHAS components had been applied instead of just one ("New Assessment System Holds Potential for Evaluating Performance," Washington, DC: GAO, March 2002). The table shows that 532 PHAs were "troubled" overall or in one area (16.8%), 827 were high performers (26.1%), and 1,808 were standard performers (57.1%).

A 2005 report from the GAO confirmed that HUD continued to have major problems ("Major Management Challenges at the Department of Housing and Urban

TABLE 5.4

Public Housing Assessment System (PHAS) designations, fiscal year 2001

PHAS designation	Number of authorities designated under one indicator	Number of authorities that could be designated under four indicators
Overall troubled[a]		90
Troubled in one area[a]		442
Substandard physical		169
Substandard financial		249
Substandard management[b]	45	24
Standard performer	3,122	1,808
High performer[a]		827
Total	**3,167**	**3,167**

[a]HUD designated no high performers for fiscal year 2001. The only troubled performers were those that were troubled in the management area.
[b]When performance is assessed using all four indicators, housing authorities that are troubled in more than one area become overall troubled. Some of the 45 housing authorities that were troubled in the management area alone under one indicator moved into the overall troubled category when their physical and financial condition were taken into account. As a result, only 24 housing authorities remained troubled in the management area alone under all four indicators.

SOURCE: "Table 1. PHAS Designations for Fiscal Year 2001 under Partial and Full Implementation," in *Public Housing: New Assessment System Holds Potential for Evaluating Performance*, GAO-02-282, U.S. General Accounting Office, March 2002, http://www.gao.gov/new.items/d02282.pdf (accessed March 10, 2005)

Development," GAO, February 23, 2005). According to the report, HUD had made some progress in addressing management problems. However, since "some of HUD's corrective actions are still in the early stages of implementation and additional steps are needed to resolve ongoing problems," its rental housing assistance programs remain "high risk."

HOPE VI

As a result of the 1992 recommendations of the National Commission on Severely Distressed Public Housing, Congress authorized $300 million for an urban revitalization demonstration program in the FY 1993 Appropriations Act. The program came to be named HOPE VI. The acronym stands for Housing Opportunities for People Everywhere. Up to that point, HUD had four different HOPE initiatives; no HOPE V was ever launched (James Bovard, "HUD's Biggest Farce?" *Free Market*, vol. 18, no. 11, November 2000).

The aim of HOPE VI was to eliminate or upgrade the 86,000 deteriorated units identified by the Commission. In the FY 1993–2002 period, HUD reported revitalization grants totaling $5.04 billion and expended $335.6 million on demolitions. In its FY 2004 budget summary, HUD claimed budget authority for FY 2003 of $574 million. HUD documented that 55,000 housing units had been demolished and 140,000 approved for demolition under HOPE VI and other programs, and no new funding was required for FY 2004 as the agency worked through its existing backlog. In FY 2005, $110 million in funds were available to public housing authorities for revitalization programs.

Critiques and Implications

The findings of the National Commission in 1992 and the launch of an initiative like HOPE VI (aimed at demolishing public housing) illustrates the sometimes troubled history of public housing. HOPE VI itself has been severely criticized by advocacy groups. A 2002 report entitled *False HOPE* (prepared by the National Housing Law Project, the Poverty & Race Research Action Council, Sherwood Research Associates, and Everywhere and Now Public Housing Residents Organizing Nationally Together, June 2002) found that HOPE VI:

1. Appeared headed toward eliminating twice the number of units found to have been "severely distressed" by the National Commission

2. Has eliminated rather than increased units available to the lowest income population

3. Has made it very difficult for residents to participate in program decisions

4. Has not improved the "living environment" of those in HOPE VI sites, and

5. Has failed to provide data on project outcomes

Data on the number of public housing units available to house low-income people support the general charge that the number of units has declined from nearly 1.37 million in 1998 to 1.22 million in 2003, a drop of 150,000 units. If people who inhabit units slated for demolition are not able to find accommodation under HUD Section 8 Voucher programs, they are at greater risk of becoming homeless.

VOUCHERS

How Voucher Programs Work

Voucher programs pay a portion of the rent for qualifying families. Only low-income families are eligible, specifically those with incomes lower than half of an area's median income. Under some circumstances, families with up to 80% of the local median income may also qualify; such cases may involve, for instance, families displaced by public housing demolition. The family pays 30% of its income in rent. Vouchers are issued by the Public Housing Agency, which executes assistance contracts with the landlord, who must also qualify.

Two major voucher programs are available: tenant-based and project-based. In tenant-based programs, the voucher "follows" the tenant when the tenant moves to another qualifying unit. In project-based programs, the voucher "attaches" to a project. Families are directed to participating projects after they qualify. Tenants cannot automatically transfer their voucher in a project-based dwelling to another—but they may qualify for tenant-based vouchers after they move.

In addition to these two basic programs, HUD also has five other voucher programs. Conversion vouchers are used to help tenants relocate when public housing is demolished. Family unification vouchers are used to help families stay together. Homeownership vouchers assist families in purchasing a first home or another home if the family has not lived in a house in the past three years. Participants must be employed and have an income of at least minimum wage. Vouchers for people with disabilities and welfare-to-work vouchers assist the elderly or non-elderly disabled and families transitioning from welfare to work.

In all of these programs, the housing supplied is privately owned and operated and rents paid are at or below fair market rent (FMR). HUD determines the FMR in every locality of the nation by an annual survey of new rental contracts signed in the past fifteen months. The FMR is set as the fortieth percentile of rents paid, meaning that 40% paid a lower rent and 60% paid a higher rent. HUD has chosen the fortieth percentile to increase housing choices while keeping budgets at reasonable levels. Table 5.5 presents FMRs used by HUD in a sample of cities around the country in 2005. Rents in certain cities are calculated at the fiftieth percentile under new HUD rules that went into effect in 2001 for thirty-nine markets, which resulted in a raise in the FMR in these localities.

Of the cities in Table 5.5, the highest FMR for 2005 was in Boston, Massachusetts ($1,266 per month). The lowest FMR was in Louisville, Kentucky ($553 per month).

Voucher Usage

As shown in Table 5.6, the amount of subsidized housing and Section 8 housing vouchers declined across all categories between 2003 and 2005. Project-based Section 8 housing has declined dramatically because funding for new construction stopped in 1983 with some minor exceptions (including construction/rehabilitation aimed at supporting homeless programs). Support of housing in such units continues, but the housing stock is going out of use through demolitions and conversions. Thus in 2005 the vast majority of Section 8 housing vouchers were tenant-based.

Characteristics of Voucher Residents

Although tenant-voucher residents have a fractionally higher average household income than public housing residents, they also have a larger family size. Therefore, two-thirds of voucher users (66%) and a little more than

TABLE 5.5

Fair market rental rates for selected metropolitan areas, 2005

[In dollars]

Area definition	Fair market rental rate, 2005
Albany-Schenectady-Troy, NY	679
Albuquerque, NM	699
Atlanta, GA	834
Bergen-Passaic, NJ	1,132
Boston, MA	1,266
Cincinnati, OH-KY-IN	652
Columbus, OH	640
Dayton-Springfield, OH	595
Denver, CO	888
Detroit, MI	805
Honolulu, HI	1,087
Houston, TX	733
Kauai County, HI	1,061
Louisville, KY-IN	553
Maui County, HI	1,149
McAllen-Edinburg-Mission, TX	593
Nashville, TN	654
Newark, NJ	1,020
New York, NY	1,075
Omaha, NE	650
Philadelphia, PA	914
Salt Lake City, UT	682
Springfield, MA	772
Tulsa, OK	640
Tuscon, AZ	673
Washington, DC	1,187

SOURCE: Adapted from "Survey Results," in *Fair Market Rents for the Voucher Choice Housing Program and Moderate Rehabilitation Single Room Occupancy Program Fiscal Year 2005*, Department of Housing and Urban Development, February 28, 2005, http://www.huduser.org/Datasets/FMR/FMR2005R/Revised_FY2005_FMR_Preamble.pdf (accessed March 12, 2005)

TABLE 5.6

Subsidized units available under public housing and voucher programs, 1998, 2003, and 2005

	1998	2003	2005
Public housing	1,300,493	1,241,466	1,220,937
Section 8 tenant vouchers	1,391,526	2,077,336	1,803,013
Section 8 project-based vouchers/certificates	1,001,939	817,274	9,833

SOURCE: Created by Melissa Doak for Information Plus from "Basic Counts," in *A Picture of Subsidized Households in 1998*, U.S. Department of Housing and Urban Development, August 28, 1998, and *Resident Characteristics Report*, U.S. Department of Housings and Urban Development, March 2005, http://www.hud.gov/offices/pih/systems/pic/50058/rcr/index.cfm (accessed April 11, 2005)

half (56%) of public housing residents have an extremely low income for their family size (See Table 5.7). The shift of the subsidized population from public housing toward voucher housing represents not an improvement so much as a shift in policy, whereby the provision of housing in the future appears to be headed for privatization. Barbara Sard has argued in the HUD journal *Cityscape: A Journal of Policy Development and Research* ("Housing

TABLE 5.7

Selected characteristics of subsidized housing populations, 2005

	Public housing	Tenant vouchers
Average income	$10,725	$11,080
Percent with income of:		
$0	5	4
$1–5,000	16	13
$5,001–10,000	41	39
$10,001–15,000	18	20
$15,001–20,000	9	12
$20,001–25,000	5	6
Above $25,000	7	6
Percent below 30% of median income	56	66
Average monthly payment	$243	$253
Race		
White	50	52
Black	46	44
American Indian/Alaska Native	1	1
Asian	2	3
Ethnicity		
Hispanic	21	17
Not-Hispanic	79	83
Average household size	2.2	2.6
Percent with 4 or more people	18	25
Percent with 2 bedrooms	30	37

SOURCE: Adapted from *Resident Characteristics Report*, U.S. Department of Housing and Urban Development, March 2005, http://www.hud.gov/offices/pih/systems/pic/50058/rcr/index.cfm (accessed April 11, 2005)

Vouchers Should Be a Major Component of Future Housing Policy for the Lowest Income Families," vol. 5, no. 2, 2001) that tenant-based voucher programs give low-income people choices in housing and avoid problems of concentrating all poor people in housing projects.

OTHER HOUSING ASSISTANCE PROGRAMS

The two biggest low-income housing programs in the United States are public housing and the Section 8 programs. Section 8 funds are distributed under HUD's Housing Certificate Fund. Other HUD programs fund housing for people living with AIDS (Housing Opportunities for Persons with AIDS, or HOPWA), elderly people, Native Americans and Native Hawaiians, and persons with disabilities. A new 2005 program, the Prisoner Reentry Initiative, helped ex-prisoners find housing as well as with job training and other services.

The homeownership voucher program provides vouchers to participants in the tenant-voucher programs who meet income and eligibility requirements to help them buy their first homes. The program assisted 2,000 low-income families from 2002 through 2005; in 2006 the program plans to assist 3,000 families with purchasing homes.

In 2004 the Self-Help Homeownership Opportunity Program (SHOP) supported the construction of 5,200 new homes for low-income people. Other HUD programs aim to increase privately owned low-income housing

stock. FHA provides mortgage insurance for multi-family projects, and the Low-Income Housing Tax Credit program, available to developers who provide a portion of their projects at low rents, added an estimated 100,000 low-income units in 2003. Funding under HUD's Community Development Block Grant program also has money for low-income housing.

HUD maintains demographic and income data only on participants in the major programs. For that reason, information on the characteristics of participants in many other HUD subsidy programs aimed at low-income people is unavailable. The programs cited above do not include mortgage insurance and other FHA programs aimed to assist the more affluent general population to own a home.

Federal Home Loan Bank

Federal law requires each of the twelve district Federal Home Loan Banks to establish an Affordable Housing Program. Member banks then provide grants and below-market loans to organizations for the purchase, construction, and/or rehabilitation of rental housing. Only 20% of the units created with these funds have to be affordable for and occupied by very low-income households.

In addition, the Federal Home Loan Banks offer a loan program called the Community Investment Program. This provides long-term funding at fixed rates to develop rental housing or finance first-time home purchases for families and individuals with incomes up to 115% of the area's median income. This means that middle-income people can build or buy homes using these funds, but the expenses are considered part of the low-income housing assistance budget.

Rural Housing Programs

A variety of rural housing programs are administered by the Rural Housing Service (RHS), a division of the U.S. Department of Agriculture. (Table 5.8 lists program data from 1979–99.) These programs make federal money available for housing in rural areas, which are considered places with populations of 50,000 or less. Eligibility for rural housing programs is similar to that of subsidized urban programs. The requirements vary from region to region, and applicants must meet minimum and maximum income guidelines. The subsidies come in the form of grants or low-interest loans to repair substandard housing; subsidized mortgages for low-income home ownership; and grants to cover down payment and purchasing costs of low-income homes.

Table 5.8 shows the various programs that were available under RHS funding in millions of dollars and the number of households helped in 1999. In 2003, $1.6 billion was appropriated; of that, $721 million went to

TABLE 5.8

Data on Rural Housing Service's housing programs, 1979–99

[Dollars in millions]

RHS housing program	Total dollars spent, fiscal year 1979	Total dollars spent, fiscal year 1994	Total dollars spent, fiscal year, 1999	Number of households helped, fiscal year 1999	Type of assistance
Single-family housing direct loans (sec. 502)	$2,870.0*	$1,656.8*	$966.9*	15,000	Loans subsidized as low as 1 percent interest
Single-family housing guaranteed loans (sec. 502)		$725.9*	$2,980.0*	38,600	No money down, no monthly mortgage insurance loans
Single-family home repair grants and loans (sec. 504)	$33.7	$52.7	$46.8	9,021	Grants for elderly and loans subsidized as low as 1 percent interest
Single-family housing mutual self-help grants (sec. 523)	$5.6	$12.8	$25.4	1,350	Grants to nonprofit and public entities to provide technical assistance
Multifamily direct rural rental housing loans (sec. 515)	$869.5*	$512.4*	$114.3*	2,181	Loans to developers subsidized as low as 1 percent interest
Multifamily housing guaranteed loans (sec. 538)			$74.8*	2,540	Guaranteed loans for developing moderate-income apartments
Multifamily housing farm labor grants and loans (secs. 516/514)	$68.8	$56.3	$33.2	622	Grants and loans subsidized at 1 percent interest
Multifamily housing preservation grants (sec. 533)		$23.0	$7.2	1,800	Grants to nonprofit organizations, local governments, and Native American tribes, usually leveraged with outside funding
Multifamily housing rental assistance (sec. 521)	$423.0	$446.7	$583.4	42,000	Rental assistance to about one-half the residents in RHS rental and farm labor units

*Dollar amounts represents private-sector loan levels guaranteed by RHS or loans made directly by RHS during the year. Actual federal outlays are much lower because they cover the subsidy cost, not the face value of the loans or guaranteed loans. The subsidy cost is the estimated long-term cost to the government of a direct or guaranteed loan calculated on a net present value basis, excluding administrative costs.

SOURCE: William B. Shear, "Table 1. Data on RHS's Housing Programs," *Rural Housing Service: Opportunities to Improve Management*, GAO-03-911T, U.S. General Accounting Office, June 19, 2003, http://www.gao.gov/new.items/d03911t.pdf (accessed March 11, 2005)

assist renters and $4.2 million toward single-family home loan guarantees.

In the fourth quarter of 2004, homeownership in rural areas, at 76.4%, was 7.2% higher than the national rate (69.2%), but affordable housing is in short supply in rural areas. Much of the rural low-income housing where renters, migrant workers, and a high population of minorities live is substandard. There are four major areas affected by housing inadequacies: the Mississippi Delta, Native American trust lands, the Colonias bordering Mexico, and Appalachia.

Unfortunately, like HUD, RHS has been plagued by accusations of mismanagement. The GAO report "Rural Housing Services, Opportunity to Improve Management" (June 2003) found that the RHS could be improved by reducing costs and centralizing administration. A May 2004 GAO report said that the RHS had consistently overestimated its budget needs ("Rural Housing Service: Agency Has Overestimated Its Rental Assistance Budget Needs over the Life of the Program," GAO-04-752).

Projects for Assistance in Transition from Homelessness (PATH)

Projects for Assistance in Transition from Homelessness (PATH) is a federally funded program administered by the federal Center for Mental Health Services through grants to state mental health agencies. These state agencies provide PATH-funded services to homeless people with mental illness primarily through local or regional mental health service providers. PATH funds can be used for outreach, screening, diagnostic treatment, habilitation, rehabilitation, community mental health services, case management, supportive and supervisory services in residential settings, and other housing-related services.

Education for Homeless Children and Youth (EHCY)

In response to reports that over 50% of homeless children were not attending school regularly, Congress enacted the McKinney-Vento Act's Education for Homeless Children and Youth (EHCY) program in 1987. The program ensures that homeless children and youth have equal access to the same free, appropriate education, including preschool education, provided to other children. EHCY also provides funding for state and local school districts to implement the law. States are required to report estimated numbers of homeless children and the problems encountered in serving them. The McKinney-Vento Homeless Education Assistance Act, part of the No Child Left Behind Act of 2001, reauthorized the program and included the following new guidelines.

- Homeless children cannot be segregated.

- Transportation has to be provided to and from schools of origin if requested (a school of origin is the school the student attended when permanently housed, or the school in which the student was last enrolled).

- In case of a placement dispute, immediate enrollment is required pending the outcome.

- Local education agencies (LEAs) must put the "best interest of the child" first in determining the feasibility of keeping children in their school of origin.

- LEAs have to designate a local liaison for homeless children and youth.

- States have to subgrant 50% to 75% of their allotments under EHCY competitively to LEAs.

Unaccompanied Youth Services

The Runaway and Homeless Youth Program (RHYA), administered by the Department of Health and Human Services, began in 1974 and provides financial assistance to community-based crisis and referral centers that serve runaway and homeless youth and their families. Transitional Living Program for Older Homeless Youth was created in 1988 as part of RHYA to assure long-term assistance to this segment of the homeless ("Family and Youth Services Bureau—Transitional Living Program for Older Homeless Youth," U.S. Department of Health and Human Services http://www.acf.dhhs.gov/programs/fysb/tlp.htm, March 10, 2004). Services are geared to the following areas:

- Living accommodations that are safe and stable

- Skill building on two levels: life-skills such as housekeeping, budgeting, and food preparation, and interpersonal skills such as relationship-building, decision-making, and stress management

- Education area addresses furthering secondary and post secondary achievement, job preparation, and substance abuse education

- Mental and physical health care, which includes counseling, health assessment, and treatment in emergencies

CHAPTER 6
THE LAW, THE COURTS, AND THE HOMELESS

The process of renewal and rebuilding that accompanies an influx of middle-class or affluent people into deteriorating areas is called gentrification. It typically displaces earlier—and usually poorer—residents, and often destroys ethnic communities (Tom Wetzel, "What Is Gentrification?" 2004, http://www.uncanny.net/~wetzel/gentry.htm). While gentrification has positive aspects—reduced crime, new investment in the community, and increased economic activity—these benefits are generally enjoyed by the newcomers while the existing residents are marginalized. When a neighborhood is gentrified, the visible homeless come to be seen as a blight on the quality of life of the new residents. The homeless can drive away tourists and frustrate the proprietors of area businesses. The widening gap between the haves and the have-nots in American society is evident in the plight of homeless people. As more and more privately owned, federally subsidized apartment buildings and former "skid rows" were gentrified during the economic boom of the 1990s, more of the poorest people were forced into homelessness.

Recent years have seen an increase in the enactment of laws and ordinances intended to regulate the activities of homeless people. Moreover, in some areas homeless children even found themselves placed outside the regular public school system and segregated in special schools for the homeless. Advocates for the homeless contend that such practices deny the homeless their most basic human, legal, and political rights.

Some local ordinances prevent the homeless from sleeping on the streets or in parks, although there may not be enough shelter beds to accommodate every homeless person every night. The homeless may be turned out of shelters to fend for themselves during the day, yet local ordinances prevent them from loitering in public places or resting in bus stations, libraries, or public buildings. Begging or picking up cans for recycling may help

the homeless to support themselves, yet often there are restrictions against panhandling (begging) or limits on the number of cans they can redeem. To see the homeless bathe or use the toilet in public makes people uncomfortable; consequently, laws are passed to prohibit such activities.

Are the homeless targeted by these laws and consequently denied their civil rights? Do such ordinances criminalize homelessness by singling out the minority (the unhoused) but not the majority (the housed)? For example, drinking alcoholic beverages in public is illegal, but the police may selectively enforce the law against street people while ignoring other drinkers, such as tourists. Ordinances disallowing life-sustaining activities performed by homeless individuals may be said to exclude the homeless from equal protection under the law.

Most measures regulating the behavior of the homeless are enacted at the community level. Sometimes the most restrictive of these laws have been challenged in federal court on the grounds that they violate the rights of the homeless people they seek to regulate. For example, a federal court may be asked to determine whether begging or panhandling is considered protected conduct under the First Amendment (freedom of speech).

A LAW CONCERNING THE EDUCATION OF HOMELESS CHILDREN

The 1987 McKinney-Vento Homeless Assistance Act (42 U.S.C. 11431 et seq.) is the federal law that entitles children who are homeless to a free, appropriate public education, for which federal funding is provided to the states under Subtitle VII-B, the Education for Homeless Children and Youth Program. At the time the legislation was passed, only an estimated 57% of homeless children were enrolled in school. By 2000 the percentage had increased to 88%.

However, in implementing the legislation, school districts found that barriers arose in such areas as residency, guardian requirements, incomplete or missing documentation (including immunization records and birth certificates), and transportation. Consequently, some school districts established separate schools for homeless children. As of 2002 there were an estimated forty separate schools for the homeless nationwide, according to the National Coalition for the Homeless.

The National Law Center on Homelessness and Poverty (*Separate and Unequal: A Report on Education Barriers for Homeless Children and Youth*, Washington, DC, January 2000) complains that such programs violate the McKinney-Vento Act and are "vastly inferior" to regular public schools in terms of resources and curricula. For example, some of the schools were located in shelters or churches that violated health and safety codes, and some were not staffed by certified teachers. Most schools were one-room classrooms with students of different ages and grades together under one teacher. Most do not offer a full range of educational programs, such as special education, gifted and talented programs, or bilingual education (National Coalition for the Homeless, "School Segregation and Homeless Children and Youth: Questions and Answers," http://www.nationalhomeless.org/unequal.html).

Walter Varner, President of the National Association for the Education of Homeless Children and Youth, testified before Congress on September 5, 2000, that in his opinion, "separate [education] is never equal." (The landmark Supreme Court decision in *Brown v. Board of Education* [347 U.S. 483 (1954)] found that "the 'separate but equal' doctrine . . . has no place in the field of public education.") Varner pointed out that thousands of schools across the country had successfully eliminated barriers to the education of homeless children. Furthermore, he stated that it is "unacceptable to accommodate the prejudices of housed children against their homeless peers. . . . As the Supreme Court has said, 'private biases may be outside the reach of the law, but the law cannot, directly or indirectly, give them effect.'"

Proponents of separate schools argue they provide badly needed supportive services such as showers, clothing, hygiene items, dental and medical care, psychological counseling, and birthday parties and gifts. The schools also shield children from the embarrassment and ridicule they might expect to encounter in regular public schools.

When Congress reauthorized the Homeless Children and Youth Program in January 2002 (through the enactment of the No Child Left Behind Act [PL 107-110]), it asserted that "Homelessness alone is not sufficient reason to separate students from the mainstream school environment." The new law required that homeless children be placed in mainstream schools, and it cut off federal aid to separate schools for the homeless. However, just before the bill was signed, six schools were exempted from the new law.

Transportation became an issue for school districts providing education to homeless students. Homes for the Homeless and the Institute for Children and Poverty found that 34% of 226 students in one New York homeless shelter faced commutes of longer than an hour because their parents had opted to keep their children in the same schools they had attended before they became homeless, a right guaranteed by the new law (Nicole Brode, "New York's School Choice Leaves More Homeless Children with Hour-Plus Commutes," *Knight-Ridder/Tribune Business News*, February 10, 2003). In 2005 the Thomas J. Pappas schools for the homeless in Phoenix and Tempe, Arizona, reported that twelve buses traveled more than 1,000 miles each morning to transport children to school.

RESTRICTIVE ORDINANCES
Not in My Backyard (NIMBY)

To many people, the prospect of low-income, subsidized housing is synonymous with rising crime, falling property values, and overcrowded classrooms, and therefore cause for protest. Because of these fears, local governments often use zoning requirements to block the establishment of group-living homes and shelters for the homeless in all or part of their city. Zoning requirements are local laws regulating what kinds of buildings can be placed in different parts of a city. The use of zoning requirements to block particular developments is often called the "Not in My Backyard" (NIMBY) effect. The people in the neighborhoods are essentially saying that they do not want to have services for the homeless near them, even if they do not oppose them on principle.

In 1997 the city of Springfield, Missouri, passed a zoning ordinance that is typical of the NIMBY effect. The ordinance imposed new restrictions on the operation of emergency and transitional shelters and soup kitchens. No such facility was allowed to be located within 2,000 feet of another similar facility. Among other restrictions, the ordinance limited the capacity of emergency shelters to fifty beds, prohibited shelters from serving meals to nonshelter residents unless the shelter obtained city authorization, and required shelters to have at least one off-street parking space for every three beds. The overall effect was to keep services for the homeless small and scattered, with none of them able to provide for all of the needs of a homeless person at once.

Criminalizing the Homeless Life

Homeless people live in and move about public spaces, and many Americans believe society has a right to control or regulate what homeless people can do in those shared spaces. A city or town may introduce local ordinances or policies designed to restrict homeless people's activities, remove their belongings, or destroy their nontraditional living places. In many cities, municipal use of criminal sanctions to protect public spaces has come into conflict with efforts by civil rights and homeless advocates to prevent the criminalization of the homeless.

There have been other approaches. Several cities have proposed or created community courts specifically to handle "public nuisance" crimes. Other cities have implemented plans to privatize public property as a way of restricting the access of homeless people to certain areas.

Other localities pass ordinances that target homeless people in the hopes of driving them from the community. For example, Olympia, Washington, considered ordinances in 2000 that banned camping and car camping, established "no panhandling" and "no alcohol" zones, and strengthened trespassing laws in public parks. According to an annual report by the National Coalition for the Homeless (NCH):

> Policies of criminalization defeat their own goals of removing homeless people from public visibility because they simply create further barriers for survival and undermine individual efforts to escape homelessness. Such policies keep more people on the streets and increase problems related to homelessness. When individuals are released from jail, they are still homeless, and they have even more barriers and obstacles to overcome than before.

—National Coalition for the Homeless, "Illegal to Be Homeless," 2004

Violating Human Rights

The NCH's 2004 *Illegal to Be Homeless* report also documented what NCH termed "the widespread trend of violations of the basic human rights of people experiencing homelessness in 179 communities in forty-eight states, Puerto Rico, and the District of Columbia." The report noted that nearly all of the communities surveyed lacked sufficient shelter space to accommodate the homeless and suggested that the effort and money spent on bringing the homeless into the courthouse might better be directed toward addressing the nation's lack of affordable housing. The report stated:

> We have asserted and continue to assert that a pattern and practice of civil rights violations and unconstitutional behaviors by local government authorities, including the police and other city agencies, exists in many cities around the country. These practices exact enormous economic, social, political and individual costs and do nothing to prevent and end homelessness that plagues individuals nationwide.

Table 6.1 illustrates the anti-homeless laws that existed in some of the cities surveyed for the 2004 report. Prohibited or restricted behaviors fell under the categories of sanitation, begging, sleeping/camping, sitting/lying, loitering/loafing, and vagrancy.

Illegal to Be Homeless declared Little Rock, Atlanta, Cincinnati, Las Vegas, and Gainesville as the five "meanest cities" for the number of anti-homeless laws passed or pending, the enforcement and severity of their laws, and the "general political climate" with regard to the homeless, among other criteria. The "meanest states" were California and Florida. Two examples of the practices of these cities follow.

In Little Rock, homeless service providers were assured by police that they would not use information about locations of homeless camps to later harass homeless people. About a month later, the providers heard that the city would, in fact, use the information to do sweeps of the camps. The sweeps occurred throughout the summer, generally before major events. Advocates urged the police not to conduct huge sweeps, arguing that there were not enough shelter beds for all the homeless. While major sweeps were postponed in August 2004, the city planned to go forward with them. According to *Illegal to Be Homeless*, Mayor Jim Dailey of Little Rock hoped to "'deal with the sensitivity issues of those who truly have needs, but as far as I'm concerned we need to run off those individuals who are the chronic homeless that don't want services provided to the them' or who 'expect they're going to victimize the community with their panhandling or other crimes.'"

In Atlanta, Mayor Shirley Franklin issued an executive order in September 2003 that prohibited feeding people in public, arguing that feeding hungry people was a health hazard. Many church groups and individuals stopped offering food to hungry homeless people in city parks. In addition, arrests for "quality of life" offenses increased 239% that year. A quasi-police force known as the "Downtown Ambassadors" awaken homeless people sleeping on the street at 6:45 A.M. Sometimes homeless people were arrested for sleeping in public places. Meanwhile, the city planned to close shelters for homeless women and children.

USE OF FORCE. Just as force was used against striking coal miners at the turn of the twentieth century and against homeless and poor World War I veterans who marched on Washington during the Great Depression, violence and force have often been used to deal with the "homeless problem." In 1995 the New York City police used an armored personnel carrier and riot gear to retake two East Village tenements from a group of squatters who had resisted city efforts for nine months. Homeless people had occupied the city-owned buildings for as long as a decade and claimed that their continuous use of

TABLE 6.1

Prohibited conduct in selected cities, 2002–03

City	Sanitation		Begging			Sleeping/camping				Sitting/lying	Loitering/loafing		Vagrancy		Other (see footnotes)
	Bathing in public waters	Urination/ defecation in public	Begging in public places city-wide	Begging in particular public places	"Aggressive" panhandling	Sleeping in public city-wide	Sleeping in particular public places	Camping in public city-wide	Camping in particular public places	Sitting or lying in particular public places	Loitering/loafing vagrancy city-wide	Loitering/loafing in particular public places	Obstruction of sidewalks/ public places	Closure of particular public places	
Albuquerque, NW	X	X			X				X				X	X	b,x,o
Atlanta, GA		X		X	X		X	X		X			X	X	a,b,f,g,l
Austin, TX	X	X	X	X	X		X	X		X	X	X		X	b
Baltimore, MD	X	X		X	X		X			X		X	X		a,c,n
Boston, MA			X	X	X	X	X	X		X		X	X		i
Buffalo, NY	X		X	X			X					X	X	X	a,b,f,g,n,q
Charlotte, NC		X		X	X	X	X		X	X			X	X	f,n
Chicago, IL				X					X				X	X	a,c,d,f
Cincinnati, OH	X	X		X	X		X	X				X	X	X	a,b,n
Cleveland, OH				X	X				X			X	X	X	a,b,d
Columbus, OH				X			X		X	X			X	X	b
Dallas, TX	X	X		X	X	X	X		X			X	X	X	a,b,d,n
Denver, CO	X	X		X	X		X		X			X	X	X	a,b,e,p
Detroit, MI		X	X	X							X		X	X	a,b,f,j
El Paso, TX				X					X			X	X	X	b,d,n
Fort Worth, TX		X	X	X			X		X		X		X	X	b
Fresno, CA	X	X		X	X				X	X		X	X	X	a,j
Honolulu, HI									X				X	X	a,b,d
Houston, TX	X	X	X	X	X		X		X	X		X	X	X	a,b,d,g,k,p,q
Indianapolis, IN	X		X	X	X	X	X	X		X	X	X	X		a,b,d,n
Jacksonville, FL	X		X	X	X		X		X				X		b
Kansas City, MO		X	X	X	X			X	X			X	X	X	b,c,g,q
Long Beach, CA	X				X		X	X		X			X		d,k
Los Angeles, CA			X		X				X			X	X	X	a,b,c,e
Memphis, TN	X			X	X	X	X		X	X			X	X	d,k
Miami, FL	X				X				X	X		X	X	X	a,b,c,e
Milwaukee, WI	X		X	X	X			X		X	X		X	X	a,b,n,j,n
Minneapolis, MN	X			X		X	X		X			X	X	X	a
Nashville, TN			X		X				X	X			X	X	a,d
New Orleans, LA			X	X		X		X				X	X		b,g,n,o
New York, NY	X	X	X	X	X	X	X		X	X		X	X	X	d,g,q
Oakland, CA	X		X	X		X	X	X		X			X	X	a,b,c,d
Oklahoma City, OK	X		X	X	X		X	X			X	X	X	X	b
Omaha, NE				X					X				X	X	a,b
Philadelphia, PA		X	X	X	X	X	X	X		X		X	X	X	a,b,d,e,f,h,i,k,o
Phoenix, AZ	X	X		X	X				X	X	X	X	X	X	a,b,e
Pittsburgh, PA	X	X		X	X		X	X				X	X	X	a,b
Portland, OR		X		X	X			X				X	X	X	a,b,j,n
Sacramento, CA		X		X	X				X			X	X	X	a,b,h
San Antonio, TX			X	X	X		X		X			X	X	X	a,b
San Diego, CA	X	X	X	X	X		X	X		X		X	X	X	b,c,d,n
San Francisco, CA	X			X					X	X			X	X	b
San Jose, CA														X	d
Seattle, WA	X	X			X				X	X	X		X	X	a,b,c,d,m
St. Louis, MO		X			X					X			X	X	a,b,c,l,m

TABLE 6.1

Prohibited conduct in selected cities, 2002–03 [CONTINUED]

City	Sanitation — Bathing in public waters	Sanitation — Urination/defecation in public	Begging — Begging in public places city-wide	Begging — Begging in particular public places	Begging — "Aggressive" panhandling	Sleeping/camping — Sleeping in public city-wide	Sleeping/camping — Sleeping in particular public places	Sleeping/camping — Camping in public city-wide	Sleeping/camping — Camping in particular public places	Sitting/lying — Sitting or lying in particular public places	Loitering/loafing — Loitering/loafing vagrancy city-wide	Loitering/loafing — Loitering/loafing in particular public places	Vagrancy — Obstruction of sidewalks/public places	Vagrancy — Closure of particular public places	Other (see footnotes)
Toledo, OH			X	X									X	X	b,d,l
Tucson, AZ	X	X	X	X	X		X		X	X		X	X	X	b,h,n
Tulsa, OK			X	X	X	X	X	X	X				X	X	a,b,k,n
Virginia Beach, VA		X	X				X			X		X	X		b,d,k
Washington, DC				X	X	✓					X				b,g,h

aSpitting.
bMinor curfew.
cHaving/abandoning merchandise carts away from premises of owner.
dFailure to disperse.
eMaintaining junk/storage of property.
fMaking music on the street/street performers.
gWashing automobile windows.
hProhibition to enter vacant building.
iRummaging.
jCreating odor.
kVehicular residence.
lWalking on highway.
mBringing paupers/insane persons into city.
nPeddling.
oPublic nuisance.
pCharging for car wash.
qWashing cars.

SOURCE: "Prohibited Conduct," in *Illegal to be Homeless: The Criminalization of Homelessness in the United States*, The National Coalition for the Homeless, August 2003, http://www.nationalhomeless.org/civilrights/crim2003/report.pdf (accessed March 17, 2005)

the buildings without the formal objection of the city gave them rights to the building, under a legal principle known as "adverse possession."

The Rationale for Restrictive and Ordinances

Local officials often restrict homeless people's use of public space to protect public health and safety—either of the general public, the homeless themselves, or both. Dangers to the public have included tripping over people and objects on sidewalks, intimidation of passersby caused by aggressive begging, and the spreading of diseases. Many people believe the very presence of the homeless is unsightly and their removal improves the appearance of public spaces. Other laws are based on the need to prevent crime. New York's campaign is based on the "broken windows" theory of criminologists James Q. Wilson and George Kelling (*Atlantic Monthly*, March 1982). They argued that allowing indications of disorder, such as a broken window, or street people, to remain unaddressed shows a loss of public order and control, as well as apathy in a neighborhood, which breeds more serious criminal activity. Therefore, keeping a city neat and orderly should help to prevent crime.

All of these are legitimate concerns to some degree. The problem, critics say, is that rather than trying to eliminate or reduce homelessness by helping the homeless find housing and jobs, most local laws try to change the behavior of the homeless by punishing them. They target the homeless with legal action, ignoring the fact that many would gladly stop living in the streets and panhandling if they had any feasible alternatives. While these laws may be effective in the sense that the shanties are gone and homeless people are not allowed to bed down in subway tunnels or doorways, the fact remains that the homeless have not disappeared. They have simply been forced to move to a different part of town, have hidden themselves, or have been imprisoned. Furthermore, many of these laws have been challenged in court as violating the legal rights of the homeless people they target.

An Argument against Criminalization as Public Policy

In "Downward Spiral: Homelessness and Its Criminalization" (*Yale Law & Policy Review*, vol. 14, no. 1, 1996), Maria Foscarinis, founder of the National Law Center on Homelessness and Poverty, argued that criminalization of the homeless is poor public policy for several reasons:

- It may be constitutionally unsound, especially in cities that are unable to offer adequate resources to their homeless residents.

- It leads to legal challenges, which may take years to resolve, regardless of outcome.

- Legal battles are costly and will deplete already scarce municipal resources that could be used on solutions to homelessness.

- Criminalization responses do not reflect public sentiment, but rather the will of a vocal, politically influential minority.

- Criminalization fosters divisiveness, pitting "us" (the housed) against "them" (the homeless).

- Like emergency relief, criminalization addresses the visible symptom of homelessness—the presence of homeless people in public space—and neglects the true causes of homelessness.

- Finally there is the fact that, in the long-term, criminalization does not and cannot work. Like all humans, homeless people must eat, sleep, and occupy space. If they are prohibited from occupying one area, they must go somewhere else.

As an alternative to criminalization, Foscarinis suggested the following:

- Police advocacy programs, in which "sweeps" are replaced by outreach units—officers assigned to go out, with service providers, to homeless people to refer them to necessary services. Unless criminal activity is involved, the police remain in the background to provide security, and the presence of service providers prevents police from being too heavy-handed or harassing.

- Standing committees composed of homeless people, advocates, a police captain, and a representative of the city government to respond to complaints about "camping" of homeless residents. The committee outreach team attempts to make alternative arrangements for the homeless. The police act only if criminal activity is involved, or if homeless people refuse alternative arrangements.

- Day-labor centers—buildings where homeless people can meet with employers to get jobs.

- One-stop access centers, which offer medical services, mental health services, social services, and job training at one location.

ALTERNATIVE STRATEGIES

Alternatives to criminalizing homeless behavior can be implemented with help from community leadership and homeless advocates, who have intimate knowledge from close contact with homelessness. In *Constructive Alternatives to Criminalization: Models to Replicate and Useful Tips to Consider* (October 2002), the National Law Center on Homelessness and Poverty (NLCHP) detailed what some cities have done about homeless problems.

Miami

After ten years in litigation, a class action suit brought by homeless persons, *Michael Pottinger, Peter Carter, Berry Young, et al. v. City of Miami* (810 F. Supp. 1551 [1992]), resulted in a financial settlement and the "no bed/no arrest" policy that other cities have adopted as a model. (No bed/no arrest means that if a person is to be arrested for an action that is a result of being homeless, that person must first be referred to an appropriate, available, and accessible shelter bed. If the person declines that bed, then he or she may be arrested.) The city of Miami used some of the settlement money to build two large shelters. Funds were raised to provide programs for the homeless, and police officers were required to undergo training on interacting with the homeless.

In analyzing the actions taken by cities to deal with homelessness, the NLCHP noted the downside to the no bed/no arrest policy: Any type of bed space can be offered to a homeless person and if that space is refused, cities often permit an arrest "rather than focusing on other more constructive long-term solutions to homelessness such as outreach or building of affordable housing."

Philadelphia

When Philadelphia proposed a "Sidewalk Behavior Ordinance" in 1998, homeless people and the mental health community formed a coalition, staged sit-ins, lobbied, and testified at city council meetings to increase public awareness of homelessness. In the end nearly $6 million was appropriated for the necessary social services in the event the ordinance was passed by voters (it was). A no bed/no citation policy (for violation of the ordinance) was adopted, and additional shelter beds and other housing opportunities were provided, with the result that there was a noticeable decline in the homeless population. The 2004 *Illegal to Be Homeless* report noted that Philadelphia has succeeded in removing nearly 75% of chronically homeless people from the streets.

Washington, D.C.

In Washington, D.C., a tax levied on business property at the rate of $0.01 per square foot was used to build the DC Downtown Day Center. Support came from those most affected by the homeless situation and resulted in services and solutions rather than fines and jail time for those in need.

Minneapolis and Fort Lauderdale

The 2004 report *Illegal to Be Homeless* also commended Minneapolis, Minnesota, and Fort Lauderdale, Florida, for their efforts to decriminalize homelessness. In Minneapolis, the City Council created a Decriminalization Task Force to "review all laws, policies, and practices that have the effect of criminalizing homelessness." The task force has recommended implementing changes in city ordinances, training police officers to help homeless people find services, repealing the vagrancy law, and allowing time for public testimony from homeless people.

In Fort Lauderdale an outreach program has been launched that sends one formerly homeless person and one police officer out to public places each afternoon, where they assess the situations of homeless people and match them with appropriate services. Some are sent to shelters, some are enrolled in long-term programs, and others are given bus tickets to reunite with family. Police take individuals to shelters rather than to jail. The impact of criminalization on the homeless has been significantly decreased through this program.

CONSTITUTIONAL RIGHTS

The U.S. Constitution and its amendments, especially the Bill of Rights, guarantee certain freedoms and rights to all citizens of the United States, including the homeless. As more and more cities move to deal with homelessness by aggressively enforcing public place restrictions, the restrictions are increasingly being challenged in court as unconstitutional. Sometimes a city ordinance has been declared unconstitutional; at other times, the courts have found that there were special circumstances that allowed the ordinance to stand.

There are numerous ways in which ordinances affecting the homeless can violate their rights. Many court challenges claimed that the law in question was unconstitutionally broad or vague. Others claimed that a particular law denied the homeless equal protection under the law or violated their right to due process, as guaranteed by the Fifth and Fourteenth Amendments. There have also been cases based on a person's right to travel, and others that claimed restrictions on the homeless constituted "cruel and unusual punishment," which is prohibited by the Eighth Amendment. Many cities have ordinances against panhandling, but charitable organizations freely solicit in public places. As a result, according to those challenging the ordinances, the right to free expression under the First Amendment is available to organizations but denied to the homeless.

The appearance of poverty should not deny an individual's right to be free from unreasonable search and seizure, as guaranteed by the Fourth Amendment. Often homeless people's property has been confiscated or destroyed (camping gear, personal possessions) without warning because they were found on public property. Unfortunately the state of homelessness is such that even the most personal living activities have to be performed in public. Denying these activities necessary for survival may infringe on an individual's rights under the Eighth Amendment.

The Fourteenth Amendment right to equal protection under the law may be at issue when the homeless are cited for sleeping in the park, but others lying on the grass sunning themselves or taking a nap during a picnic, for instance, are not.

Testing the Laws in Court

Some court cases test the law through civil suits, and others challenge the law by appealing convictions in criminal cases. Many advocates for the homeless, or the homeless themselves, have challenged laws that they believed infringed on the rights of homeless people.

NO BED, NO ARREST. The concept of "no bed, no arrest" first arose out of a 1988 class action suit filed by the Miami Chapter of the American Civil Liberties Union on behalf of about 6,000 homeless people living in the city of Miami. The city had a practice of "sweeping" the homeless from the areas where the Orange Bowl Parade and other related activities were held. The complaint alleged that the city had

> a custom, practice and policy of arresting, harassing and otherwise interfering with homeless people for engaging in basic activities of daily life—including sleeping and eating—in the public places where they are forced to live. Plaintiffs further claim that the City has arrested thousands of homeless people for such life-sustaining conduct under various City of Miami ordinances and Florida Statutes. In addition, plaintiffs assert that the city routinely seizes and destroys their property and has failed to follow its own inventory procedures regarding the seized personal property of homeless arrestees and homeless persons in general.

In *Michael Pottinger, Peter Carter, Berry Young, et al. v. City of Miami* (810 F. Supp. 1551 [1992]), the U.S. District Court for the Southern District of Florida ruled that the city's practices were "cruel and unusual," in violation of the Eighth Amendment's ban against punishment based on status. (Only the homeless were being arrested.) Furthermore, the court found the police practices of taking or destroying the property of the homeless to be in violation of Fourth and Fifth Amendment rights of freedom from unreasonable seizure and confiscation of property.

The city appealed the district court's judgment. Ultimately, a settlement was reached in which the city of Miami agreed that a homeless person observed committing a "life-sustaining conduct" misdemeanor may be warned to stop, but if there is no available shelter, no warning is to be given. If there is an available shelter, the homeless person is to be told of its availability. If the homeless person accepts assistance, no arrest is to take place.

USING LIBRARIES. Richard Kreimer, a homeless man in Morristown, New Jersey, often visited the Joint Free Library of Morristown. The library personnel objected to his presence, claiming his behavior was disruptive, and his body odor so offensive that it kept patrons from using some of the areas of the library. After the librarians documented the problems for a period of time, the Library Board of Trustees passed a Library Patron Policy that, among other things, allowed librarians to ask people to leave if their hygiene was unacceptable to community norms.

In 1990 Kreimer filed suit in the Federal District Court for New Jersey against the library, the Board of Directors, the Morristown Bureau of Police, and other library and municipal officials. The suit alleged that the policy rules were "overbroad" (that is, they failed to specify what actions would be objectionable), "vague," and a violation of Kreimer's First Amendment right of access to information and his Fourteenth Amendment rights of equal protection and due process, as well as his rights under the New Jersey Constitution.

The district court upheld Kreimer's complaint that the policy violated his First and Fourteenth Amendment rights. The library appealed the decision to the Court of Appeals, and the court reversed the decision, validating the library's policy, finding that a library, by its very nature, cannot support all First Amendment activities, such as speech-making and interactive debate. Therefore, a library is a "limited public forum," and the rules of the Morristown Library were appropriate to its limited functions of reading, studying, and using library materials. (*Kreimer v. Bureau of Police for Morristown*, 958 F.2d 1242 [3rd Cir. 1992]).

LOITERING OR WANDERING. In 2000 homeless street dwellers and shelter residents of the Skid Row area (the plaintiffs) sought a temporary restraining order (TRO) against the Los Angeles Police Department (the defendants), claiming their First and Fourth Amendment rights were being violated. The plaintiffs alleged they were being stopped without cause and their identification demanded on threat of arrest, that they were being ordered to "move along" although they were not in anyone's way, that their belongings were being confiscated, and that they were being ticketed for loitering. In *Justin v. City of Los Angeles* (No. CV-00-12352 LGB, 2000 U.S. Dist. Lexis 17881 [C.D. Cal. Dec. 5, 2000]), Judge Lourdes Baird denied a TRO that would have prevented the defendants from asking the plaintiffs to "move along." The TRO was granted with reference to the following actions when in the Skid Row area:

- Detention without reasonable suspicion

- Demand of identification upon threat of arrest

- Searches without probable cause

- Removal from sidewalks unless free passage of pedestrians was obstructed

- Confiscation of personal property that was not abandoned

- Citation of those who may "annoy or molest" if interference was reasonable and free passage of pedestrians was not impeded

LIVING IN AN ENCAMPMENT. In 1996 advocates for the homeless sought an injunction against a Tucson, Arizona, resolution barring homeless encampments from city-owned property on Eighth Amendment and Equal Protection grounds. The court, in *Davidson v. City of Tucson* (924 F. Supp. 989), held the plaintiffs did not have standing to raise a cruel and unusual punishment claim, as they had not been convicted of a crime and no one had been arrested under the ordinance. The Equal Protection claim failed because the court did not consider homeless people a suspect class and the right to travel did not include the right to ignore trespass laws or remain on property without regard to ownership.

SITTING OR LYING ON THE SIDEWALK. In 1995 homeless persons challenged Cincinnati, Ohio, ordinances prohibiting sitting or lying on sidewalks and solicitation on First and Fourteenth Amendment grounds. In 1998, in *Clark v. Cincinnati* (No. 1-95-448, S.D. Ohio, October 25, 1995), determining that the ordinances likely infringed on the plaintiffs' First Amendment right to freedom of speech, the U.S. District Court issued a preliminary injunction to stop the city from enforcing the ordinances, except for the specific provision of the sidewalk ordinance that prohibited lying down.

LOITERING IN A TRAIN STATION. In 1995 plaintiffs challenged Amtrak's policy of arresting or ejecting persons who appeared to be homeless or loitering in Penn Station in New York City, even though the individuals were not apparently committing crimes. The district court, in *Streetwatch v. National R.R. Passenger Corp.* (875 F. Supp. 1055), determined that Amtrak's rules of conduct were unacceptably vague and that their enforcement impinged on plaintiffs' rights to freedom of movement and due process.

PANHANDLING. One of the notable court cases addressing panhandling involved Jennifer Loper, who moved from her parents' suburban New York home to beg on the streets of New York City. From time to time she and her friend William Kaye were ordered by police to move on, in accordance with the city ordinance stating: "A person is guilty of loitering when he: '(1) Loiters, remains or wanders about in a public place for the purpose of begging.'" In 1992 Loper and Kaye sued the city, claiming that their free speech rights had been violated and that the ordinance was unconstitutional. A district court declared the ordinance unconstitutional on First Amendment grounds. On appeal, the police department argued that begging has no expressive element that is protected by the First Amendment. In *Loper v. New York City Police Department* (999 F.2d 699 [2d Cir. 1993]), the U.S. Court of Appeals, Second Circuit declared the city's ban on begging invalid, noting that the regulations applied to sidewalks, which have historically been acknowledged to be a public forum. The Court agreed that the ban deprived beggars of all means to express their message. Even if a panhandler does not speak, "the mere presence of an unkempt and disheveled person holding out his or her hand or a cup to receive a donation itself conveys a message of need for support and assistance."

ZONING THE HOMELESS OUT OF DOWNTOWN. In 1998 Alan Mason, a homeless man, sought an injunction, damages, and relief against the city of Tucson and the city police for "zoning" homeless people. The suit alleged that homeless people were arrested without cause, were charged with misdemeanors, and were then released only if they agreed to stay away from the area where they had been arrested. Mason himself had been restricted from certain downtown areas, including state, local, and federal courts (including the court in which his case was tried); voter registration facilities; a soup kitchen; places of worship; and many social and transportation agencies.

The plaintiff argued that such restrictions violated his constitutional right to travel, deprived him of liberty without due process in violation of the Fifth Amendment, and implicated the Equal Protection clause of the Fourteenth Amendment. In July 1998 the district court, in *Mason v. Tucson* (D. Arizona, 1998), granted a temporary injunction against enforcing the law, saying the zone restrictions were overbroad. The case was subsequently settled out of court.

HOMELESS COURT

One solution to the increasing backlog of court cases involving petty offenses committed by the homeless is the Homeless Court Program, founded in 1996 by Steven R. Binder, Deputy Public Defender for San Diego County. The program is now a model for other jurisdictions. In a typical program, a courtroom is set up in a shelter or in a Health Care for the Homeless office, and defendants charged with criminal misdemeanor warrants are tried in the presence of a judge, a clerk, a public defender, and a prosecutor who are familiar with the problems of the homeless. The guiding principle is rehabilitation, not punishment. According to Justin Graf of the American Bar Association, in an online review of Binder's *The Homeless Court Program: Taking the Court to the Streets* (Washington, DC: American Bar Association Commission on Homelessness and Poverty, 2002):

> The key players involved in the program realize that outstanding criminal warrants often preclude homeless people from accessing vital services such as employment, housing, public benefits, and treatment for mental health and/or substance abuse problems. As such, the court seeks to address the legal problems of the homeless participants as well as linking them with appropriate services and treatment programs.

CHAPTER 7
THE HEALTH OF THE HOMELESS

LIVING IN PUBLIC: INCREASED HEALTH PROBLEMS

Health problems are recognized as both causes and effects of homelessness. For example, a health problem that prevents an impoverished person from working can result in a loss of income that leads to homelessness. For those living on the streets, lack of adequate shelter and proper facilities for maintaining personal hygiene can exacerbate illness. Alcoholism, mental illnesses, diabetes, and depression become visible and more pronounced in homeless people. Other serious illnesses (tuberculosis [TB], for example) are almost exclusively associated with the unhealthy living conditions brought on by poverty. In general, experts agree that homeless people suffer from more types of illnesses, for longer periods of time, and with more harmful consequences than housed people. In addition, according to "Homelessness and Health," a 2004 policy statement by the National Health Care for the Homeless Council (NHCHC), health care delivery is complicated by the patient's homeless status, making management of such chronic diseases as diabetes, HIV, and hypertension more difficult. Virtually all Americans suffer illness and disease at some time in their lives, but for people experiencing homelessness and poverty, illness often leads to serious health concerns or premature death.

The Homeless/Morbidity Connection

One way of measuring the health of a population is to measure its morbidity rate—the rate of incidence of a disease or a mental or substance abuse disorder. The homeless often exhibit two or more conditions simultaneously, a phenomenon known as comorbidity or co-occurring disorders. Researcher Mary Ann Burg, in "Health Problems of Sheltered Homeless Women and Their Dependent Children" (*Health and Social Work*, 1994), explored the relationship between ill health and poverty and categorized the health problems of homeless

women and their dependent children living in shelters. Burg's study revealed three general classifications of illnesses related to homelessness:

- Illnesses resulting from homelessness
- Illnesses intensified by the limited health care access of the homeless
- Illnesses associated with the psychosocial burdens of homelessness

Poor health has also been reported as a cause of homelessness. In a frequently cited national survey of homeless patients (James D. Wright and Eleanor Weber, *Homelessness and Health*, Washington, DC: McGraw-Hill, 1987), 13% of the patients said that poor physical health was a factor in becoming homeless. Of people responding in the affirmative, half said health was a "major factor" and 15% said that it was the "single most important" factor. Wright and Weber also found that up to 40% of the homeless suffered from a major mental illness. In the case of the mentally ill and the alcoholic and drug-addicted homeless, the authors asserted that the failure of America's health care system must bear a major share of the blame for their homelessness.

David P. Folsom et al. found that 15% of patients treated for serious mental illness were homeless at some point during a one-year period ("Prevalence and Risk Factors for Homelessness and Utilization of Mental Health Services among 10,340 Patients with Serious Mental Illness in a Large Public Mental Health System," *American Journal of Psychiatry*, vol. 162, February 2005). The authors emphasized that homelessness among the mentally ill was associated with two other factors: substance use disorders and a lack of Medicaid insurance. The authors wrote,

> Although it would be naïve to assume that treatment for substance abuse disorders and provision of Medicaid insurance could solve the problem of homelessness

among persons with serious mental illness, further research is warranted to test the effect of interventions designed to treat patients with dual diagnoses and to assist homeless persons with serious mental illness in obtaining and maintaining entitlement benefits.

The Homeless/Mortality Connection

Mortality refers to the proportion of deaths to population. San Francisco, estimated to have one of the largest homeless populations in the country (6,248 in January 2005, down 28% from a high of 8,640 in October 2002), has been tracking homeless mortality data since 1985. Since 1988 the annual number of homeless deaths has exceeded 100 and reached 169 in the one-year period ending June 30, 2003 (a rate of one death every other day). The following year, homeless deaths decreased to 101. In an analysis of deaths among San Francisco's homeless (Ricardo Bermúdez et al., *San Francisco Homeless Deaths Identified from Medical Examiner Records: December 1996–November 1997*), the authors noted that it was obvious from this and previous reports that the homeless had a higher mortality rate than the housed population. The homeless die at younger ages; in 1997 the average age of death among the homeless was 43.3 years, compared with 72.6 years for the general population. The leading cause of death was substance abuse (50% of all deaths); 31% of deaths were caused by illicit drug use and 19% by alcohol use.

James O'Connell, a physician with the Boston Health Care for the Homeless program, concluded in "Death on the Streets" (*Harvard Medical Alumni Bulletin*, Winter 1997) that while the causes of the higher morbidity and mortality rates among Boston's homeless people were complex, there were elements of the homeless life that encourage early death. Some of these were: exposure to extremes of weather and temperature; crowded shelter living, which increases the spread of communicable diseases such as TB and pneumonia; violence; the high frequency of medical and psychiatric illnesses; substance abuse; and inadequate nutrition. A 2001 study of 558 deaths among the homeless population in Boston found that within one year prior to death, 27% of homeless people had no outpatient visits, emergency department visits, or hospitalizations (S. W. Hwang et al., "Health Care Utilization among Homeless Adults Prior to Death," *Journal of Health Care for the Poor and Underserved*, vol. 21, 2001). The authors concluded that even homeless people at high risk of death were underutilizing health care services.

A 2003 study of homeless deaths in King County, Washington, identified seventy-seven people who had died while homeless in the county that year (*King County 2003: Homeless Death Review*, Seattle: Health Care for the Homeless Network, 2004). Major causes of death included acute intoxication (26%), cardiovascular disease (17%), and homicide (9%). Most of the homeless deaths involved several illnesses prior to death; on average, those who died had three health conditions prior to death.

In a study of deaths among homeless women in Toronto, Angela M. Cheung and Stephen W. Hwang found that homeless women aged eighteen to forty-four were ten times more likely to die than women in the general population of Toronto ("The Risk of Death among Homeless Women: A Cohort Study and Review of the Literature," *Canadian Medical Association Journal*, vol. 170, 2004). Another key finding of the study was that the risk of death among young homeless women was nearly the same as the risk of death among men of the same age.

The Causes

The following socioeconomic conditions contribute to the greater prevalence of illness and early death among the poor and homeless population:

- Poor diet
- Inadequate sleeping locations
- Contagion from overcrowded shelters
- Limited facilities for daily hygiene
- Exposure to the elements
- Exposure to violence
- Social isolation
- Lack of health insurance

The Severity of the Problem

There is a growing belief in the health care field that homelessness needs to be considered in epidemic terms— that massive increases in homelessness may result in a hastened spread of illness and disease, overwhelming the health care system. John Lozier, in *The Health Care of Homeless Persons* (Boston Health Care for the Homeless Program, 2004) wrote that "Primary care clinics for indigent people generally operate beyond their capacity, are not well-located to serve people staying in shelters, and are not prepared to deal with the complex conditions often presented by homeless people." He conveyed the sense of many public health officials that the health care system was facing a crisis due to homelessness when he wrote, "The public health system, which made great strides in the twentieth century by eliminating unhealthy living conditions, seems ill-equipped to contend with the teeming shelters that are a throwback to the nineteenth century."

Researcher W. R. Breakey recognized the morbidity rates among the homeless as a major public health concern. In a 1997 article in the *American Journal of Public Health* ("It's Time for the Public Health Community to

FIGURE 7.1

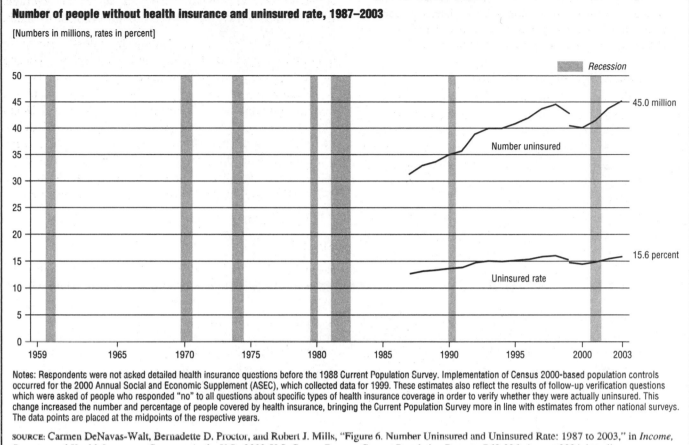

Number of people without health insurance and uninsured rate, 1987–2003

[Numbers in millions, rates in percent]

Notes: Respondents were not asked detailed health insurance questions before the 1988 Current Population Survey. Implementation of Census 2000-based population controls occurred for the 2000 Annual Social and Economic Supplement (ASEC), which collected data for 1999. These estimates also reflect the results of follow-up verification questions which were asked of people who responded "no" to all questions about specific types of health insurance coverage in order to verify whether they were actually uninsured. This change increased the number and percentage of people covered by health insurance, bringing the Current Population Survey more in line with estimates from other national surveys. The data points are placed at the midpoints of the respective years.

SOURCE: Carmen DeNavas-Walt, Bernadette D. Proctor, and Robert J. Mills, "Figure 6. Number Uninsured and Uninsured Rate: 1987 to 2003," in *Income, Poverty, and Health Insurance Coverage in the U.S.: 2003*, U.S. Census Bureau, Current Population Reports, P60-226, August 2004, http://www.census.gov/prod/2004pubs/p60-226.pdf (accessed February 18, 2005)

Declare War on Homelessness"), Breakey proposed that homelessness be responded to with the same urgency as an epidemic of an infectious disease. He urged public health officials to address larger issues—socioeconomic elements such as housing availability and wages—in order to effectively treat afflicted individuals.

The scope of health issues regarding the impoverished and homeless in the United States is related in part to the number of uninsured Americans. Figure 7.1 shows that in 2003, the number of uninsured people was higher than it had been in decades. At that time, forty-five million people were uninsured. Table 7.1 shows the percentage of people who were without health insurance coverage in 2002, by state. Texas (25.8%) and New Mexico (21.1%) had the highest percentages of uninsured people, while Minnesota (7.9%) had the lowest. (See Table 7.1.) In twenty states, the proportion of people without health insurance coverage rose between 2001 and 2003; in only two states, did the proportion drop. (See Figure 7.2.)

People without insurance are less likely to seek medical care. In "Out of Pocket Medical Spending for Care of Chronic Conditions" (*Health Affairs*, November–December 2001), S.W. Hwang et al. noted that "among chronically ill persons the uninsured had the highest out-of-pocket spending and were five times less likely to see a medical provider in a given year."

The Health Costs of Street Living

The rates of both chronic and acute health problems are disproportionately high among the homeless population. With the exception of obesity, strokes, and cancer, homeless people are far more likely than the housed to suffer from every category of chronic health problems. Conditions that require regular, uninterrupted treatment, such as TB, human immunodeficiency virus/acquired immunodeficiency syndrome (HIV/AIDS), diabetes, hypertension, malnutrition, severe dental problems, addictive disorders, and mental disorders, are extremely difficult to treat or control among those without adequate housing.

Street living comes with a set of health conditions that living in a home does not. Human beings without shelter tend to fall prey to parasites, frostbite, leg ulcers, and infections. Homeless people are also at greater risk of physical and psychological trauma resulting from muggings,

TABLE 7.1

Percentage of people without health insurance coverage, 2002

[242,360 represents 242,360,000. Based on the Current Population Survey (CPS) and subject to sampling error]

State	Total persons covered (1,000)	Total persons not covered		Children not covered	
		Number (1,000)	Percent of total	Number (1,000)	Percent of total
U.S.	242,360	43,574	15.2	8,531	11.6
AL	3,876	564	12.7	122	10.8
AK	516	119	18.7	26	13.3
AZ	4,526	916	16.8	218	14.7
AR	2,252	440	16.3	67	10.0
CA	28,761	6,398	18.2	1,352	14.0
CO	3,756	720	16.1	165	14.4
CT	3,027	356	10.5	71	8.1
DE	719	79	9.9	19	9.8
DC	498	74	13.0	10	8.6
FL	13,586	2,843	17.3	563	14.5
GA	7,072	1,354	16.1	279	12.3
HI	1,101	123	10.0	24	7.4
ID	1,067	233	17.9	50	13.6
IL	10,737	1,767	14.1	373	11.3
IN	5,303	797	13.1	158	9.8
IA	2,626	277	9.5	42	5.9
KS	2,404	280	10.4	57	8.1
KY	3,498	548	13.6	122	12.6
LA	3,627	820	18.4	140	11.9
ME	1,125	144	11.3	22	7.9
MD	4,728	730	13.4	140	9.9
MA	5,827	644	9.9	88	5.9
MI	8,752	1,158	11.7	175	6.9
MN	4,657	397	7.9	72	5.8
MS	2,322	465	16.7	83	10.9
MO	4,939	646	11.6	69	5.0
MT	767	139	15.3	32	15.0
NE	1,530	174	10.2	25	5.6
NV	1,703	418	19.7	114	19.7
NH	1,141	125	9.9	15	4.8
NJ	7,408	1,197	13.9	210	9.7
NM	1,452	388	21.1	73	14.5
NY	16,241	3,042	15.8	461	9.9
NC	6,794	1,368	16.8	261	12.7
ND	564	69	10.9	11	7.4
OH	9,938	1,344	11.9	239	8.2
OK	2,876	601	17.3	102	11.6
OR	2,999	511	14.6	95	11.3
PA	10,809	1,380	11.3	290	10.2
RI	952	104	9.8	11	4.7
SC	3,497	500	12.5	69	6.9
SD	659	85	11.5	15	7.7
TN	5,058	614	10.8	95	6.8
TX	15,973	5,556	25.8	1,352	22.4
UT	2,000	310	13.4	71	9.3
VT	553	66	10.7	8	5.7
VA	6,156	962	13.5	221	12.3
WA	5,151	850	14.2	137	9.0
WV	1,496	255	14.6	40	10.3
WI	4,938	538	9.8	63	4.6
WY	402	86	17.7	17	14.2

SOURCE: "Table 140. Persons With and Without Health Insurance Coverage by State: 2002," in *Statistical Abstract of the United States: 2004–2005*, U.S. Census Bureau, http://www.census.gov/statab/www/sa04api.pdf (accessed March 31, 2005)

Homeless people may also lack the ability to access some of the fundamental rituals of self-care: bed rest, good nutrition, and good personal hygiene. The luxury of "taking it easy for a day or two," for example, is almost impossible for homeless people; they must often keep walking or remain standing all day in order to avoid criminal charges.

Unwell homeless people also remain untreated longer than their sheltered counterparts because obtaining food and shelter takes priority over health care. As a result, relatively minor illnesses go untreated until they develop into major emergencies, requiring expensive acute care treatment and long-term recovery.

The Urban Institute analyzed the results of the 1996 National Survey of Homeless Assistance Providers and Clients, the only survey of its kind (studies of the homeless tend to focus on local populations). The analysis showed that in the year preceding the survey, 25% of the clients studied had needed medical attention but were not able to see a doctor or a nurse. The study also revealed that newly housed people were even less likely to receive medical help when needed (26%) (*Homelessness: Programs and the People They Serve—Findings of the National Survey of Homeless Assistance Providers and Clients*, Urban Institute, December 1999).

The authors attributed the higher rate of health problems among newly housed people to several factors, including:

1. The loss of convenient health care in centers or shelters

2. The habit of enduring untreated ailments, and/or

3. a lack of health care benefits (common among people below the poverty level)

Figure 7.3 shows that the lower the income range of a household, the greater possibility the household would be uninsured. Among households with an annual income of less than $25,000 in 2003, almost a quarter (24.2%) were uninsured. Moreover, between 2002 and 2003, the percentage of uninsured people rose in every income bracket except the highest one.

The results of a study published in February 2000 (L. Gelberg et al., "The Behavioral Model for Vulnerable Populations: Application to Medical Care Use and Outcomes for Homeless People," *Health Services Research*) on the prevalence of certain disease conditions among homeless adults revealed that 37% suffered from functional vision impairment, 36% from skin/leg/foot problems, and 31% tested positive for TB. The authors of the study indicated that homeless people who had a community clinic or private physician as a regular source of care exhibited better health outcomes. The research

beatings, and rape. With no safe place to store belongings, proper storage or administration of medications becomes difficult. In addition, some homeless people with mental disorders may use drugs or alcohol to self-medicate, and those with addictive disorders are more susceptible to HIV and other communicable diseases.

FIGURE 7.2

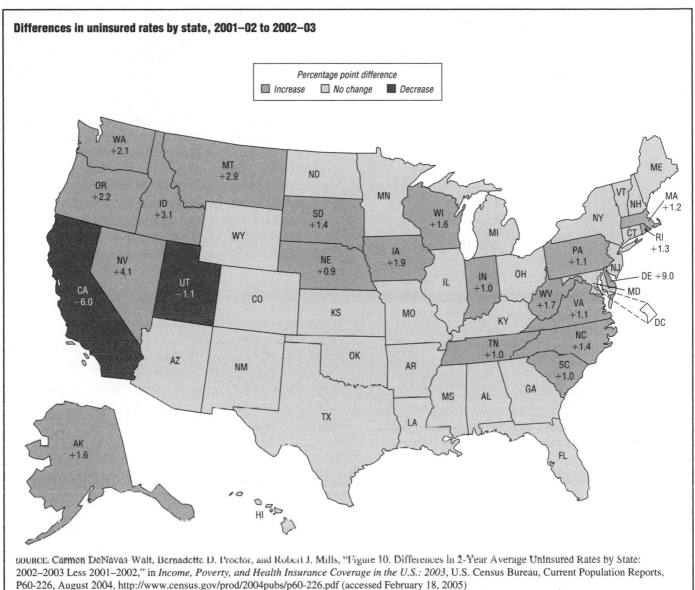

Differences in uninsured rates by state, 2001–02 to 2002–03

Percentage point difference
■ Increase □ No change ■ Decrease

SOURCE: Carmen DeNavas-Walt, Bernadette D. Proctor, and Robert J. Mills, "Figure 10. Differences in 2-Year Average Uninsured Rates by State: 2002–2003 Less 2001–2002," in *Income, Poverty, and Health Insurance Coverage in the U.S.: 2003*, U.S. Census Bureau, Current Population Reports, P60-226, August 2004, http://www.census.gov/prod/2004pubs/p60-226.pdf (accessed February 18, 2005)

study also suggested that clinical treatment of the homeless be accompanied by efforts to help them find permanent housing.

PHYSICAL AILMENTS OF HOMELESS PEOPLE

A March 2000 survey of the homeless in Hartford, Connecticut, performed by the Institute of Outcomes Research for the Hartford Community Health Partnership (E. B. O'Keefe et al., *Hartford Homeless Health Survey*), counted 1,365 homeless persons on the evening of December 13, 1999. The vast majority (87%) of survey respondents reported a prior diagnosis of at least one of seventeen chronic conditions. The most prevalent of these chronic conditions were drug and alcohol abuse, depression and other mental illnesses, hypertension, chronic bronchitis and emphysema, HIV/AIDS, asthma, and arthritis. Comparing the responses from the homeless survey against the

rates for the general Hartford population revealed that homeless people suffered twice the rate of depression (41%) as the general population (23%) and three times the rate of chronic bronchitis and emphysema (22.7%). While these chronic diseases exist throughout the general population, difficulty in providing treatment to the homeless makes them worse, as do hunger and malnutrition.

Gillian Silver of the Johns Hopkins Bloomberg School of Public Health and Rea Pañares summarized one study's findings regarding the health problems faced by homeless women, who comprised about one-third (32%) of the homeless population. This group was prone to the same physical ailments reported by the general homeless population in Hartford but also reported high rates of gastrointestinal problems, neurological disorders, chronic obstructive pulmonary disease, and peripheral vascular disease. (See Table 7.2.)

FIGURE 7.3

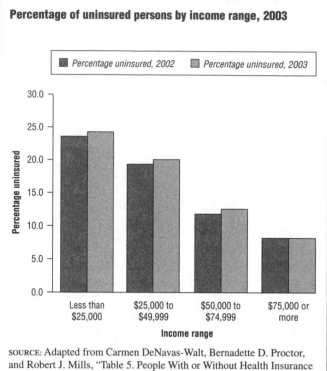

Percentage of uninsured persons by income range, 2003

- ■ Percentage uninsured, 2002
- ■ Percentage uninsured, 2003

SOURCE: Adapted from Carmen DeNavas-Walt, Bernadette D. Proctor, and Robert J. Mills, "Table 5. People With or Without Health Insurance Coverage by Selected Characteristics: 2002 and 2003," in *Income, Poverty, and Health Insurance Coverage in the U.S.: 2003*, U.S. Census Bureau, Current Population Reports, P60-226, August 2004, http://www.census.gov/prod/2004pubs/p60-226.pdf (accessed February 18, 2005)

Tuberculosis

Several kinds of acute, nonspecific respiratory diseases are common among homeless people. These diseases are easily spread through group living in overcrowded shelters without adequate nutrition. Tuberculosis (TB), a disease at one time almost eliminated from the general American population, has become a major health problem among the homeless. This disease is associated with exposure, poor diet, alcoholism, HIV, injection drug use, and other illnesses that lower the body's resistance to infection. TB is spread by lengthy personal contact, making it a potential hazard not only to shelter residents but also to the general public.

From 1953 to 1984 the United States experienced a decrease of 73.6% in the number of reported TB cases (from 84,304 cases to 22,255 cases). However, in 1984 the number of TB cases began to rise, reaching 25,701 cases in 1990. According to the Centers for Disease Control and Prevention (CDC), rising homelessness and poverty account, in part, for the resurgence of TB. Poor ventilating systems and the inability to quarantine victims allowed it to become prevalent. In 2003 the CDC found that 6.3% of the homeless population were infected with TB. (See Table 7.3.) State-by-state breakdowns gave some indication of the contagious nature of the disease. In 2003, for example, Montana reported that 28.6% of its

homeless population tested positive for TB, while New Hampshire, North Dakota, Rhode Island, Vermont, and Wyoming had no cases of TB among the homeless.

Clinical data from the federally funded Health Care for the Homeless program (HCH), part of the Bureau of Primary Health Care, found prevalence rates for TB to be 100 to 300 times higher among the homeless than among the overall population. An additional contributing factor was the emergence of drug-resistant strains of TB. Experts reported that to control the spread of TB, the homeless must receive frequent screenings for TB, and the infected must get long-term care and rest. A campaign for increased public awareness, particularly among members of the medical community, was launched in 1990 to identify and screen those at the greatest risk for TB. Some researchers tested pilot programs to better identify and treat homeless persons infected with TB (P. M. Kong et al., "Skin-Test Screening and Tuberculosis Transmission among the Homeless," *Emerging Infectious Diseases*, vol. 8, 2002). Other studies investigated how best to help homeless adults adhere to treatment for latent TB infection (J. P. Tulsky et al., "Can the Poor Adhere? Incentives for Adherence to TB Prevention in Homeless Adults," *International Journal of Tuberculosis and Lung Disease*, vol. 8, 2004). The number of reported TB cases in the United States declined to 14,511 in 2004.

Malnutrition

Homeless people face a daily challenge to fulfill their basic need for food. They often go hungry. This was borne out in an analysis of the findings of the 1996 *National Survey of Homeless Assistance Providers and Clients* by Martha R. Burt et al. (*Homelessness: Programs and the People They Serve*, Urban Institute, August 1999). Clients of homeless assistance programs were found to have higher levels of food problems than poor people in general; 28% reported not getting enough to eat sometimes or often, compared with 12% of poor American adults. More than one-third of the homeless clients had been hungry in the past thirty days but did not eat because they had no money for food (39%), and 40% reported going at least one whole day without eating. Undernourishment and vitamin deficiency can cause or aggravate other physical conditions.

Meg Wilson found in a study published in 2005 that despite being homeless, many homeless women practiced "health-promoting behaviors" ("Health-Promoting Behaviors of Sheltered Homeless Women," *Family and Community Health*, vol. 28, January-March 2005). However, because of their homelessness, they had difficulty getting adequate nutrition.

The diet of the homeless is generally not balanced or of good quality, even among those who live in shelters or cheap motels. Homeless people often rely on ready-cooked meals,

TABLE 7.2

Health problems faced by homeless women, 2000

Health Issue	Key findings
Chronic disease	• The most common chronic physical conditions (excluding substance abuse) are hypertension, gastrointestinal problems, neurological disorders, arthritis and other musculoskeletal disorders, chronic obstructive pulmonary disease, and peripheral vascular disease.
Infectious disease	• The most common infectious diseases reported were chest infection, cold, cough, and bronchitis; reporting was the same for those formerly homeless, currently homeless, and other service users. • Homeless patients with tuberculosis were more likely to present with a more progressed form than nonhomeless. • Widespread screening for TB in shelters may miss most homeless persons because many do not live in the shelter, and instead present in emergency departments.
STDs/HIV/AIDS	• A mobile women's health unit in Chicago reported that of 104 female homeless clients, 30 percent had abnormal Pap smears—14 percent with atypia and 10 percent with inflammation; the incidence of chlamydia was 3 percent, gonorrhea 6 percent, and trichomoniasis 26 percent. • HIV infection was found to be 2.35 times more prevelant in homeless, drug-abusing women than homeless, drug-abusing men.
Stress	• Homeless mothers reported higher levels of stress, depression, and avoidance and anti-cognitive copying strategies than low-income, housed mothers.
Nutrition	• Currently and formerly homeless clients are more likely to report not getting enough to eat (28 and 25 percent reprectively) than among all U.S. households (4 percent) and among poor households (12 percent). • Contrary to their opinions, homeless women and their dependents were consuming less than 50 percent of the 1989 recommended daily allowance for iron, magnesium, zinc, folic acid, and calcium. • Subjects of all ages consumed higher than desirable quantities of fats. • The health risk factors of iron deficiency anemia, obesity, and hypercholesterolemia were prevelant.
Smoking	• More than half of both homeless mothers and low-income housed mothers were current smokers, compared with 22.6 percent of female adults 18 years and over.
Violence	• Poor women are at higher risk for violence than women overall; poverty increases stress and lowers the ability to cope with the environment and live safely. • In a study of 436 sheltered homeless and poor housed women: 84 percent of these women had been severely assaulted at some point in their lives; 63 percent had been severely assaulted by parental caretakers while growing up; 40 percent had been sexually molested at least once before reaching adulthood; 60 percent had experienced severe physical attacks by a male intimate partner, and 33 percent had been assaulted by their current or most recent partner. • A study of 53 women homeless for at least three months in the past year demonstrated that this group is at a very high risk of battery and rape, with 91 percent exposed to battery and 56 percent exposed to rape.
Substance abuse	• Homeless women comprise a subpopulation at high risk for substance abuse; rates of substance use disorder range from 16 percent to 67 percent. There exists an imbalance between treatment need and treatment access. • Some homeless people with mental disorders may use drugs or alcohol to self-medicate.
Mental health/depression	• A case-control study of 100 homeless women with schizophrenia and 100 nonhomeless women with schizophrenia found that homeless women had higher rates of a concurrent diagnosis of alcohol abuse, drug abuse, antisocial personality disorder, and also had less adequate family support. • Many homeless women with serious mental illness are not receiving care; this is due to lack of perception of a mental health problem and lack of services designed to meet the needs of homeless women.

SOURCE: Gillian Silver and Rea Panares, "Table 2. Summary of Study Findings Related to Health Problems Faced by Homeless Women," in *The Health of Homeless Women: Information for State Mental and Child Health Programs*, Women's and Children's Health Policy Center, Johns Hopkins Bloomberg School for Public Health, 2000, http://www.jhsph.edu/WCHPC_/Publications/homeless.PDF (accessed March 31, 2005).

fast-food restaurants, garbage cans, and the sometimes-infrequent meal schedules of free food sources, such as shelters, soup kitchens, and drop-in centers. Many soup kitchens serve only one meal a day, and many shelters that serve meals—and not all of them do—serve only two meals a day.

BARRIERS TO ADEQUATE NUTRITION. People who live below the poverty level, including the homeless, are eligible for food stamps, but many people are not aware that they are eligible. In her speech before the New York City Coalition against Hunger on June 16, 2003, public advocate Betsy Gotbaum described an investigation into the reasons why New Yorkers' participation in the food stamp program was declining even though the city had endured high unemployment as a result of the national recession that began in March 2001, combined with the further blow to the city's economy caused by the terrorist attacks of September 11, 2001. The investigation revealed that welfare participants who had left the welfare rolls following the 1996 welfare reform legislation were not aware that they could still receive food stamps.

Even if people were aware of their eligibility, they were required to fill out a seventeen-page form to receive benefits. This is the type of barrier that prevents the poor and homeless from accessing or effectively using federal assistance programs.

In 2004 the U.S. Conference of Mayors reported that nearly all (96%) of the twenty-seven cities they surveyed reported an increase in requests for emergency food assistance over the course of the year by an average of 14%. Over half (56%) of those requesting food assistance were children or their parents. Fewer than half (44%) of the cities reported that their facilities were able to provide an adequate amount of food. Officials cited unemployment or underemployment, low-paying jobs, high housing, utility, and transportation costs, medical or health costs, reduced public benefits, and high child-care costs as causes of hunger in their cities.

Alcoholism, drug use, mental illness (especially severe depression), and physical illness contribute to nutritional deficiencies or lack of appetite. Some soup kitchens

TABLE 7.3

Tuberculosis cases by homeless status,[a] 2003

Reporting area	Total cases	Cases with information on homeless status[a]		Cases among homeless persons	
		Number	(%)	Number	(%)
United States	14,874	14,555	(97.9)	913	(6.3)
Alabama	258	258	(100.0)	12	(4.7)
Alaska	57	57	(100.0)	9	(15.8)
Arizona	295	281	(95.3)	35	(12.5)
Arkansas	127	122	(96.1)	3	(2.5)
California	3,227	3,198	(99.1)	226	(7.1)
Colorado	111	111	(100.0)	6	(5.4)
Connecticut	111	98	(88.3)	2	(2.0)
Delaware	33	33	(100.0)	2	(6.1)
District of Columbia	79	79	(100.0)	14	(17.7)
Florida	1,046	1,045	(99.9)	76	(7.3)
Georgia	526	511	(97.1)	27	(5.3)
Hawaii	117	117	(100.0)	1	(0.9)
Idaho	13	9	(69.2)	—	—
Illinois	633	623	(98.4)	21	(3.4)
Indiana	143	143	(100.0)	4	(2.8)
Iowa	40	40	(100.0)	1	(2.5)
Kansas	75	74	(98.7)	8	(10.8)
Kentucky	138	138	(100.0)	7	(5.1)
Louisiana	260	255	(98.1)	26	(10.2)
Maine	25	25	(100.0)	6	(24.0)
Maryland	268	268	(100.0)	4	(1.5)
Massachusetts	261	260	(99.6)	15	(5.8)
Michigan	243	239	(98.4)	7	(2.9)
Minnesota	214	214	(100.0)	8	(3.7)
Mississippi	128	124	(96.9)	6	(4.8)
Missouri	131	128	(97.7)	7	(5.5)
Montana	7	7	(100.0)	2	(28.6)
Nebraska	28	28	(100.0)	2	(7.1)
Nevada	107	106	(99.1)	13	(12.3)
New Hampshire	15	15	(100.0)	0	(0.0)
New Jersey	495	494	(99.8)	17	(3.4)
New Mexico	49	48	(98.0)	5	(10.4)
New York state[b]	340	338	(99.4)	12	(3.6)
New York City	1,140	973	(85.4)	60	(6.2)
North Carolina	374	374	(100.0)	37	(9.9)
North Dakota	6	6	(100.0)	0	(0.0)
Ohio	229	227	(99.1)	15	(6.6)
Oklahoma	163	161	(98.8)	7	(4.3)
Oregon	106	106	(100.0)	8	(7.5)
Pennsylvania	336	331	(98.5)	8	(2.4)
Rhode Island	46	46	(100.0)	0	(0.0)
South Carolina	254	252	(99.2)	12	(4.8)
South Dakota	20	20	(100.0)	1	(5.0)
Tennessee	285	277	(97.2)	27	(9.7)
Texas	1,594	1,589	(99.7)	104	(6.5)
Utah	39	39	(100.0)	1	(2.6)
Vermont	9	9	(100.0)	0	(0.0)
Virginia	332	322	(97.0)	9	(2.8)
Washington	250	248	(99.2)	38	(15.3)
West Virginia	21	20	(95.2)	1	(5.0)
Wisconsin	66	65	(98.5)	1	(1.5)
Wyoming	4	4	(100.0)	0	(0.0)
American Samoa[c]	...	...	...	...	...
Fed. States of Micronesia[c]	...	...	...	...	...
Guam[c]	61	59	96.7	0	(0.0)
N. Mariana Islands[c]	45	45	100.0	0	(0.0)
Puerto Rico[c]	115	115	100.0	5	(4.3)
Republic of Palau[c]	9	9	100.0	0	(0.0)
U.S. Virgin Islands[c]	...	...	...	...	...

[a]Homeless within past 12 months. Percentage based on 52 reporting areas (50 states, New York City, and the District of Columbia). Counts and percentages shown only for reporting areas with information reported for ≥75% of cases.
[b]Excludes New York City.
[c]Not included in U.S. totals.

SOURCE: "Table 30. Tuberculosis Cases and Percentages by Homeless Status: 59 Reporting Areas, 2003," in *Reported Tuberculosis in the United States, 2003*, Centers for Disease Control and Prevention, National Center for HIV, STD, and TB Prevention, 2003, http://www.cdc.gov/nchstp/tb/surv/surv2003/PDF/Table30.pdf (accessed March 31, 2005)

and shelters exclude persons under the influence of drugs or alcohol from partaking of meals at their facilities. Intoxicated persons may not be interested in food and can lose a substantial amount of weight as a result. Some advocates for the homeless suggest providing vitamin and mineral supplements to homeless substance abusers.

Skin and Blood Vessel Disorders

Frequent exposure to severe weather, insect bites, and other infestations make skin lesions fairly common among the homeless. Being forced to sit or stand for extended periods results in many homeless people being plagued with edema (swelling of the feet and legs), varicose veins, and skin ulcerations. This population is more prone to conditions that can lead to chronic phlebitis (inflammation of the veins). A homeless person with circulatory problems who sleeps sitting up in a doorway or a bus station can develop open lacerations that may become infected or maggot-infested if left untreated.

Regular baths and showers are luxuries to most homeless people, so many suffer from various forms of dermatitis (inflammation of the skin), often due to infestations of lice or scabies (a contagious skin disease caused by a parasitic mite that burrows under the skin to deposit eggs, causing intense itching). The lack of bathing increases the opportunity for infection to develop in cuts and other lacerations.

AIDS

The CDC reported that in 2003, between 850,000 and 950,000 Americans were living with HIV, the virus that causes AIDS, and 405,926 of those had full-blown AIDS (*HIV/AIDS Surveillance Report 2003*, vol. 15, March 2005). AIDS diagnoses increased in 2002 for the first time in ten years and increased another 1% between 2002 and 2003. In November 2002 the Food and Drug Administration approved a rapid test for HIV infection that can provide results in twenty minutes. U.S. Health and Human Services Secretary Tommy G. Thompson explained the significance of the test: "Each year, 8,000 HIV-infected people who come to public clinics for HIV testing do not return a week later to receive their test results . . . . With this new test, in less than a half an hour they can learn preliminary information about their HIV status, allowing them to get the care they need to slow the progression of their disease and to take precautionary measures to help prevent the spread of this deadly virus."

The CDC estimates that up to one-fourth of people infected with HIV are not aware of their condition. The CDC is working with health officials to make the rapid test widely available, particularly in places where likely victims reside, such as homeless shelters, drug treatment centers, and jails.

A study of AIDS patients in San Francisco found that poor people die sooner from AIDS ("Study: Disparity between Rich and Poor Mortality: Poor, Disadvantaged People Develop AIDS Faster," *AIDS Alert*, August 2003). Within five years of diagnosis, fewer than 70% of people living in the city's poorest neighborhoods were still alive, compared with more than 85% of people who lived in the richest neighborhoods. Poor people with HIV usually have a number of co-occurring disorders, such as drug dependence, mental illness, and unstable housing arrangements. The lack of affordable and appropriate housing can be an acute crisis for these individuals, who need a safe shelter that provides protection and comfort, as well as a base from which to receive services, care, and support.

The University of California at San Francisco, in *HIV Prevention: Looking Back, Looking Ahead* (1995), stated that almost half the homeless are estimated to have two or more of the risk factors associated with HIV—unprotected sex with multiple partners, injection drug use, sex with an injection drug user (IDU), or the exchange of unprotected sex for money or drugs. One-fourth report three or more risk factors. Having multiple sex partners is a risk for HIV, but it is extremely difficult for homeless people to form safe or stable intimate relationships due to drug use, mental illness, violence, or transient living conditions. Many homeless women are victims of rape or battery, and many women and children engage in "survival sex" or the exchange of sex for money, drugs, food, or housing.

THE MENTAL HEALTH OF HOMELESS PEOPLE

Before the 1960s people with chronic mental illness were often committed involuntarily to state psychiatric hospitals. The development of medications that could control the symptoms of mental illness coincided with a growing belief that involuntary hospitalization was warranted only when a mentally ill person posed a threat to him- or herself or to others. Gradually, large numbers of mentally ill people were discharged from hospitals and other treatment facilities. Because the community-based treatment centers that were supposed to take the place of state hospitals were often either inadequate or nonexistent, many of these people ended up living on the streets.

According to Folsom and his colleagues, 15% of patients treated for serious mental illness in California's mental health system were homeless at some point during a one-year period (*American Journal of Psychiatry*, vol. 162, February 2005). Twenty percent of patients with schizophrenia, 17% of patients with bipolar disorder, and 9% of patients with depression were homeless. The authors found that mentally ill people are at a much higher risk of homelessness than the general population.

Many homeless people do not realize how ill they are and how dependent they are on regular treatment. Others no longer believe the system can or will help them. This seems to have been borne out by a 1999 survey of 301 homeless adults in Buffalo, New York (O. Acosta and P. A. Toro, "Let's Ask the Homeless People Themselves: A Needs Assessment Based on a Probability Sample of Adults," *American Journal of Community Psychology*, vol. 28, 2000). When researchers asked homeless people what their greatest needs were, respondents listed affordable housing, safety, education, transportation, medical/dental treatment, and job training/placement. Formal mental health and substance abuse services were rated as unimportant by comparison, easy to obtain, and not very satisfactory to people who had used them.

In a 1998 study of 132 homeless adults (E. M. Reichenbach et al., "The Community Health Nursing Implications of the Self-Reported Health Status of a Local Homeless Population," *Public Health Nurse*, December 1998), researchers explored the personal characteristics and the health and health-related concerns of homeless health clinic clients. The study examined the significant differences in health and well being between homeless shelter residents and nonshelter residents. The homeless population studied featured a majority of males with an average age in the mid-thirties, a high rate of unemployment, and a low rate of health insurance. One-third of respondents reported their own health status as fair or poor. Joint problems and cardiovascular disease were the two most common physical ailments mentioned, while depression was the most common self-identified mental health problem. The most common fear mentioned by study participants was loneliness, but homeless people staying in shelters reported this fear much less often than those who did not stay in shelters.

Table 7.2 describes a study of 100 homeless women with schizophrenia and 100 non-homeless women with schizophrenia. The study, summarized by Silver and Pañares, found that homeless schizophrenic women had higher rates of co-occurring disorders, including alcohol and/or drug abuse and antisocial personality disorder.

Silver and Pañares noted that families with children comprise about 40% of the total homeless population, and the vast majority (about 90%) are female-headed. The authors reported on a study of 436 sheltered homeless and low-income housed mothers. The study found that 84% of all of these women had a history of having been severely assaulted at some point in their lives. Research has shown that mothers with a history of abuse are more likely to have children with mental health problems.

Perceptions of Mental Illness and the Homeless

Homeless people may be looked upon as mentally ill when their "abnormal" actions may actually be behavior caused by social and economic problems. For example,

some homeless women act strangely and neglect personal hygiene as a way to protect themselves from attack. A 1988 report on homeless women in San Francisco (C. J. Cooper, "Brutal Lives of Homeless S.F. Women," *San Francisco Examiner*, December 18, 1988) revealed a high rate of rape and sexual assault—some of the women had been raped as many as seventeen times. The report stated that to protect themselves from attack, homeless women would wear ten pairs of panty hose at once and bundle up in layers of clothing.

Prevalence and Treatment

There is some debate over the rate of mental disorders among homeless populations, but there is general agreement that it is greater among the homeless than the general population. The 2004 U.S. Conference of Mayors study revealed that an average of 23% of the homeless in the twenty-seven surveyed cities were mentally ill. The National Resource and Training Center on Homelessness and Mental Illness reported in "Get the Facts: Why Are So Many People with Serious Mental Illnesses Homeless?" that a disproportionate percentage of the homeless population suffers from serious mental illnesses of the most "personally disruptive" kind, "including severe, chronic depression; bipolar disorder; schizophrenia; schizoaffective disorders; and severe personality disorders." An estimated 20% to 25% of the homeless population is afflicted, compared with only 4% of the general population.

Mentally ill homeless people present special problems for health care workers. They may not be as cooperative and motivated as other patients. Because of their limited resources, they may have difficulty getting transportation to treatment centers. They frequently forget to show up for appointments or take medications. They are often unkempt. The addition of drug abuse can make them unruly or unresponsive. Among people with severe mental disorders, those at greatest risk of homelessness are both the most severely ill and the most difficult to help.

SUBSTANCE ABUSE

The abuse of alcohol and other drugs has long been recognized as a major factor contributing to the problems of the homeless. According to the National Coalition for the Homeless, in *No Open Door: Breaking the Lock on Addiction Recovery for Homeless People* (December 1998), the number of addictive disorders per capita within the homeless population is nearly twice that of the general population, and even higher in certain localities. The 2004 Conference of Mayors report estimated that 30% of homeless people in the twenty-seven cities surveyed were substance abusers.

Being intoxicated or high in public is considered socially unacceptable. Housed substance abusers have the luxury of staying out of public scrutiny when in such a condition. Homeless people, however, may have no place else to be except outside; many homeless shelters refuse to provide shelter to intoxicated persons. Consequently, homeless substance abusers are often more visible than those in the general population. In addition, studies published in the 1970s and 1980s often used lifetime rates of substance abuse, rather than current rates, and tended to focus on single, homeless men, which led to inflated statistics. The overall effect has been to create a false impression among many people that most or all of the homeless are drunks and drug addicts.

Young homeless people are at the greatest risk for substance abuse problems. Children, either in families or on their own, are the fastest-growing segment of the homeless population. In "Substance Use among Runaway and Homeless Youth in Three National Samples" (*American Journal of Public Health*, 1997), researchers J. M. Greene, S. T. Ennett, and C. L. Ringwalt found that 81% of street youth (children under eighteen who have been on their own for an extended period of time) and 67% of homeless youth in shelters were using alcohol. In addition, 75% of street youth and 52% of sheltered youth were using marijuana, and 26% of street youth and 8% of sheltered youth were using crack cocaine. Among housed youth, 64% used alcohol, 25% used marijuana, and 2% used crack cocaine.

Dual Diagnosis and Substance Abuse

The National Institute of Mental Health and the National Institute on Alcohol Abuse and Alcoholism report that mental illness and substance abuse frequently occur together; clinicians call this dual diagnosis. Experts state that in the absence of appropriate treatment, persons with mental illness often resort to "self-medication," using alcohol or drugs to silence the voices or calm the fears that torment them. Homeless people with dual diagnoses are frequently excluded from mental health programs because of treatment problems created by their substance abuse and are excluded from substance abuse programs due to problems in treating their mental illness. Experts explain that the lack of an integrated system of care plays a major role in their recurrent homelessness. They stress that transitional or assisted housing initiatives for homeless substance abusers must realistically address the issue of abstinence and design measures for handling relapses that do not place people back on the streets.

Welfare Reform and Substance Abusers

Some people fear that welfare policy changes have increased homelessness among impoverished people with addiction disorders. In 1996 Congress passed the Personal Responsibility and Work Opportunity Reconciliation Act (PL 104-193), which, among other things, denies Social Security Income and Social Security Disability Insurance benefits and, by extension, Medicaid to people whose addictions are a "contributing factor" in their disability. More than 200,000 people were affected by the cutoff. In "Welfare Reform and Housing: Assessing the Impact to Substance Abuse" (T. L. Anderson et al., *Journal of Drug Issues*, Winter 2002), the authors discussed their study of the effects of terminating the benefits to addicts "at a time of diminishing social services and a housing market explosion." Former benefit recipients reported increased homelessness and were found to be at increased risk of drug and alcohol use, criminal participation, and criminal victimization.

SPECIAL POPULATION CONCERNS
Children

While a quarter of all homeless people may suffer from mental illness, and many more have past or current drug or alcohol addictions, these common stereotypes of the homeless do not fit the homeless population of children under eighteen years of age, who make up from 8% to 12% of the homeless.

One research team (E. R. Danseco and E. W. Holden, "Are There Different Types of Homeless Families? A Typology of Homeless Families Based on Cluster Analysis," *Family Relations*, 1998) sought to identify different types of homeless families and to examine children from these families. The researchers studied 180 families, with a total of 348 children, participating in a comprehensive health care program for children of homeless families. The results showed that homeless children consistently exhibited greater behavior problems and showed a trend of poorer cognitive, academic, and adaptive behaviors than children in the general population.

Similar results were found in a 1999 Urban Institute study. Its findings demonstrated that poor children were less involved in school than their wealthier peers—41% of children above 200% of the poverty level had a high engagement in school, versus 34% of children below that level. Lower-income children had 4% more behavioral and emotional problems, skipped school 7% more often, were expelled or suspended more than twice as often, and reported fair or poor health more than three times as frequently as higher-income children.

According to "Child and Youth Health and Homelessness," a 2004 policy statement of the National Health Care for the Homeless Council, homeless children experience a variety of behavioral and/or health disorders, including depression, developmental delay, asthma, respiratory infections, and gastrointestinal problems. Homeless children may also lack preventive care, such as immunizations, which leaves them vulnerable to preventable diseases. Failure to treat certain childhood conditions early (ear infections, for example) can lead to a lifetime of health problems. They also frequently suffer from malnutrition. In addition, the NHCHC policy statement noted that the condition of homelessness in childhood is a risk factor for adult homelessness.

Unaccompanied Youth

Unaccompanied youth is the term used to describe children under the age of eighteen who are either runaways (away without permission), thrownaways (told or forced to leave or abandoned), or street youth (long-term runaways or thrownaways). The 2004 Conference of Mayors report estimated that 5% of homeless people are unaccompanied youth. The National Runaway Switchboard estimates that between 1.3 and 2.8 million runaway and homeless youth live on America's streets and that one out of every seven children will run away before the age of eighteen. Many of these children are escaping physical and sexual abuse, strained family relationships, addiction of a family member, and/or parental neglect.

Access to health care at traditional health care centers is complicated for this segment of the homeless population by parental permission requirements, lack of insurance, and a reluctance to trust health care professionals. They often do not receive preventive health care or seek treatment for illnesses or injuries.

Veterans

According to the Veterans Health Administration, in 1990 veterans were present in shelters at a rate of 149 per 100,000 compared with 126 per 100,000 of other males (*Data on the Socioeconomic Status of Veterans and on VA Program Usage*, Washington, DC, May 2001). The National Coalition for Homeless Veterans, citing Department of Veterans Affairs (VA) sources, stated on its Web site in 2005 that of homeless veterans 2% were female, 45% suffered from mental illness, and half abused drugs or alcohol. An estimated 299,321 veterans were homeless on any single night; over the course of a year, more than 500,000 were homeless at least one night. The majority were single. Almost half (47%) of homeless veterans served in Vietnam. The 2004 Conference of Mayors report stated that 10% of homeless people in the twenty-seven surveyed cities were veterans.

To some, the homelessness of veterans is hard to understand. Since World War II, U.S. veterans have been offered a broad range of benefits, including educational assistance, home loan guarantees, pension and disability payments, and free health care. In fact, veterans consistently have higher median incomes, lower rates of poverty and unemployment, and better education than U.S. males in similar age groups. Veterans, those observers claim, should be less vulnerable to homelessness than other Americans. The belief that combat-related stress leads some veterans to become homeless has received much attention. Health care professionals believe that there may be a link between the persistence of post-traumatic stress disorder in veterans and the stresses of street living, though research on this topic is as yet inconclusive.

The Veterans Administration operates numerous outreach programs designed specifically to help homeless veterans in areas of health, housing, and employment. Among those that address the health concerns of homelessness are:

- Health Care for Homeless Veterans (HCHV), which offers comprehensive health and psychiatric evaluations, treatment, and referrals at 135 locations nationwide.

- Domiciliary Care for Homeless Veterans (DCHV), a residential treatment and rehabilitation program operating at thirty-five VA medical centers in twenty-six states. Services include screening and assessment; medical and psychiatric examinations, treatment, vocational counseling, and post-discharge support.

- Drop-In Centers, providing daytime environments where homeless veterans can eat, shower, do laundry, and participate in organized activities that promote life skills.

- Stand Downs, comprising one- to three-day programs that offer safe haven for homeless veterans. According to the fact sheet "VA Programs for Homeless Veterans" (VA, March 2002), "Stand Downs give homeless veterans a temporary place of safety and security where they can obtain food, shelter, clothing and a range of community and VA assistance. In many locations VA provides health screenings, referral and access to long-term treatment, benefits counseling, ID cards and linkage with other programs to meet their immediate needs."

Victims of Violence

VIOLENCE TOWARD HOMELESS WOMEN. Angela Browne and Shari Bassuk, in a study funded by the National Institute of Mental Health and the Maternal and Child Health Bureau, found that lifetime prevalence rates of physical and sexual assault among homeless women were particularly high. The study, "Intimate Violence in the Lives of Homeless and Poor Housed Women: Prevalence and Patterns in an Ethnically Diverse Sample" (*American Journal of Orthopsychiatry*, April 1999), which surveyed both homeless and very poor, housed women, found that although violence by intimate male partners was high in both groups, homeless women experienced violence at a somewhat higher rate (63.3%) than poor, housed women (58%).

Homeless women (41%) were also more likely than housed women (33%) to report a male partner threatening suicide. More than one-third (36%) of homeless women said their partner had threatened to kill them, compared to 31% of poor, housed women. Almost 27% of homeless women and 19.5% of poor, housed women needed or received medical treatment because of physical violence. Table 7.2 summarizes other studies related to violence and homeless women.

HATE CRIMES. According to the National Coalition for the Homeless (NCH), homeless advocates have demanded that crimes against homeless people be defined as hate crimes, which may result in harsher penalties in federal courts. Determining how many of these crimes occur is difficult. Some factors that have an effect on the accuracy of the count are:

- The bodies of the victims are not always discovered.

- Bodies may be badly decomposed, preventing accurate identification of the cause of death.

- Local authorities may rule causes of death other than violence.

- Survivors do not always report crimes, and murdered victims cannot tell their own stories.

In April 2003 the NCH released the results of a four-year study of hate crimes and violence committed against homeless people (*Hate, Violence, and Death on Main Street, USA: A Report on Hate Crimes and Violence against People Experiencing Homelessness from 1999–2002*, Washington, DC). The NCH identified 123 deaths and eighty nine nonlethal attacks on homeless people over the four-year period that they considered hate crimes. The crimes occurred in ninety-eight cities in thirty-four states and in Puerto Rico. According to the NCH, the five most dangerous cities for people experiencing homelessness are Denver, Las Vegas, Rapid City (South Dakota), Toledo, and New York.

In "Hate Crimes and Violence against People Experiencing Homelessness" (June 2005), the NCH recommended the following actions to address the problem of violence against homeless individuals:

- "A public statement by the U.S. Department of Justice acknowledging that hate crimes and/or violence against people experiencing homelessness is a serious national trend."

- A Department of Justice database to "track hate crimes and/or violence against people who are experiencing homelessness."

- Justice Department guidelines "for local police on how to investigate and work with people experiencing homelessness" and recommendations for improvements to state law that would "better protect against violence directed against people experiencing homelessness, including tougher penalties."

- "Inclusion of housing status in the pending state and federal hate crimes legislation."

- "Sensitivity/Awareness training at police academies and departments nationwide for trainees and police officers on how to deal effectively and humanely with people experiencing homelessness in their communities."

- "A U.S. Government Accountability Office (GAO) study into the nature and scope of hate crimes and/or violent acts and crimes that occur against people experiencing homelessness."

PROBLEMS IN TREATING THE HOMELESS

To understand why health care may not be readily available to the homeless population, one must look at American health care in general. In "U.S. Health-Care System Faces Cost and Insurance Crises: Rising Costs, Growing Numbers of Uninsured and Quality Gaps Trouble World's Most Expensive Health-Care System" (*The Lancet*, August 2, 2003), Michael McCarthy described a system "lurching towards crisis." Costs continue to rise, as do the numbers of people who do not have insurance. The Census Bureau noted in 2004 that the number of Americans living below the poverty line increased by 1.3 million in 2004, and the number of uninsured Americans grew by 1.4 million.

McCarthy noted that while most hospitals by law must provide care for the indigent, in reality an uninsured patient is less likely to receive any care at all and, if hospitalized, is less likely to receive the same quality of care as an insured patient. He cited a 2002 study by the U.S. National Academy of Sciences Institute of Medicine (*Care without Coverage: Too Little, Too Late*, National Academies Press). That study found that "uninsured patients who are hospitalized for a range of conditions are more likely to die in the hospital, to receive fewer services when admitted, and to experience substandard care and resultant injury than are insured patients."

Medicaid

Medicaid is the federal health insurance program for low-income families with children, among others. In "'I Abhor the Status Quo': HHS Secretary Tommy G. Thompson's Plan to Revamp the Healthcare Industry" (Michael T. McCue, *Managed Healthcare Executive*, March 2003), Tommy Thompson, Secretary of Health and Human Services, described Medicaid as an outdated system that does not adequately serve the mentally or chronically ill, people with substance abuse problems, or childless adults (who make up a significant portion of the homeless population).

Medicare payments to physicians were cut in the early 2000s. Projections prepared by the Office of the Actuary for the Centers for Medicare and Medicaid Services indicated that Medicare will reduce payment rates to physicians by about 5% each year for seven years, beginning in 2006 ("Johnson Announces Hearing on Medicare Payments to Physicians," Press Release, Committee on Ways and Means, Subcommittee on Health, February 3, 2005). As a result of these cuts, some medical providers turned Medicaid patients away. A survey by the American Medical Association found that the number of physicians who said they planned to participate in the Medicare program in 2003 was down to 83%, 9% lower than the previous year (92%). Almost one-quarter of physicians had scaled back on the number of Medicare patients they would treat (American Medical Association: "Research Brief on Medicare Physician Payment Cut Survey," 2002). As a result, access to health care for many low-income people has been compromised.

HEALTH CARE FOR THE HOMELESS

In 1987 Congress passed the Stewart B. McKinney Homeless Assistance Act (PL 100-77) to provide services to the homeless, including job training, emergency shelter, education, and health care. Title VI of the Act funds Health Care for the Homeless (HCH) programs. HCH has become the national umbrella under which most homeless health-care initiatives operate. In 1994 there were 119 HCH programs in the United States; by 2005, 172 programs provided health care to about 600,000 people each year. In the year 2000 the government appropriated $88 million for HCH programs, almost double the $46 million appropriation of 1987, the first year of the program. The president's proposed FY 2006 budget included approximately $175 million for HCH programs.

Nonprofit private organizations and public entities, including state and local government agencies, may apply for grants from the program. The grants may be used to continue to provide services for up to one year to individuals who have obtained permanent housing if services were provided to them when they were homeless.

The goal of the HCH program is to improve health status for homeless individuals and families by improving access to primary health care and substance abuse services. HCH provides outreach, counseling to clients explaining available services, case management, and linkages to services such as mental health treatment, housing, benefits, and other critical supports. Access to around-the-clock emergency services is available, as well

TABLE 7.4

Profile of clients served by Health Care for the Homeless programs, 2003

Characteristic	Percent
Male	59.0
Female	41.0
Age 0–14	11.0
Age 15–19	4.0
Age 20–44	53.0
Age 45–64	28.0
Age 65	2.0
African American	37.0
White	35.0
Hispanic	19.0
Asian/Pacific Islander	2.0
Native American/Alaskan Native	2.0
Lived in shelter	43.0
Lived on the street	11.0
No medical insurance	71.0
Enrolled in Medicaid	22.0
Enrolled in Medicare	3.0
Private insurance	2.0
Other public insurance	3.0
Living at or below poverty level	92.0

SOURCE: Adapted from data provided by the U.S. Department of Health and Human Services, Health Resources and Services Administration, Bureau of Primary Health Care, 2005, http://bphc.hrsa.gov/hchirc/about/prog_successes.htm (accessed March 31, 2005)

as help in establishing eligibility for assistance and obtaining services under entitlement programs.

Table 7.4 shows characteristics of people treated in HCH centers in 2003. The majority of clients (59%) were male. Almost two-thirds (60%) of homeless clients were members of minority groups: African-Americans made up 37%; Hispanics, 19%; Asians/Pacific Islanders, 2%; and Native Americans/Alaskan natives, 2%.

Clients between the ages of twenty and forty-four represented the largest portion of people served by the HCH programs (53%), followed by individuals between the ages of forty-five and sixty-four (28%), children up to age fourteen (11%), and teenagers between the ages of fifteen and nineteen (4%). Homeless persons over sixty-five comprised 2% of clients served.

Of clients seen in HCH centers, 43% lived in shelters at some point during treatment, while 11% lived on the street. The remainder lived in transitional housing, with family or acquaintances, or in some other type of temporary living arrangement. The majority (71%) of HCH users had no medical care coverage. Of those who had some type of insurance, 22% were enrolled in Medicaid, 3% were enrolled in Medicare, 2% had private insurance, and 3% had some other type of insurance.

IMPORTANT NAMES
AND ADDRESSES

America's Second Harvest
35 East Wacker Dr.
Suite 2000
Chicago, IL 60601
(312) 263-2303
1-800-771-2303
URL: http://www.secondharvest.org/

Association of Gospel Rescue Missions
1045 Swift St.
Kansas City, MO 64116-4127
1-800-4-RESCUE
FAX: (816) 471-3718
URL: http://www.agrm.org/

Center on Budget and Policy Priorities
820 First St. NE
Suite 510
Washington, DC 20002
(202) 408-1080
FAX: (202) 408-1056
E-mail: center@cbpp.org
URL: http://www.cbpp.org/

Children's Defense Fund
25 E St. NW
Washington, DC 20001
(202) 628-8787
E-mail: cdfinfo@childrensdefense.org
URL: http://www.childrensdefense.org/

Fannie Mae Foundation
4000 Wisconsin Ave. NW
North Tower, Suite One
Washington, DC 20016-2804
(202) 274-8000
FAX: (202) 274-8100
URL: http://www.fanniemaefoundation.org/

Food Research and Action Center
1875 Connecticut Ave. NW
Suite 540
Washington, DC 20009
(202) 986-2200
FAX: (202) 986-2525

E-mail: webmaster@frac.org
URL: http://www.frac.org/

Habitat for Humanity International
121 Habitat St.
Americus, GA 31709-3498
(229) 924-6935 x2551 or x2552
E-mail: publicinfo@habitat.org
URL: http://www.habitat.org/

**Health Care for the Homeless
Information Resource Center**
Bureau of Primary Health Care
U.S. Department of Health and Human
Services
Parklawn Building
5600 Fishers Ln.
Rockville, MD 20857
URL: http://bphc.hrsa.gov/hchirc/

Homes for the Homeless
36 Cooper Square
6th Floor
New York, NY 10003
(212) 529-5252
FAX: (212) 529-7698
E-mail: info@homesforthehomeless.com
URL: http://www.homesforthehomeless.com/

Housing Assistance Council
1025 Vermont Ave. NW
Suite 606
Washington, DC 20005
(202) 842-8600
FAX: (202) 347-3441
E-mail: hac@ruralhome.org
URL: http://www.ruralhome.org/

Institute for Research on Poverty
University of Wisconsin-Madison
1180 Observatory Dr.
3412 Social Science Bldg.
Madison, WI 53706-1393
(608) 262-6358
FAX: (608) 265-3119

E-mail: irpweb@ssc.wisc.edu
URL: http://www.irp.wisc.edu/

Interagency Council on Homelessness
451 Seventh St. SW
Suite 2100
Washington, DC 20410
(202) 708-4663
FAX: (202) 708-1216
URL: http://www.ich.gov/

National Alliance of HUD Tenants
42 Seaverns Ave.
Boston, MA 02130
(617) 267-9564
FAX: (617) 522-4857
E-mail: naht@saveourhomes.org
URL: http://www.saveourhomes.org/

National Alliance to End Homelessness
1518 K St. NW
Suite 410
Washington, DC 20005
(202) 638-1526
E-mail: naeh@naeh.org
URL: http://www.endhomelessness.org

**National Center for Homeless
Education**
P.O. Box 5367
Greensboro, NC 27435
1-800-308-2145
FAX: (336) 315-7457
E-mail: homeless@serve.org
URL: http://www.serve.org/nche/

**National Coalition for Homeless
Veterans**
333 1/2 Pennsylvania Ave. SE
Washington, DC 20003-1148
1-800-VET-HELP
FAX: (202) 546-2063
E-mail: nchv@nchv.org
URL: http://www.nchv.org/

National Coalition for the Homeless
2201 P St. NW
Washington, DC 20037
(202) 462-4822
FAX: (202) 462-4823
E-mail: info@nationalhomeless.org
URL: http://www.nationalhomeless.org/

National Health Care for the Homeless Council
P.O. Box 60427
Nashville, TN 37206-0427
(615) 226-2292
FAX: (615) 226-1656
E-mail: council@nhchc.org
URL: http://www.nhchc.org/

National Housing Conference
1801 K St. NW
Suite M-100
Washington, DC 20006-1301
(202) 466-2121
FAX: (202) 466-2122
E-mail: nhc@nhc.org
URL: http://www.nhc.org/

National Housing Law Project
614 Grand Ave.
Suite 320
Oakland, CA 94610
(510) 251-9400
FAX: (510) 451-2300
E-mail: nhlp@nhlp.org
URL: http://www.nhlp.org/

National Law Center on Homelessness and Poverty
1411 K St. NW
Suite 1400
Washington, DC 20005
(202) 638-2535

FAX: (202) 628-2737
E-mail: nlchp@nlchp.org
URL: http://www.nlchp.org/

National Low Income Housing Coalition
727 15th St. NW
6th Floor
Washington, DC 20005
(202) 662-1530
FAX: (202) 393-1973
E-mail: info@nlihc.org
URL: http://www.nlihc.org/

National Resource and Training Center on Homelessness and Mental Illness
7500 Old Georgetown Rd.
Suite 900
Bethesda, MD 20814
1-800-444-7415
E-mail: nrtcinfo@cdmgroup.com
URL: http://www.nrchmi.samhsa.gov/

National Rural Housing Coalition
1250 Eye St. NW
Suite 902
Washington, DC 20005
(202) 393-5229
FAX: (202) 393-3034
E-mail: nrhc@nrhcweb.org
URL: http://www.nrhcweb.org/

National Student Campaign against Hunger and Homelessness
233 North Pleasant St.
Suite 32
Amherst, MA 01002
(413) 253-6417
1-800-NO-HUNGR
FAX: (413) 256-6435
E-mail: info@studentsagainsthunger.org
URL: http://www.nscahh.org/

Urban Institute
2100 M St. NW
Washington, DC 20037
(202) 833-7200
E-mail: paffairs@ui.urban.org
URL: http://www.urban.org/

U.S. Conference of Mayors
Task Force on Hunger and Homelessness
1620 Eye St. NW
Washington, DC 20006
(202) 293-7330
FAX: (202) 293-2352
E-mail: info@usmayors.org
URL: http://www.usmayors.org/uscm/

U.S. Department of Education
Education for Homeless Children and Youths
400 Maryland Ave. SW
Washington, DC 20202
1-800-USA-LEARN
FAX: (202) 401-0689
E-mail: customerservice@inet.ed.gov
URL: http://www.ed.gov/programs/homeless/resources.html?exp=0

U.S. Department of Housing and Urban Development
451 Seventh St. SW
Washington, DC 20410
(202) 708-1112
URL: http://www.hud.gov/

U.S. Government Accountability Office
441 G St. NW
Washington, DC 20548
(202) 512-3000
E-mail: webmaster@gao.gov
URL: http://www.gao.gov/

RESOURCES

Many different organizations study the homeless and the poor. Notable among them for their many large studies on homelessness is the Urban Institute. This organization's ongoing studies of the homeless are among the largest and most comprehensive in the United States. Their publications were a major source of information for this volume, especially: *The 1996 National Survey of Homeless Assistance Providers and Clients: A Comparison of Faith-Based and Secular Non-Profit Programs* (2002), *America's Homeless II: Populations and Services* (2000), *Homelessness: Programs and the People They Serve—National Survey of Homeless Assistance Providers and Clients* (December 1999), and *On the Bottom Rung: A Profile of Americans in Low-Income Working Families* (October 2000).

Three other excellent sources of information on the national homeless population are the National League of Cities, the U.S. Conference of Mayors, and the Association of Gospel Rescue Missions. The publication *The State of America's Cities 2004: The Annual Opinion Survey* (National League of Cities, 2004) contains valuable data on the scope of urban homelessness and how cities and regions try to deal with it. *Hunger and Homelessness Survey: A Status Report on Hunger and Homelessness in America's Cities* (U.S. Conference of Mayors, 2004) and *2004 Snap Shot Survey of the Homeless* (Association of Gospel Rescue Missions, 2004) also provide a great deal of information on the homeless population.

The many organizations that advocate for the homeless and their issues are also crucial sources for this book. The National Coalition for the Homeless is certainly one of the most important of these organizations. Their publication *Illegal to Be Homeless: The Criminalization of Homelessness in the United States* (2004) is particularly recommended. The National Low Income Housing Coalition is another advocacy organization with useful information on homelessness, including *Out of Reach: The Growing Gap between Housing Costs and Income of Poor People in the United States* (September 2000) and *Rental Housing for America's Poor Families: Farther Out of Reach Than Ever, 2002* (2002).

Applied Survey Research, Economic Policy Institute, Joint Center for Housing Studies of Harvard University, Health Care for the Homeless, National Coalition for Homeless Veterans, Millennial Housing Commission, National Multi Housing Council, and the National Law Center on Homelessness and Poverty all provide extensive coverage of important aspects of the housing and homelessness issues.

The federal government, though it has done relatively few studies on the homeless since the 1980s, remains the premier source of facts on many issues closely related to homelessness, including poverty, employment, welfare, and housing. Some particularly excellent sources of information from the U.S. Census Bureau are: *Emergency and Transitional Shelter Population: 2000* (October 2001), *Historical Poverty Tables* (October 2001), *Income, Poverty, and Health Insurance Coverage in the United States: 2003* (August 2004), *Poverty in the United States: 2001* (September 2002), and *Statistical Abstract of the United States: 2004–2005* (2004). Other publications of the federal government include: *Household Data Annual Averages* (Department of Labor, 2004), *The Employment Situation: February 2005* (Bureau of Labor Statistics, March 2005), *Homelessness: Improving Program Coordination and Client Access to Programs* (General Accounting Office, March 2002), *Fair Market Rents for the Housing Choice Voucher Program and Moderate Rehabilitation Single Room Occupancy Program, Fiscal Year 2005* (Department of Housing and Urban Development, February 2005), and *Rural Housing Service: Opportunities to Improve Management* (General Accounting Office, June 2003). In addition to these specific publications, Thomson Gale recommends that anyone who is interested in homelessness and related issues make use of the latest reports from the Census Bureau, the Department of Health and Human Services, and the Department of Housing and Urban Development.

INDEX

DeNavas-Walt, Carmen
  children in poverty, 26
  poverty rates by race/ethnicity, 27
  poverty rates by region, 29
*Department of Housing and Urban
  Development: Status of Achieving Key
  Outcomes and Addressing Major
  Management Challenges* (U.S. General
  Accounting Office), 47
Depression, 73, 77, 79, 82, 83
Diet, 78–79, 81
Disposable income
  national savings rate as percent of
    disposable income, 36 (*f*3.8)
  savings and, 35–36
"Dissenting Statement to the Report of
  the Millennial Housing Commission"
  (Rector), 47
Dolbeare, Cushing N.
  federal government's funding for
    housing, 46
  lack of affordable units, 44
Domiciliary Care for Homeless Veterans
  (DCHV), 84
"Downtown Ambassadors," 65
"Downward Spiral: Homelessness and Its
  Criminalization" (Foscarinis), 68
Drever, Anita, 3
Drop-in centers, 84
Drug use
  drug abuse by homeless people,
    82–83
  risk factors of AIDS, 81
Dual diagnosis, 83
Duration, of homelessness, 21

E
Economy, 26
Education
  earnings, mean, by highest degree
    earned, 31 (*t*3.4)
  Education for Homeless Children and
    Youth program, 61–62
  family income ranges of least/most
    educated, 32 (*f*3.5)
  homeless children and youth,
    enrollment/attendance, 21*t*
  homeless children in school, 49
  of homeless children, youth, 21
  of homeless people, 20
  income level and, 29–30, 32
  poverty rate and, 27
  segregation of homeless children,
    63–64
Education for Homeless Children and
  Youth (EHCY) program
  description of, 61–62
  requirement of report on homeless
    children, 48
  segregation of homeless children in
    schools, 63–64

*Education for Homeless Children and Youth
  Program* (U.S. Department of
  Education), 14
Eighth Amendment
  Constitutional rights of homeless, 69
  homeless encampments and, 71
  "no bed/no arrest" policy and, 70
*Emergency and Transitional Shelter
  Population: 2000* (U.S. Census Bureau)
  count of homeless, 7, 48
  on S-Nights, 5–6
Emergency Relief and Construction
  Act, 51
Emergency Shelter Grants (ESG)
  description of, 54
  function of, 53
  HUD McKinney-Vento programs,
    requirements of, 54*t*
Emergency shelters
  demand/need for, 15–16
  emergency, transitional shelters,
    population in, 15 (*t*2.3)
  homeless living in, 48
  population in emergency, transitional
    shelters, 8*t*
Emerging Infectious Diseases (journal), 78
Emphysema, 77
Employment
  educational attainment/income level,
    29–30, 32
  employment/unemployment in
    families, by race and Hispanic
    ethnicity, 2002–03 annual
    averages, 37 (*f*3.10)
  family income ranges of least/most
    educated, 32 (*f*3.5)
  homeless and, 39
  household income, 29
  jobs in low wage industries, 32
  mean earnings by highest degree
    earned, 2002, 31 (*t*3.4)
  minimum wage jobs, 32, 34
  money income, earnings by selected
    characteristics, 30*t*–31*t*
  percent change in employment by
    industrial sector, 32 (*f*3.6)
  unemployment, 36–37
  unemployment rate, seasonally
    adjusted, 37 (*f*3.9)
  wage/salary workers paid hourly rates
    equal to or less than prevailing
    minimum wage, by occupation
    and industry, 2004, 33*t*–34*t*
  welfare reform and, 38
  work for homeless, 39–41
Employment Characteristics of Families
  (U.S. Bureau of Labor Statistics), 37
"Employment for Homeless People: What
  Works, Fall 2000" (Health Care for
  the Homeless Information Resource
  Center), 39
Encampment, homeless, 71

English Poor Laws of 1601, 1
Ennett, S. T., 83
ESG. *See* Emergency Shelter Grants
Ethnicity. *See* Race/ethnicity
*Evaluation of Continuums of Care for
  Homeless People* (U.S. Department of
  Housing and Urban Development)
  homelessness assessment, 13
  number of homeless people, 14
Everywhere and Now Public Housing
  Residents Organizing Nationally
  Together, 58
"Existing-Home Sales Hold Steady in
  January" (Bresnahan), 43
Expenditures
  federal expenditures on housing, 55
  HUD budget authority for homeless
    and public housing programs, 55*t*

F
Fair market rent (FMR)
  fair market rental rates for selected
    metropolitan areas, 59 (*t*5.5)
  rents in voucher programs, 59
Faith-based organizations, 11
False HOPE (National Housing Law
  Project, Sherwood Research Associates,
  and Everywhere and Now Public
  Housing Residents Organizing
  Nationally Together), 58
*Families on Welfare in the Post-TANF
  Era: Do They Differ from Their Pre-
  TANF Counterparts?* (Urban Institute),
  38–39
Family
  employment/unemployment in
    families, by race and Hispanic
    ethnicity, 37 (*f*3.10)
  family poverty rates, selected
    indicators, 29*f*
  gender of homeless and, 17–18
  household income by, 29
  poverty, people, families in, by selected
    characteristics, 25*t*
  poverty rate and, 24, 26
  poverty threshold and, 23
  poverty threshold by size of family,
    number of related children under
    18 years of age, 24*t*
  structure of homeless population,
    18, 20
  in subsidized housing, 55
  unemployment and, 37
  welfare reform and, 38–39
Family and Community Health (journal), 78
"Family and Youth Services Bureau—
  Transitional Living Program for Older
  Homeless Youth" (U.S. Department
  of Health and Human Services), 62
Family unification vouchers, 59
Farmers Home Administration
  (FmHA), 52

National Resource and Training Center on Homelessness and Mental Illness, 82

National R.R. Passenger Corp., Streetwatch v., 71

National Runaway Switchboard, 84

National Survey of Homeless Assistance Providers and Clients (U.S. Census Bureau)
  health costs of street living, 76
  homeless population estimates, 13
  malnutrition of homeless people, 78

National Multi Housing Council/ National Apartment Association, 47

Native Americans
  homeless population, 18
  public housing residents, 57

NCH. *See* National Coalition for the Homeless

NHCHC. *See* National Health Care for the Homeless Council

"New Assessment System Holds Potential for Evaluating Performance" (Government Accountability Office), 57

New Deal, 2

"A New Era for Affordable Housing" (Murphy), 47

New Jersey, 70

New York City (NYC)
  court case about loitering in train station, 71
  court case about panhandling, 71
  homeless population in, 15
  Street News newspaper of, 39, 40
  use of force against homeless, 65, 68

New York City Police Department, Loper v., 71

New York, homeless population in, 15

New York Metropolitan Transportation Authority, 40

New York Times, 40

New York University (NYU), 43

"New York's School Choice Leaves More Homeless Children with Hour-Plus Commutes" (Brode), 64

Newspapers, street, 39–40

NIMBY ("Not In My Backyard") effect
  description/example of, 64
  resistance to low-income housing, 47

NIMH (National Institute of Mental Health)
  funding for NYU study, 43
  on substance abuse, 83

"The 1990 Census Shelter and Street Night Enumeration" (U.S. Census Bureau), 5

Nixon, Richard, 52

NLCHP. *See* National Law Center on Homelessness and Poverty

NLIHC (National Low Income Housing Coalition)
  lack of affordable units, 44
  Out of Reach, 2004, 46

"No bed/no arrest" policy, 69, 70

No Child Left Behind Act of 2001, 61, 64

No Open Door: Breaking the Lock on Addiction Recovery for Homeless People (National Coalition for the Homeless), 82

North American Street Newspaper Association (NASNA), 39

Northeast
  homeless population in, 15
  poverty rate in, 29

"Not In My Backyard" (NIMBY) effect
  description/example of, 64
  resistance to low-income housing, 47

Nunez, Ralph da Costa, 23

NYU (New York University), 43

O

O'Connell, James, 74

Office of Policy Development and Research, Department of Housing and Urban Development, 45–46

Ohio, 71

O'Keefe, E. B., 77

Olympia (WA), 65

An Open Letter on Revising the Official Measure of Poverty ("Conveners of the Working Group on Revising the Poverty Measure"), 24

Ordinances, restrictive
  alternatives to criminalization, 68–69
  Constitutional rights and, 69–71
  criminalization as public policy, argument against, 68
  criminalization of homeless life, 65
  human rights violations, 65, 68
  NIMBY effect, 64
  rationale for, 68
  regulation of homeless, 63

Orshansky, Mollie, 23

"Out of Pocket Medical Spending for Care of Chronic Conditions" (W. Hwang et al.), 75

Out of Reach, 2004 (National Low Income Housing Coalition), 46

P

Pacific Islander Americans. *See* Asian and Pacific Islander Americans

Pañares, Rea, 77, 82

Panhandling (begging)
  court case about, 71
  ordinances about, 63

PATH (Projects for Assistance in Transition from Homelessness), 61

Penn Station (NYC), 71

Personal Responsibility and Work Opportunity Reconciliation Act
  welfare reform from, 38
  welfare reform/substance abusers, 83

PHAs (public housing agencies), 57–58

PHAS (Public Housing Assessment System)
  components of, 57
  designations, 58*t*

Philadelphia (PA), 69

Physical ailments, of homeless people, 77–79, 80

Physical assault, 84–85

Physical disabilities, homeless with, 53

Police
  advocacy programs, 68
  hate crimes against homeless and, 85

Poor
  based on official poverty rate, 24, 26
  low-income housing for, 43–47
  people, families in poverty, by selected characteristics, 25*t*
  welfare reform and, 38–39

Poorhouse, 1

Post, Patricia A., 22

Posttraumatic stress disorder, 84

Poverty
  family poverty rates, selected indicators, 29*f*
  health of children and, 83
  health problems and, 73
  HIV/AIDS and, 81
  homelessness and, 14–15, 23
  housing for poor, 43–47
  income, percent change in mean income, share of aggregate income, by population fifths, 36 (*f*3.7)
  measurement of, 23–24
  national savings rate as percent of disposable income, 36 (*f*3.8)
  number in poverty and poverty rate, 28 (*f*3.2)
  number of people in, 15 (*t*2.2)
  people, families in poverty, by selected characteristics, 25*t*
  poor, demographics of, 24, 26–27, 29
  poverty rates by age, 28 (*f*3.3)
  poverty rates, official/experimental, by age, 27*f*
  poverty threshold by size of family, number of related children under 18 years of age, 24*t*
  savings, bankruptcies, 35–36
  share of aggregate income received by each fifth and top five percent of families, 35*t*
  subsidized housing and, 55
  wealth, distribution of, 34
  welfare reform, 38–39

Poverty in the United States: Current Population Reports (U.S. Census Bureau)
  poverty rates by race/ethnicity, 27
  poverty rates by region, 29
  poverty rates of children, 26